America's History is *His* Story:

Daily Reflections on Our Godly American Heritage

Books by R.G. Yoho

America's History is *His* Story
Long Ride to Yesterday
Boot Hill Valley

Kellen Malone Series
Death Comes to Redhawk
Death Rides the Rail

Coming Soon!
Nightfall Over Nicodemus
The Evil Day
Palo Duro
Return to Matewan

**For more information
visit:** www.SpeakingVolumes.us

America's History is *His* Story:

Daily Reflections on Our Godly American Heritage

R.G. Yoho

SPEAKING VOLUMES, LLC
NAPLES, FLORIDA
2023

America's History is His Story:

Copyright © 2012 by R.G. Yoho

All rights reserved. No part of this book may be reproduced or transmitted in any form or by any means without written permission.

ISBN 979-8-89022-044-8

I dedicate this book to my Lord and Savior.

Forward

"The Americans are here…" was the chatter that spread quickly through a humble little town in Northern Ukraine.

I was there to conduct a Gospel meeting along with two other men.

A town official would not open the doors of a public building to allow the crowd to enter so we could have our meeting.

The official said, "In America, you would not allow a communist to gather a crowd and speak so freely, why should we?"

But little did he know that in America, he could, and our tax dollars would even pay for his protection, because in America we enjoy the freedom of speech.

What makes America different from other countries of the world?

America's History is His Story, by R.G. Yoho, will take you from the granite walls of the Constitutional Congress, to dusty country cornfields; from bloody battlefields to the blood-stained cross of the risen Saviour proving that the principles of Biblical Christianity are indelibly etched in the pages of American history and that our founding fathers believed that freedom is an unalienable right granted to us by our Creator.

Once this truth is removed from history, we will never be able to learn from history.

R.G. will challenge your mind, thrill your soul, and burden your heart as you read this one of a kind, colorful, witty and historical daily devotional.

Read it with your family and pass along the stories because America's history is His Story.

Oliver Araiza, Evangelist

Prologue

President Ronald Reagan said, "Always remember that you are Americans, and it is your birthright to dream great dreams in this sweet and blessed land, truly the greatest, freest, strongest nation on Earth."

Americans have been granted an exceptional birthright of freedom, success, and prosperity, which came to us through our Godly American heritage.

In the book of Genesis, we see Esau foolishly selling his precious birthright to his brother for little more than a bowl of stew.

Increasingly, we in America are also witnessing our fellow citizens and our politicians trading away our precious birthright of freedom. We have willingly surrendered our birthright to historians and the media, allowing them to make their false claims and denials about our Christian heritage.

Unfortunately, too many Americans have tasted of this evil stew.

The simple truth is this: you cannot understand the greatness of America without understanding the story of Christ. The two are inseparable.

The United States of America has always been an exceptional nation, because it was founded on Christianity.

Our founding documents are steeped with the words and principles of Scripture. They influence our laws. We can often see them in the writings and speeches of our presidents, George Washington, John Adams, Thomas Jefferson, and Abraham Lincoln.

America's history *is* Christ's story, from which I derive the title.

Patrick Henry said, "It cannot be emphasized too strongly or too often that this great nation was founded, not by religionists, but by Christians; not on religions, but on the Gospel of Jesus Christ."

Some of the stories you will read in this book are about people who would make no claim of having a personal relationship with the Lord. However, their wondrous experiences and boundless success are only further proof of God's blessing on our nation.

Unfortunately, those who write our history books have deliberately sought to purge any trace of our Godly American heritage from the pages of our schools' textbooks. Moreover, they also wish to convince American citizens that these truths exist only in the minds of misguided fools.

But ultimately, they are only fooling themselves.

A failure to acknowledge our country's deeply religious origins isn't only a denial of the facts; it is a deliberate and deceitful act to hide the truth from America.

C.K. Chesterton said, "These are the days when a Christian is expected to praise every creed except his own."

Only recently have we seen a groundswell of Americans, such as those in the Tea Party and others, people who strongly wish to embrace our patriotic values and reclaim the truths of our Founding.

These modern-day American patriots, people of faith and advocates of smaller government, are constantly slandered and mischaracterized by politicians and the media, who often call them "racists."

Obviously, these accusations are strategically designed to employ the tactics of Communist revolutionary Vladimir Lenin, who once said, "A lie told often enough becomes the truth."

These people are certainly not racists.

They are simply good and decent American citizens, who routinely pay their taxes and try to consistently obey our laws. Many of them faithfully attend their places of worship. They are our friends and neighbors, our co-workers and business people. These good-hearted men and women are united in their desire to see America return to the timeless principles and traditions of our Founders.

However, we have seen a hateful, California Congresswoman telling these law-abiding members of the Tea Party that they "can go straight to hell."

These are the obstacles we now seek to overcome in America, when we see sitting members of Congress, arrogantly ridiculing those they deceitfully claim to serve.

These are the ones who wish to suppress the truth about our nation.

President Donald Trump said, "I have embraced crying mothers who have lost their children because our politicians put their personal agendas before the national good. I have no patience for injustice, no tolerance for government incompetence, no sympathy for leaders who fail their citizens."

John Adams stated, "If men through fear, fraud, or mistake, should in terms renounce and give up any essential natural right, the eternal law of reason and the great end of society, would absolutely vacate such renunciation; the right to freedom being the gift of God Almighty, it is not in the power of man to alienate this gift and voluntarily become a slave."

The truth of America's religious heritage is there for every citizen to discover. That is what I hope to do with this book.

As you read it, I trust you will be moved by things contained within its pages; I certainly was!

If you embrace the power of the Christian faith, if you love the United States, if you cherish your family, and if you respect our military personnel, then you should love this book. Every single page is brimming with the qualities of faith, family, and freedom.

We can all be thankful for the United States of America, this great and marvelous land, a product of God's almighty and gracious hand, in which we were indeed privileged to call our own.

May the Lord continue to bless the United States of America! And may we always continue to remember Him…

Because America's history is His Story!

January 1

"If I could have entertained the slightest apprehension that the Constitution framed by the Convention where I had the honor to preside, might possibly endanger the religious rights of any ecclesiastical Society, certainly I would never have placed my signature to it."

–George Washington

The great general and statesman, George Washington presided over the Constitutional Convention, which gave us that precious and time-honored document, which governs our nation. At the same time, it was important to him to preserve the rights and liberties of every citizen to practice whatever religion they saw fit.

Washington, a man of deep and abiding faith, made sure that nothing produced from their convention would ever limit the faith of those who call this nation their home.

In addition, it was also critical to the "Father of our Country" that government should never be permitted to interfere or hinder the individual exercise and practice of religious faith.

The Constitution of our United States of America does not ban our rights to religious liberty; the Constitution defends them.

America's history is His story!

January 2

"It was wonderful to see the change soon made in the manners of our inhabitants. From being thoughtless or indifferent about religion, it seemed as if all the world were growing religious, so that one could not walk through the town in an evening without hearing psalms sung in different families of every street." –Benjamin Franklin

Franklin, the author of *Poor Richard's Almanack*, became a good friend of George Whitefield, one of the preachers responsible for America's Great Awakening.

Whitefield possessed an amazing voice, allowing him to be heard by crowds that would occasionally number in the thousands. It was reported that Whitefield's preaching could be understood for approximately a mile away.

Whenever Whitefield preached, lives were forever altered.

In his initial quote, Franklin made note of the transformation in the city, as a result of Whitefield's ministry. The undeniable signs of revival were all around him.

In fact, a number of historians believe it was the ministry of George Whitefield, and other preachers of the Great Awakening, that ultimately prepared Americans for their struggle for freedom. Moreover, the spiritual transformation his preaching brought to their lives, gave them the courage and moral fiber to endure the hardships the American Revolution would soon require of them.

American independence wasn't simply a triumph of the human spirit; it was also a glorious, unshackling of the soul.

America's history is His story!

January 3

"It cannot be emphasized too strongly or too often that this great nation was founded, not by religionists, but by Christians; not on religions, but on the gospel of Jesus Christ. For this very reason peoples of other faiths have been afforded asylum, prosperity, and freedom of worship here." –Patrick Henry

America's History is His Story:

The man who boldly declared, "Give me liberty or give me death," realized that our nation was founded on the principles of Scripture. Henry also knew that this unique and precious form of government offered a shelter and a haven for all, a place where each citizen could practice his individual faith or beliefs, without fear of restraint or persecution from the government.

Moreover, it was this foundation of religious freedom that made us unique throughout the annals of history. The United States is truly special. No other nation, founded on such a specific set of religious principles, has ever been so willing to grant each individual the right to worship so freely.

Our leaders in Washington often deny our heritage as a Christian nation. Many of those in the press corps also question our religious underpinnings. Still, their denials don't change the facts.

Who are you going to believe about our country's foundations? Do you choose to believe those who seek to rewrite history; or do you believe Patrick Henry, one of the men responsible for creating it?

America's history is His story!

January 4

"No people can be bound to acknowledge and adore the Invisible Hand which conducts the affairs of men more than the people of the United States." –George Washington

The father of our country, George Washington understood that this country couldn't have been founded without the remarkable guidance and intervention of Almighty God.

After having led a rag-tag band of meagerly-clothed, poorly-fed, and ill-equipped soldiers through the horrors of war, while facing a much more equipped and experienced army, Washington gained the eventual triumph over the most powerful military force on the face of the earth.

Moreover, the general knew his victory was won through the remarkable power of prayer and Divine providence.

Although Washington didn't think the people of our country should be required to follow the Lord's guidance, our nation's first president placed the Savior in a prominent place in his own personal life.

Perhaps, you should do the same.

America's history is His story!

January 5

"Is life so dear, or peace so sweet, as to be purchased at the price of chains and slavery? Forbid it, Almighty God! I know not what course others may take; but as for me, give me liberty or give me death."

–Patrick Henry

During the Second World War, Hitler's German army mounted a daring, but foolish offensive, known as the Battle of the Bulge.

Through their attack, the Germans hoped to drive a wedge between the British and American forces. Located right in the middle of this fighting was Bastogne, Belgium, a place where all the roads seemed to converge.

Ordering them to defend the city at all costs, Allied Commander Dwight Eisenhower sent troops from the 101st Airborne to Bastogne.

In charge of those forces was General Anthony McAuliffe.

Surrounding the city was a heavily armored German army, whose commander ordered the surrender of U.S. forces stationed there. He gave the Americans two hours to comply with his terms or they would be annihilated by German artillery.

When presented with the German demands, General McAuliffe responded only with a single-word reply:

"Nuts!"

Although they paid a heavy price for defending the city, General McAuliffe's troops were not defeated. Nor did they surrender. By the grace of God, Bastogne was held by the Americans, and the German offensive was soon defeated.

America's history is His story!

January 6

"Before any man can be considered a member of civil society, he must be considered as a subject of the Governor of the Universe."
–James Madison

Born the son of a Virginia slave and a white plantation owner, Barney L. Ford escaped slavery when he was twenty-six. His flight to freedom would take him to Chicago, where he met his wife, who helped Barney choose his last name.

Their travels would take them to Nicaragua, where Barney and his wife chose to stay and open their first hotel, which turned out to be a profitable venture.

Still longing for the promise of riches in the Colorado goldfields, Barney was unable to take the stage because he was a black man. Unshackled by circumstances or the color of his skin, the relentless former slave reached the Colorado mines by way of a wagon train, signing on with the travelers as a barber.

Unable to file papers on his own claim because he was black, Ford was persuaded to register the claim under his lawyer's name. The unscrupulous attorney later double-crossed him and stole the mine from the former slave. And although the claim jumper personally never found any gold there, apparently Barney escaped with enough gold dust to bankroll his next round of successful business investments.

Barney Ford established a restaurant and hotel in Denver and Cheyenne. His Inter-Ocean Hotel was one of the most prominent hotels in the West. Barney's story is further proof that America was a country where a resourceful man, of any color, could fully realize his dreams of success and liberty.

America's history is His story!

January 7

"The laws of nature are the laws of God, whose authority can be superseded by no power on earth." –George Mason

A delegate to the Constitutional Convention, George Mason steadfastly refused to sign the document, because he wisely feared a strong central government would eventually abuse the rights of individual citizens.

Mason is also called the "Father of the Bill of Rights," because he was largely responsible for the first ten amendments to the Constitution, which greatly limited the power of the government to interfere in our daily lives.

A vocal opponent of slavery, this remarkable Founding Father believed his fellow men should be shackled to no one. Mason believed our servitude should never be to individuals or to the government, but only to the Lord.

Mason shared the opinion of Thomas Paine, who said, "Government even in its best state is but a necessary evil, in its worst state, an intolerable one."

In these days when governments increasingly seek to take the place of God in our daily lives, it is essential that our love of country must always remain secondary to our allegiance to Him.

America's history is His story!

January 8

"In the Name of the Great Jehovah and the Continental Congress."
–Ethan Allen

During the American Revolution, a well-educated frontiersman named Ethan Allen became the Commander of the Green Mountain Boys.

In 1775, under Allen's leadership—and with the assistance of Connecticut Colonel Benedict Arnold—the daring troops of the Green Mountain Boys staged a surprise attack on Fort Ticonderoga, an outpost which was under British control.

When Allen boldly ordered the fort to be surrendered to the American troops, the British commander asked Allen what authority gave him the power to demand their surrender.

In response to the British commander's question, Ethan Allen spoke those magnificent words: "In the Name of the Great Jehovah and the Continental Congress."

After a time, the British commander emerged, fully dressed, and reluctantly surrendered his fort and his sword to these American soldiers, led by Ethan Allen.

America's history is His story!

January 9

"We are spending less time in the classroom on the Bible, which should be the principle text in our schools…The Bible states these great moral lessons better than any other manmade book." –Fisher Ames

Fisher Ames is a name unknown to many of you.

However, Ames was a Congressman from Massachusetts when James Madison was carefully engaged in drafting our Constitution.

It was Ames who proposed the wording of the Constitution's First Amendment, which proclaimed our God-given freedom of religion.

The First Amendment begins with the words, "Congress shall make no law…"

Fisher Ames clearly understood religion was a precious gift, a human right which needed to be protected from needless political tampering. It was his contribution to the First Amendment, which protects our freedom today and preserves our rights to worship.

This little-known Founder of our country is just one bright thread in the fabric of our remarkable Christian heritage.

America's history is His story!

January 10

"The only foundation for…a republic is to be laid in religion. Without this there can be no virtue, and without virtue there can be no liberty."
–Benjamin Rush

Benjamin Rush was one of the signers of the Declaration of Independence, 56 men who pledged to each other "our Lives, our Fortunes, and our sacred Honor."

America's History is His Story:

The ones who signed this document were brave and virtuous men, patriots who boldly risked everything to form this great republic.

During our war for independence, Rush, a physician, was named the Surgeon General of the Continental Army. Later, this man of great virtue started the nation's first free medical clinic and led the fight against slavery.

Clearly, his life reflected the words he spoke.

A nation founded on the principles of individual freedom must demand a lot from its people. The United States cannot thrive without a virtuous people.

Throughout our nation's history, faith has always been our vessel of liberty and virtue has been its sail.

America's history is His story!

January 11

"For my own part, I sincerely esteem it a system which without the finger of God, never could have been suggested and agreed upon by such a diversity of interests." –Alexander Hamilton

It is clear that Alexander Hamilton knew that the Constitution was truly a special document, something unique throughout history.

The Constitution was not Divinely inspired in the same way the Scriptures were inspired. However, it is certainly hard to argue with those who would suggest the profound influence of God in its creation.

Hamilton was correct.

Those who gathered at the Constitutional Convention were some of the most learned and accomplished men to ever assemble in one room. But despite their renown, they were simply men, occasionally separated by differing opinions and heartfelt objections.

Somehow, they set aside those differences and tabled their pride long enough to create a blueprint upon which a great nation would be governed.

Summoning the very best of themselves, while at the same time they sought the Lord's daily blessings in prayer, these men rose above themselves to establish a country, which has been a beacon of freedom for over two centuries.

America's history is His story!

January 12

"In vain, without the Bible, we increase penal laws and draw intrenchments around our institutions. Bibles are strong intrenchments. Where they abound, men cannot pursue wicked courses, and at the same time enjoy quiet conscience." –James McHenry

A member of the Continental Congress and one of the signers of the Constitution, James McHenry knew the importance of Scripture to the betterment of society.

Increasingly, we have seen the Lord and the Bible removed from our public institutions. Therefore, is it any wonder crime and tragedy have multiplied in our nation?

We misuse the phrase "separation of church and state," like it's a statement of faith or lifted from the Constitution. It isn't!

We remove any mention of the Ten Commandments or the Lord from our public schools and we wonder why these school shootings multiply. However, once the tragedy occurs, once the body bags have been removed, our *brilliant* educators suddenly decide it's time to invite God back to our schools.

They suddenly organize gatherings and prayer vigils, strangely with no mention of separation of church and state.

The idea is a fallacy. Despite what you may have heard, our Founding Fathers intended our government to be influenced by faith. They intended religion to be an essential part of the public discourse.

America's history is His story!

January 13

"But by the all-powerful dispensations of Providence, I have been protected beyond all human probability or expectation; for I had four bullets through my coat, and two horses shot under me, yet escaped unhurt, although death was leveling my companions on every side of me." –George Washington

During the French and Indian War, a young George Washington survived many close calls with the enemy in 1755. Delivering orders for General Braddock, who was later killed by those same enemies, Washington was somehow spared from the bullets which killed every other mounted officer.

One of the Indians who witnessed the battle stated: "Washington was never born to be killed by a bullet! I had seventeen fair fires at him with my rifle, and after all could not bring him to the ground."

Apparently, the Lord had a greater purpose for young George Washington. The Indians claimed Washington was protected by "The Great Spirit."

Washington and those who opposed him in battle were cognizant of the fact that the hand of God rested upon him.

Approximately two decades later, the mighty General Washington would command the Continental Army in the fight for independence and guide his troops to victory. He would lead the United States, a nation created in that historic struggle.

The life of George Washington was obviously shielded by the hand of God.

America's history is His story!

January 14

"I have returned. By the grace of Almighty God, our forces stand again on Philippine soil—soil consecrated by the blood of our two peoples."
–Douglas MacArthur

Not only was Gen. Douglas MacArthur the Commander of the Allied Forces in the Pacific in World War II, he was also a man of great faith.

Like Gen. George Washington before him, Gen. MacArthur was seemingly protected by the hand of God to serve a greater purpose.

During the occupation of Veracruz in 1914, young Douglas MacArthur was attacked by a party of Mexican horsemen. In the course of the battle, he took three bullet holes in his clothes. Unscathed by the attack, MacArthur shot several of his attackers.

In a later attack, he received another bullet hole in his clothes.

Apparently, the young man who would lead our nation's defeat of the brutal Japanese Imperial Army had the hand of God upon his life. In order to gain the ultimate triumph, the United States needed his leadership in a time of war.

Like Gen. Washington, Gen. Douglas MacArthur wasn't bulletproof. However, any man is truly invincible if the Lord has a plan for his life.

Clearly, there was no *earthly* reason why these two future generals were not killed as young men. Therefore, it is reasonable to assume their lives were designed by a guiding power to fulfill a greater purpose.

America's history is His story!

January 15

"The cause of America is in a great measure the cause of all mankind. Where, say some, is the king of America? I'll tell you, friend. He reigns above." –Thomas Paine

In the darkest days of British tyranny by King George, writer and author Thomas Paine penned the words which greatly inspired the American Revolution.

Even Mr. Paine couldn't realize the great truth of his statement.

The war for independence didn't simply benefit the American colonists; it benefitted all mankind.

The United States of America has been the launching pad of liberty and innovation ever since it was conceived. America has been the nation sending missionaries all over the globe to spread the Gospel. Whenever there is a catastrophe or a natural disaster, the people of the United States are the first ones on the scene to help.

Beleaguered peoples everywhere look to these shores for leadership.

Although much of the world claims they do not like us, it is just because many of them are also jealous of us. They long to share our freedoms, to share our abundance, and to enjoy the blessings that God has bestowed upon us.

And who can blame them?

America's history is His story!

January 16

"I could say a thousand things to you if I had leisure. I could dwell on the importance of piety and religion, of industry and frugality, of prudence, economy, regularity and even Government, all of which are essential to the well being of a family. Religion in a family is at once its brightest ornament and its best security." –Samuel Adams

In God's divine order, the Lord established the home before He instituted the church. That alone should demonstrate its significance.

To some it may sound trite, but the hand that rocks the cradle truly *is* the hand that rules the world!

America has been a great country because it has been built on the values and virtues of the home. It has been grounded in the principles of love and family. It is rooted in the traditions of home and hearth.

Is it any wonder the country's recent moral decline seems to coincide with the dissolution of the traditional family? It is the children who suffer the most when Dad and Mom cannot live together in harmony.

According to national statistics, the children of single parent families are much more likely to suffer from poverty, lower test scores, and higher rates of crime.

If the United States is to maintain its status as a world power, then it is crucial the American home return to the high standard of prominence it once formerly enjoyed.

America's history is His story!

January 17

"It must be felt that there is no national security but in the nation's humble, acknowledged dependence upon God and his overruling providence." –Franklin Pierce

America's History is His Story:

In his inaugural address, Franklin Pierce, our nation's 14th president humbly acknowledged our nation's security rested not on the power of this land's highest elective office. Rather, our nation's ultimate security rests solely in the hands of God.

Throughout our nation's history, the United States has been protected by the greatest military forces the world has ever seen.

From Crispus Attucks to Antietam, from the Ardennes to Afghanistan, the American fighting man has stood in defense of liberty. The American soldier is daring and innovative. He is courageous and humble. Despite their occasional bouts with fear, they remain formidable.

Our armed forces continue to be the envy of the world, the desire of every would-be dictator and tyrant who ever cast on evil eye on humanity.

However, you cannot read the history of the American Revolution or the accounts of World War II and not come to the conclusion that God was often with us in battle.

It is more than patriotism that causes a soldier to lay down his life for generations yet unborn. It is God's purest love, inspiring a man in uniform to selflessly give his life for his brothers-in-arms.

America's history is His story!

January 18

"America seeks no empires built on blood and force. No ambition, no temptation, lures her to thought of foreign domination. The legions which she sends forth are armed, not with the sword, but with the Cross. The higher state to which she seeks the allegiance of all mankind is not human, but of Divine origin. She cherishes no purpose, save to merit the favor of Almighty God." –Calvin Coolidge

Unlike the Greek or Roman empires, which arrogantly sought to conquer the entire known world, the United States has never been a country to deliberately misuse its military in the pursuit of global domination.

Moreover, what other country in world history has ever rebuilt the nations destroyed in our times of warfare?

Nobody but America!

Following World War II, the United States instituted the Marshal Plan, an ambitious economic plan to rebuild much of war-torn Europe. The United States has always been, as Abraham Lincoln so aptly stated, "the last best hope of earth."

Two days after the attack on the World Trade Center, none of the victims had been found alive and the spirits of rescue workers were shaken. However, among the carnage, one of those rescuers discovered a 20-foot, steel I-beam, in the shape of a cross.

That cross, which has now been relocated beside St Peter's Church in New York City, became a symbol of hope for all Americans.

Since the Pilgrims landed on Plymouth Rock, the cross has been a precious symbol of hope to our nation. It inspired brave men to tame a vast continent. It has been America's backbone, our inspiration, and the eternal symbol of our faith.

America's history is His story!

January 19

"All the distinctive features and superiority of our republican institutions are derived from the teachings of Scripture." –Edward Everett

America's History is His Story:

Educator and politician, Edward Everett was known as one of the outstanding orators of his day. However, his two-hour speech to dedicate a new military cemetery at Gettysburg was greatly overshadowed by a humble, two-minute address given by President Abraham Lincoln.

In what has arguably become the most famous political speech in our nation's history, Lincoln called our country, "this nation—under God."

Both of these men, Lincoln and Everett, understood that this country had been blessed by the Lord and influenced by His Word.

When Lincoln said, "all men are created equal," he was acknowledging the fact that humanity is not a random act of nature. We are the products of a Divine Creator, who affords the same unalienable rights to every individual.

In addition, Lincoln was also reiterating the principles of another president, Thomas Jefferson, who penned the Declaration of Independence.

Lincoln's desire to free the slaves was borne of the same principles which inspired Jefferson's vision of freedom for the colonists. The philosophies of these two great men, from two vastly different generations, were ultimately conceived in the pages of God's unchanging word.

America's history is His story!

January 20

"Being thus arrived in a good harbor, and brought safe to land, they fell upon their knees and blessed the God of Heaven who had brought them over the vast and furious ocean, and delivered them from all the perils and miseries thereof, again to set their feet on the firm and stable earth, their proper element." –William Bradford

The Pilgrims who landed on these shores were brave and committed followers of Christ. Crossing the Atlantic Ocean was a daring and risky proposition.

Sailing through often-hostile waters on tiny wooden ships was always a treacherous venture. Many of those vessels routinely failed to reach their destinations.

"We on this continent should never forget," Robert J. McCracken said, "that men first crossed the Atlantic, not to find soil for their plows but to secure liberty for their souls."

However, the promise of freedom, the ability to worship how they desired, and the chance to build a culture and society grounded in their faith, those things ultimately made the Pilgrims' journey a venture worth taking.

Bradford, governor of the Plymouth Colony, believed the Pilgrims were protected by Divine providence. This conviction inspired the writing of his book, "Of Plymouth Plantation."

Like William Bradford and his fellow pilgrims, men of faith are often inspired to set out on great and noble journeys. Those brave souls who landed on Plymouth Rock planted not only the seeds which yielded their future crops. They also sowed the seeds of faith and religious freedom in a burgeoning land, a fertile soil known as America.

America's history is His story!

January 21

"In what light soever we regard the Bible, whether with reference to revelation, to history, or to morality, it is an invaluable and inexhaustible mine of knowledge and virtue." –John Quincy Adams

America's History is His Story:

In Marietta, Ohio, a local organization was responsible for building the "Liberty Ship," a structure resembling a 17th Century, sea-going vessel. The creator of this structure planned to display it in parades and any number of other gatherings.

It is hoped that the vessel will become a symbol of inspiration and also, a teaching tool, something to educate young and old alike in the largely-forgotten principles of liberty and our Godly American heritage.

The vessel is equipped with two anchors. One of them symbolizes our Constitution, the document upon which our nation is governed. The other anchor signifies the Word of God, the unbendable steel upon which our country was founded.

Without the eternal anchor of God's word, our ship of state may drift into danger. It will wander aimlessly, wherever the winds and turbulent storms of life may take it.

The unchanging Word of God and the United States Constitution are essential to keeping our republic from drifting away from the eternal values and traditions that have made us strong.

America's history is His story!

January 22

"The citizen is a better businessman if he is a Christian gentleman, and, surely, business is not the less prosperous and successful if conducted on Christian principles." – Grover Cleveland

Surprisingly to some, the Bible has a lot to say about business and how it should be conducted. The Lord talks about the responsibilities and duties of masters and servants, and the principles regarding how employers and employees should treat each other.

It matters not what the endeavor, following God's plan always leads to success. And the Lord often sends famine to individuals *and* nations which forsake His guidance.

Many of this country's greatest industrialists founded their businesses on Godly principles. Influenced by the teachings of Christ, a number of these entrepreneurs donated a large portion of their wealth to others.

The United States has always been a giving country. Americans of every social and economic level give of their time and money to those who have been met with a natural disaster or have suffered some other economic heartbreak.

As long as America followed Godly teachings, our country thrived economically. It was only when we deliberately wavered from those Scriptural principles that bankruptcy and bailouts became the order of the day.

America's history is His story!

January 23

"Wherever there is a human being, I see God-given rights inherent in that being, whatever may be the sex or complexion."
–William Lloyd Garrison

Despite the fact our government allowed slavery at its inception, the United States is the only country in the history of the world to ever go to war with itself over the issue.

Approximately 625,000 Americans were killed during our brutal Civil War. Over one-fourth of the male population, under the age of 25, were annihilated in this bloody, national conflict.

America's History is His Story:

The Scriptural influence and moral upbringing of the people in our republic couldn't allow the continuation of human bondage of one man to another.

Slavery was abolished in this country because our churches and their pulpits cried out against this evil and showed the country a better way. The same Lord and Savior, who broke the chains of spiritual bondage, also inspired men and women to strike down the scourge of human bondage as well.

Slavery still exists in other parts of the world. But it is the glorious light of the Gospel which showed America the path out of this moral darkness.

America's history is His story!

January 24

"This Biblical story of the Promised Land inspired the founders of America. It continues to inspire us." –Dwight D. Eisenhower

America's first settlers were immersed in the Scriptures from an early age. Often with the Bible as their only source of reading material, by candlelight and the blaze of open hearths, these colonists and settlers learned to read from the pages of the Bible. They followed its precepts. They schooled their children in its passages.

Naturally, those who grew up reading the story of Moses and the Jews eventually came to see this country as *their* Promised Land.

Pioneers and frontiersmen such as Daniel Boone often braved this rugged wilderness, seeking to find their place, another land flowing with milk and honey. They eventually pushed westward, exploring new lands, bringing friends and loved ones with them on their exodus.

Like the children of Israel, a name Boone even gave to one of his sons, these settlers faced hardships in the wilderness. Inspired by the tales of Moses, they continued their wilderness journeys.

The Word of God and the stories contained within its pages inspired Americans to push forward, to explore and populate this vast continent, from sea to shining sea.

This country was indeed *their* Promised Land.

America's history is His story!

January 25

"This Christian religion is, above all the religions that ever prevailed or existed in ancient or modern times, the religion of wisdom, virtue, equity, and humanity." –John Adams

One of the great tragedies of our culture has been the idea that those who firmly embrace their Christianity are somehow less intellectual than those who have chosen a more secular lifestyle. Nothing could be more at odds with the truth.

Not only is the Word of God the bedrock upon which our nation was built, the Scriptures are also the foundation of all human truth.

In Proverbs 1:7, the Bible tells us, "the fear of the Lord is the beginning of knowledge."

In the early days of our nation's history, the Bible was America's principle textbook, its primary source of literature, and a trusted primer in human relations.

Princeton, Yale, and Harvard all had their origins in the church. These universities were started by preachers, in the interest of spreading the Gospel. And for all our so-called *intelligence* of these modern times, the entrance requirements for those schools were much higher than they are today.

America's most prominent universities were established by churches, preachers, and the Word of God. Moreover, it can never be stated loudly enough: there is no true education apart from the Lord.

America's history is His story!

January 26

"The fundamental basis of this nation's laws was given to Moses on the Mount. The fundamental basis of our Bill of Rights comes from the teachings we get from Exodus and St. Matthew, from Isaiah and St. Paul. I don't think we emphasize that enough these days. If we don't have a proper fundamental moral background, we will finally end up with a totalitarian government which does not believe in rights for anybody except the State." –Harry S. Truman

Like many of our presidents, President Truman was fully aware of America's Christian heritage. He also knew our system of government would never function properly without a moral people.

There is certainly nothing wrong with an economy built on capitalism. It is not a crime when anyone seeks profit from the fruit of his labors. Money is not the root of all evil; the love of money *is*!

Our economy functions best when it is governed by those who routinely base their actions on moral principles.

Those who put the Lord first in their business dealings will not defraud their fellow man. They will not abuse their employees. They will not seek to steal that which others rightfully earned.

Our government leaders must not do those things as well.

Unlike other nations, our Republic thrived because it was built on godly principles. We have only experienced economic hardships in America when we strayed from those ideals.

America's history is His story!

January 27

"If thou wouldst rule well, thou must rule for God, and to do that, thou must be ruled by Him. Those who will not be governed by God will be ruled by tyrants." –William Penn

In the pages of Scripture, we see where the children of Israel are often protected by the hand of God. However, every time they strayed from following His guidance, the Jewish people soon found themselves persecuted and enslaved by evil rulers.

This same scenario is often seen repeated in the book of Judges. The Lord graciously selected judges who would deliver his people from death and bondage. Yet despite God's goodness to them, the people still chose, over and over again, to stray from His established path.

The United States became a great nation because we were founded on godly principles. Increasingly, our leaders refuse to submit themselves to His guidance and many of our people arrogantly refuse to bow before His will.

Is it any wonder that so many of those in Washington regard themselves as gods, refusing to listen to the petitions of those they once served? Much too often, our leaders have become tyrants.

If we once again allow the Lord to steer the ship of state, then we will most certainly find the shelter of His peaceful harbor. However, should we continue to rely on our own wisdom, then our nation, like many of those before us, may eventually be crushed upon the rocky shoreline.

America's history is His story!

January 28

"Christianity works while infidelity talks. She feeds the hungry, clothes the naked, visits and cheers the sick, and seeks the lost, while infidelity abuses her and babbles nonsense and profanity."

–Henry Ward Beecher

The United States is unique among all the nations in world history. Unlike godless Communism that offers much to its citizens and delivers nothing but pain, hunger, oppression, and death, America's Christian heritage offers its citizens life, freedom, and salvation.

It has also been a beacon of light to the world.

When Europe was facing an onslaught of godless tyranny, it was America that responded to their calls for help.

Wearing the uniform of the United States military, our men scaled the cliffs, they stormed the beaches, and they braved the ravages of hostile machine gun fire.

Out of the millions who served, not all of them returned home. Those who paid the ultimate price are interred on American soil, in foreign lands, in places such as France, Belgium, Luxembourg, England, and Italy.

Row after row of white crosses mark the landscape, crosses that symbolize our losses in the eternal struggle for freedom. When worldwide freedom was in danger, our Christian nation didn't just talk. We responded.

America's history is His story!

January 29

"That I am not a member of any Christian Church, is true, but I have never denied the truth of the Scriptures; and I have never spoken with intentional disrespect of religion in general, or of any denomination of Christians in particular. I do not think I could, myself, be brought to support a man for office whom I knew to be an open enemy of, and scoffer at religion." –Abraham Lincoln

The preceding words were Abraham Lincoln's answer to those who said he wasn't a Christian.

Often referred to as "Honest Abe," Lincoln, our 16th president, was a man of impeccable character. He was also a man who was deeply private about the matter of his personal faith.

From his writings, it is obvious that Lincoln was intimately familiar with the writings of Scripture. It is also abundantly clear the president had been influenced by those things he read.

While leading a great nation, torn asunder by the brutal Civil War, Lincoln was appreciative of the faith and prayers of others. He even sent a letter to a couple of Iowa Quakers, thanking them for the petitions offered up in his behalf.

Although there will always be speculation regarding the faith of Abraham Lincoln, there can be no question this great man was profoundly influenced by Scripture. It also cannot be disputed that the Lord granted our nation a man for such a time as this.

America's history is His story!

January 30

"The Christian religion is no longer the badge of weaklings and enthusiasts, but of distinction, enforcing respect." –William McKinley

America's History is His Story:

Those who embrace the Christian faith have often suffered persecution. In fact, that is the reason why many of our earliest settlers migrated to this continent. Those brave and hardy souls desired the freedom to worship the Lord according to the dictates of their own hearts.

And although the meek may inherit the earth, they didn't inherit much of anything in the New World. These settlers had to earn their daily bread in a brutal and primitive environment.

The Pilgrims endured many hardships in order to thrive in America. Surviving the long journey across unforgiving seas was only the beginning of the challenges they faced as a people.

They endured death, hunger, disease, and loneliness. However, they willingly faced these hardships for the privilege to worship God, free from the Church of England.

History teaches us Christianity grew and flourished under the threat of Roman persecution. In addition, Christianity also thrived in the hardships of the New World.

These early Christians also gave us the framework and leadership to establish one of the greatest Republics in human civilization.

America's history is His story!

January 31

"Slavery as an institution is a moral and political evil in any country. I think, however, a greater evil to the white than to the black race."
–Robert E. Lee

Before General Robert E. Lee led the forces of the Confederacy, President Lincoln offered him command of the Union army. The agonizing decision Lee faced kept him awake throughout the night.

In this period of our nation's history, a man's allegiance was often devoted to his individual state, not to the nation as a whole.

A marvelous and devoted Christian, General Lee didn't support the institution of slavery. However, he refused to lift his sword against his own beloved Virginia.

A former slaveholder, Lee obviously became convicted of the practice. No doubt his faith figured prominently in the decision to willingly free his slaves, several years before the war.

In the Mexican-American War, this graduate of West Point had established himself as a formidable leader and a brilliant military strategist. And had General Lee chosen to lead the Union forces, it is unlikely the war would have lasted as long as it did.

In retribution for Lee leading the Confederate army, Union officials seized his family home and estate. However, a forgiving nation later compensated Lee for the property, which is now part of the beautiful Arlington National Cemetery.

America's history is His story!

February 1

"History fails to record a single precedent in which nations subject to moral decay have not passed into political and economic decline. There has been either a spiritual awakening to overcome the moral lapse, or a progressive deterioration leading to ultimate national disaster."
—Douglas MacArthur

General MacArthur's study of world history and the chronicles of military conquest provided him with all the reasons why a nation might fall.

America's History is His Story:

In the pages of Scripture and in the annals of history, we repeatedly see once-great nations eventually destroyed by moral decay.

The Roman Empire fell because the moral decline of its rulers and the people. Drunkenness and debauchery characterized their culture. Ultimately, it led to their destruction.

Following the attacks on the Twin Towers, a couple of well-known ministers were excoriated for suggesting the incident could have been the judgment of God.

Nevertheless, it is certainly a principle of Scripture that the Father chastises His children when they depart from following His statutes.

Perhaps the best illustration is the nation of Israel.

Despite the parting of the Red Sea and God's deliverance from the Egyptians, Israel soon forgot the goodness bestowed upon them. Time-after-time, they turned away from God and suffered under his judgment.

However, the Loving Father always stood ready to happily receive his children whenever they returned to Him. No doubt He would do the same for America, as well.

America's history is His story!

February 2

"Posterity—you will never know how much it has cost my generation to preserve your freedom. I hope you will make good use of it."
—President John Quincy Adams

Perhaps as well as anyone else, John Quincy Adams understood the true cost of liberty. Little more than a child during the Revolution, he saw the hardships faced by the Founding Fathers, hardships such as those faced by John Adams, his father, and his cousin, Samuel Adams.

As someone who watched the Battle of Bunker Hill from his home, John Quincy Adams fully understood the many sacrifices faced by those in his family. He realized these made liberty available to every individual.

This great man and sixth President of the United States was fully cognizant of our freedom; indeed, he was grateful for it. Therefore, it is likely John Quincy Adams would look with disdain upon anyone who failed to recognize their efforts.

We can be certain that all those who paid a price for the establishment of our freedoms would expect future generations to know them, to study them, and to give their utmost to preserve them.

We owe them no less.

America's history is His story!

February 3

"There is not a truth to be gathered from history more certain, or more momentous, than this: that liberty cannot long be separated from religious liberty without danger, and ultimately without destruction of both." –Joseph Story

Although a great shipbuilder might construct a seaworthy vessel, it cannot sail without some legitimate means of propulsion. Without a sail or an engine, the ship will simply float, aimlessly carried along with the current. Ultimately, the vessel will never arrive at its destination.

Moreover, a stationary ship will be susceptible to the danger of stormy seas and the violence of the waves beating upon it.

Although our nation is free, religious liberty is the sail that carries our nation along to its destination.

Our Christian principles are the fabric of our nation. When these are lifted up and hoisted to the top of the mast, for the whole world to see, then our country will enjoy smooth sailing, socially, spiritually, and economically.

The blessings of liberty give us freedom from tyranny. Our faith looses us from the shackles of sin. Both of them are critical to the ultimate survival of the United States.

It matters not whether we are talking about nations or individuals, there is no greater freedom than when one willingly shackles himself to a purpose greater than himself.

America's history is His story!

February 4

"Manned space flight is an amazing achievement, but it has opened for mankind thus far only a tiny door for viewing the awesome reaches of space. An outlook through this peephole at the vast mysteries of the universe should only confirm our belief in the certainty of its Creator. I find it difficult to understand a scientist who does not acknowledge the presence of a superior rationality behind the existence of the universe as it is to comprehend a theologian who would deny the advance of science." –Wernher von Braun

It has become increasingly popular in the scientific community to scoff at those who believe in God's act of creation. Fortunately, it was not always so.

Wernher von Braun, a brilliant German scientist, who emigrated to America to work in our space program, understood that the wonders of our solar system didn't come into existence by chance.

Without von Braun's knowledge and insight, NASA wouldn't have gained the technology to touch the distant reaches of space, let alone to place a man on the surface of the moon.

The Scriptures tell us in the book of Proverbs: "The fear of the Lord is the beginning of knowledge."

Perhaps those pseudo-intellectuals, who deliberately ignore the evidence of creation, are so blinded by their own vanity, that they fail to fully grasp the truths that are suspended right above their heads.

America's history is His story!

February 5

"The rights of man come not from the generosity of the state but from the hand of God." –John F. Kennedy

In his Inaugural Address to the nation, President John F. Kennedy reiterated the principles that Thomas Jefferson so wisely penned in the Declaration of Independence.

Kennedy, a veteran of World War II, lived in a time when Washington politicians of both parties readily acknowledged our nation's dependence on God.

Presidents Kennedy and Jefferson knew our rights were granted to us from the Heavenly Father, not from a legislative body. Those rights came not from the President of the United States, but from the Divine Creator. They came not from the Supreme Court, but were authored by the Supreme Judge of the Universe.

Since our rights do not have earthly origins, then they cannot be taken from us by earthly forces. It was a principle that led to our nation's Founding. It is a principle often forgotten by many of those in Washington today.

America's History is His Story:

Throughout our nation's history, the United States has been the embodiment of those rights. Perhaps it is time our nation should embrace them once again.

America's history is His story!

February 6

"America was founded by people who believed that God was their rock of safety. I recognize we must be cautious in claiming that God is on our side, but I think it's all right to keep asking if we're on His side."
–Ronald Reagan

On this day which former president Ronald Reagan was born, I think it's important to recognize this great man. Like many of his predecessors, Reagan had no doubts that our country was indeed a Christian nation.

In fact, he often fondly referred to the United States as "a shining city upon a hill," a phrase that has its origin in the pages of Holy Writ.

From his statements and his writings, there is no question that Reagan believed in the Lord. Moreover, after the assassination attempt on Reagan's life by John Hinckley, Jr., the president believed he'd been spared for a special purpose.

He also believed the United States had a special purpose among nations. While others may have doubted, Reagan's belief in God's presence on our nation never wavered. This good man was confident God had established the United States as a beacon of freedom to the world.

If our country ever perished or lost its freedom, Reagan believed freedom for all mankind would be doomed as well.

On this day we celebrate Reagan's birth, may we always heed his admonition that we, as a people, should always strive to be on the Lord's side.

America's history is His story!

February 7

"There is no leveler like Christianity, but it levels by lifting all who receive it to the lofty table-land of a true character and of undying hope both for this world and the next." –Jonathan Edwards

While many among you might know that Jonathan Edwards was a great preacher of the Gospel, only a handful of you may know that Edwards was also the third president of Princeton University.

Whenever prominent educational establishments are named, Princeton is often mentioned near the top of the list. However, the Ivy League school that once called Edwards its president now scoffs at the Gospel he preached.

As an educator, Jonathan Edwards clearly placed great importance on education in the development of an individual. However, as a preacher of the Gospel, Edwards knew Christianity, not education, was the only effective means to lift a man to a higher moral plain.

As proof of Edwards' belief, one has only to look at the success of his own home. Eleven children were born to Jonathan and Sarah Edwards. Numbered among their descendants were a host of educators, missionaries, litigators, government officials, and one Vice President of the United States.

Edwards was correct; Christianity is indeed a leveler of men. It lifts them to be better educated, better family men, and better citizens.

America's history is His story!

February 8

"God Almighty does not throw dice." –Albert Einstein

The German-born scientist, credited with developing the theory of relativity, made it possible for the United States to unlock the mysteries of atomic energy.

Often recognized as one of the greatest minds of the twentieth century, Einstein knew the wonders of this universe didn't come along by chance.

Those who believe in man-made global climate change, requiring a man-made solution, cannot believe in the infinite perfection of an all-knowing Creator.

It is vanity of the highest order to think God needs our help in repairing the inherent "flaws" in His creation.

The Creator of this universe made no mistakes; nor was He caught off guard by the actions of man. And God flawlessly designed this earth to withstand whatever man-made disasters His creation would ultimately visit upon themselves.

In the beginning, our omniscient Creator designed this planet with remarkable, regenerative powers.

God Almighty does not throw dice. He isn't short-sighted. And God certainly isn't weak or forgetful.

Most of all, those in our country need to realize that God doesn't need our help to fix the errors He didn't make.

America's history is His story!

February 9

"As an eye-witness, I assert it to be a fact beyond contradiction that there is not an official, or any other person, from emperors, down to

the lowest coolies in China and Japan, who are not indebted every day to the work of our American missionaries." –George Eugene Belknap

This Navy Commodore and Rear Admiral recognized the fact that America has repeatedly been the nation responsible for taking the Gospel to a lost and dying world.

The "Lost Colony" of Roanoke is one of the great mysteries of our nation's history. When John White returned from Europe three years later, he found absolutely no trace of the 90 men, 17 women, and 11 children he left in Roanoke.

Just a few brief years later, English settlers established another colony at Jamestown. Unlike the colony at Roanoke, Jamestown not only survived; it thrived.

What was the difference in the two colonies? Why did Jamestown survive, but Roanoke was forever lost to history?

The Roanoke colony was strictly an economic enterprise. Its sole purpose was to make a profit for its financiers.

However, Jamestown was not only an economic enterprise; it was also an evangelistic mission. Its declared purpose was to share the Gospel with the Natives of the New World, in addition to turning a profit.

As we have learned from our country's history, the United States grew and thrived economically because its founding was truly based on Christian principles, religious freedom, and the desire to share the Gospel.

America's history is His story!

February 10

"Up to January, 1865, it was estimated that nearly 150,000 soldiers had been converted during the progress of the war, and it was believed that fully one-third of all the soldiers in the field were praying men, and

members of some branch of the Christian church. In the army of General Lee, while it lay on the upper Rappahannock, the revival flame swept through every corps, division, brigade, and regiment."

–William W. Bennett

During the Civil War, William Bennett was a chaplain in Robert E. Lee's Army of Northern Virginia.

Bennett later wrote about a great religious awakening, an event that took place in the Confederate ranks in the midst of this bloody carnage.

Despite our current-day habit of assigning only an evil purpose to the Confederate forces, many of these soldiers were devoted Christians, strongly opposed to the institution of slavery.

This brutal conflict often separated friends and loved ones. It destroyed families. It stained our countryside with blood and divided our Union.

Perhaps it was the Word of God, its message taking root in the hearts of those soldiers—North and South alike—that made it possible for a great nation to eventually heal the wounds of war.

And despite the assassination of its president, the United States would once again assume our lofty status as a country. In the wake of this conflict, which resulted in freedom for every citizen, of every skin color, God would raise up an even greater nation.

America's history is His story!

February 11

"I only regret I have but one life to give for my country." –Nathan Hale

These are the final recorded words of Nathan Hale, a spy for the Continental Army, hanged by the British during the American Revolution.

Pat Tillman was a professional football player, enjoying a bright and promising career with the Arizona Cardinals. However, in the aftermath of the attacks on the World Trade Center, Tillman's love of country caused him to give up the wealth, fame, and prominence of an NFL career to join the United States Army.

In 2004, this football star-turned-Army Ranger not only sacrificed a bright NFL career; Tillman also sacrificed his life in the preservation of freedom, when he was killed in the rugged terrain of Afghanistan.

Dwelling in Heaven with the Father, the Son of God had all the wealth of the world at his disposal. However, His great love for a lost and dying world caused the Lord to give up the glories of Heaven.

Jesus came to this earth and was sacrificed on the cross. He willingly gave His life so that all mankind might have freedom from sin.

The United States has been blessed by having an abundance of men, who were willing to give their lives to pay for our freedom. Our country was also blessed by having a Savior, who willingly gave His life to purchase our redemption.

America's history is His story!

February 12

"I have been driven many times upon my knees by the overwhelming conviction that I had nowhere else to go. My own wisdom, and that of all about me, seemed insufficient for that day." –Abraham Lincoln

America's History is His Story:

His likeness engraved on the side of Mount Rushmore, Abraham Lincoln didn't only cast a massive shadow from the side of a mountain; America's 16th president, born on this day in 1809, was also a giant among men.

Probably no president in our nation's history ever faced a more challenging set of circumstances than those confronted by President Abraham Lincoln.

Within two months of the day he was elected to lead our nation, and before his inauguration, seven states seceded from the Union.

As Commander-in-Chief, Lincoln was forced to make many difficult decisions, the likes of which hadn't been seen since George Washington was chosen to lead the Continental Army.

And despite the questions about his faith, Lincoln made no secret of his reliance on the Word of God and the remarkable power of prayer to guide his overwhelming decisions.

On this day we remember the birth and life of this great man, maybe we should also remember and emulate the Almighty source of Lincoln's strength.

A man always stands tallest when he is upon his knees.

America's history is His story!

February 13

"Who can doubt that God created us to be happy, and thereto made us to love one another." –Francis Marion

When discussing the history of the American Revolution, there is probably not a more colorful character than Francis Marion.

Often known as the "Swamp Fox, this general of the South Carolina militia was known for his swift and brutal attacks on British Regular troops. Then, just as quickly as he struck the enemy, his band of volunteers fled back into the swamps.

His troops, composed of black and white volunteers, received no salary. Marion's men often supplied their own food, horses, and armaments. Sometimes they looted the provisions of British loyalists and collaborators.

Marion's battle tactics, which were the forerunner of modern guerilla warfare, often struck fear in the hearts of British soldiers. Hated as much as he was feared by the Redcoats, all of their attempts to capture him proved to be fruitless.

Despite the criticism of Francis Marion by some modern historians, it must be pointed out that his militia's contributions to the Continental Army were critical to our ultimate victory over the British. Like all of those who carried the banner in the cause of liberty, the Swamp Fox deserves our gratitude.

America's history is His story!

February 14

"Let my neighbor once persuade himself that there is no God, and he will soon pick my pocket, and break not only my leg but my neck."
–William Linn

Elected Chaplain of the Congress in 1789, William Linn knew it was only the existence of God that prevented man from taking that which belongs to another. And if there is no God to Whom we must answer, then there is no morality. There is no truth. Moreover, there is no judgment for our actions.

America's History is His Story:

Our Founding Fathers believed in God. Therefore, they didn't believe one individual had the right to deny another individual that which he rightly earned.

It was one of the principles that led to the colonists' revolt. It was one of the charges listed by Thomas Jefferson in the Declaration of Independence.

Perhaps it's not a coincidence that the less our Washington politicians seem to acknowledge the existence of God, the greater their desire to pick the pockets of those they falsely claim to serve.

Once God has been eliminated from a person's mind, the less respect he has for the life and property of others.

Although God's existence is no longer recognized by many of those in Washington, our Founders' God still rules in the affairs of men. And that very same God is still watching and preparing judgment for all those who abuse his principles.

America's history is His story!

February 15

"The world about us, far more intricate than any watch, filled with checks and balances of a hundred varieties, marvelous beyond even the imagination of the most skilled scientific investigator, this beautiful and intricate creation, bears the signature of its Creator."
—Charles Milton Stine

Charles Stine, scientist and organic chemist, was the director of research for E.I. DuPont Company. Stine's vast knowledge of science made it impossible for him to believe the tortured explanations for evolution.

Increasingly in America, those who believe in creation are routinely belittled by politicians and the media. However, the true zealots are the ones who foolishly accept the principles of evolutionary theory.

Modern day science has been shamelessly compromised. Scientists and researchers have willingly bowed their knees at the idol of political ideology.

For proof of this point, one has only to look at the newspaper. Recently, e-mails were discovered and leaked to the press. These private communications showed how scientists altered the data in order to support their theories of man-made global warming.

Mr. Stine was certainly correct. Creation is a foundational truth of science. It's simply impossible for living things and heavenly bodies to spring from nothing.

I Corinthians 1:25 states: "The foolishness of God is wiser than men."

The greatest minds in human history formed this Republic. And almost without exception, these men believed in the Creator and relied upon His guidance.

Who are we to question their wisdom and the God they served?

America's history is His story!

February 16

"The sacredness of the Bible awes me, and I approach it with the same kind of reverential feeling that an ancient Hebrew might be supposed to feel who was about to touch the ark of God with unhallowed hands."
—William Cullen Bryant

America's History is His Story:

This famous American poet and long-time editor of the *New York Evening Post* stood in awe of Scripture. Bryant valued it. He reverenced it. He was influenced by it.

In these days, when we claim so many intellectual advancements, it would appear we are going backwards in our relationship to God's Word. We tamper with it. We impugn it. Increasingly, we refuse to follow its precepts.

And much like one of David's servants, Uzza, who was struck down for simply touching the Ark of the Covenant, we place our own lives and futures in jeopardy for treating Scripture lightly.

Contained within the pages of the King James Bible we will find some of the greatest literature ever penned by the hand of mortal men, inspired from on high.

For centuries, poets, artists, scientists, and true intellectuals gave the Bible a place of prominence in their life, work, and philosophy. Many great paintings, sculptures, and famous works of literature owe their existence to the stories contained within the pages of Holy Writ.

The Word of God, which was often read, studied, and practiced by our country's Framers isn't a collection of fables; this Sacred Book is a window to our past. It is the truth for today and a marvelous insight into our future.

America's history is His story!

February 17

"I loved all mankind, slaveholder not excepted, though I abhorred slavery more than ever, I saw the world in a new light. I gathered scattered pages of the Bible from the filthy street gutters, and washed and dried them, that in moments of leisure I might get a word or two of wisdom from them." –Frederick Douglass

In the 1800s, Frederick Douglas was a great abolitionist, who successfully escaped the bonds of slavery. Once free of those shackles, the elimination of slavery became the predominant cause of his life.

Douglas not only penned several versions of his autobiography, which outlined his experiences as a slave, he was also known as an outstanding orator. He often traveled around this country and across the seas, trying to further the cause of liberty for people of every race.

With great joy and passion, Douglas specifically wrote about his escape from slavery and his initial arrival in New York City.

However, the preceding words by Douglas describe another time he was freed from bondage, this time from the shackles of sin. Upon his conversion, Frederick Douglas stated that the Word of God had taught him to love all mankind.

Douglas' conversion was quite a transformation of heart for someone who had been so wronged in this life.

In fact, the Word of God didn't only transform the heart of Frederick Douglas; it also transformed a nation, the principles of Scripture inspiring America to forever end the practice of slavery.

America's history is His story!

February 18

"It is impossible to mentally or socially enslave a Bible-reading people." –Horace Greeley

Horace Greeley was a famous American newspaperman, probably best known for the phrase, "Go West, young man!" One of the founding members of the Republican Party, his pen often flamed in the abolitionist cause.

Although Mr. Greeley shared the opinion of many in America that education was the key to ending slavery, he also took it a step farther. Not only was education important, Greeley believed an intimate knowledge of Scripture would lift a man—any man—from his impoverished state.

During World War II, a young naval mechanic was captured by the Japanese on the island of Corregidor. Eventually taken by his captors to Yokohama, Dorsey Merrells was forced to work in the shipbuilding trade.

Provided with little food or water, the prisoner would pick up whatever scraps fell in the street. Dorsey once traded the cigarette butts he collected for a copy of the Bible.

Dorsey later said, "It was the greatest trade I ever made in my life."

Although he endured captivity for quite some time thereafter, Merrells proved the truth in Mr. Greeley's statement. The Word of God allowed this young American naval man, physically enslaved in a foreign land, to experience a freedom of the mind and soul.

"I have nothing at all against the Japanese," he said. "The Lord took all of that hatred and bitterness and it's gone. God got ahold of me there and I'm thankful."

America's history is His story!

February 19

"The secret of my success is that at an early age, I discovered I was not God." –Oliver Wendell Holmes

Oliver Wendell Holmes, outstanding jurist and editor, served in the Union Army during the Civil War. Appointed by President Theodore

Roosevelt, Holmes would judge for 30 years on the United States Supreme Court.

Increasingly, many of those in the judiciary fail to realize that which Holmes learned as a young man, that they are not God. These jurists and judges often fail to acknowledge that they, too, must stand before the Almighty Judge of the Universe.

God established government upon this earth. The power to execute judgment is a sacred trust. In fact, Moses chose wise men, known among the tribes, to help him judge the people. Moses personally charged them that they should judge fairly, not favoring the rich over the poor.

Since our founding, judges have been bestowed with a certain moral authority. Traditionally, our earliest Supreme Court justices didn't seek to use their position to establish policies that were in opposition to God's Word.

The Constitution should never be misused as a means to play God. Those who are entrusted with establishing justice must realize their responsibility to zealously defend the weak, the innocent, the helpless, and the voiceless, as well as to punish the guilty.

May our judiciary always remember the words of Deuteronomy: "For the judgment is God's."

America's history is His story!

February 20

"Providence has given to our people the choice of their rulers, and it is the duty, as well as the privilege and interest of our Christian nation to select and prefer Christians for their rulers." –John Jay

America's History is His Story:

John Jay was one of our Founding Fathers and the first Chief Justice of the United States Supreme Court.

America was founded as a Christian nation. Its heritage, its laws, and its foundational truths were taken directly from the pages of God's Word.

Although the toxins of political correctness and revisionist history have contaminated the waters of truth, one fact cannot be legitimately refuted: ours is a Christian nation.

Those who founded our Republic knew it would take Christian leadership to keep our nation's liberty strong and vibrant. A nation founded on freedom, morality, and individual responsibility is particularly vulnerable to oppressors who would misuse those principles for their own selfish objectives.

That is why John Jay and others like him knew it was imperative that our rulers, those who steer our nation's course, should be men of faith or people of high moral character.

In order to keep our country strong, it is essential we hold our leaders to a higher moral standard. Those who expect us to bow before their leadership must be equally willing to bow their knee before the Lord. For it is only in bringing ourselves low, will we return our nation to its former greatness.

America's history is His story!

February 21

"Here the Royal army was again stopped by a sudden rise of the waters, which had only just fallen (almost miraculously) to let the enemy over, who could not else eluded Lord Cornwallis' grasp, so close was he upon their rear." –Gen. Henry Clinton

Any careful study of America's War for Independence will leave you convinced that nothing short of the hand of God played a prominent role in our victory over King George. Numerous times during the Revolution, the forces of nature strangely seemed to work in America's favor.

On one such occasion, General Nathaniel Greene was forced to lead the retreat of his overwhelmingly-outnumbered Continental forces. Desperately racing across North Carolina with the British troops in close pursuit, the colonials' retreat to Virginia was repeatedly aided by the changing conditions of the rivers they encountered.

Three times, the British were slowed by the unpredictable waters of the Catawba, Yadkin, and Dan Rivers.

As Henry Clinton, the British Commander-in-Chief, observed, the waters of the Dan River appeared to fall, in order to aid the Colonials' escape. He also stated that the swollen, turbulent waters hindered British General Cornwallis from pursuing the fleeing, poorly equipped soldiers of General Greene.

The loss of Greene's forces would have doomed General Washington's Continental Army and their hopes for America's victory. The circumstances can only lead one to conclude that the Lord intervened for America and gave birth to our freedom.

America's history is His story!

February 22

"Without making ostentatious professions of religion, he was a sincere believer in the Christian faith, and a truly devout man." –John Marshall

These words were spoken about President George Washington by United States Chief Justice John Marshall. As someone who served with the general during those dark days at Valley Forge, Marshall probably knew our first president better than most men.

In the annals of American history, George Washington is quite possibly the greatest man our nation ever produced.

Moreover, Washington's life is a uniquely American story.

General Washington served our nation in the French and Indian War. He led the Continental Army to victory over the British. He presided over our nation's Constitutional Convention. Then, Washington became our country's first president.

Although Washington achieved great wealth, he was extremely generous in his personal dealings. While he was a man of great Christian faith, he worked to assure that all men could practice their own religion freely. And despite the fact he was elevated to great power, Washington chose to walk away from the presidency after only two terms.

George Washington was born on this day in 1732. On this day we recognize his birth, perhaps it would be wise for our nation to reaffirm those truths to which our first president clearly devoted his life.

America's history is His story!

February 23

"I sought for the key to the greatness and genius of America in her harbors, in her fertile fields and boundless forests; in her rich mines and vast world commerce; in her public school system and institutions of learning. I sought for it in her democratic Congress and in her matchless Constitution. Not until I went into the churches of America and heard her pulpits flame with righteousness did I understand the secret of her genius and power. America is great because America is

good, and if America ceases to be good, America will cease to be great." –Alexis de Tocqueville

In 1831, Alex de Tocqueville, a Frenchman, came to America to study our nation. As a result of his study, de Tocqueville wrote *Democracy in America*, which attempted to explain America's faith and society.

Although he wasn't born in America, de Tocqueville correctly determined the source of America's greatness.

Unfortunately, many of those in America have come to believe that America's greatness rests in the benevolence of a powerful government. However, the government is only great when it recognizes and acknowledges its Godly heritage.

As de Tocqueville stated, America's churches and our pulpits contain the answers to the challenges that currently inflict us as a nation. Our problems are not secular; they are spiritual. Moreover, they do not cry out for governmental solutions.

If America is once again to assume its place as the world's leader, then its citizens must once again acknowledge their dependence on Almighty God.

America's history is His story!

February 24

"It is a great comfort to trust God, even if His providence is unfavorable. Prayer steadies one, when he is walking in slippery places, even if things asked for are not given." –President Benjamin Harrison

America's History is His Story:

The preceding words were spoken by Benjamin Harrison, our 23rd president, the beneficiary of an extraordinary inheritance of honor and freedom.

His great-grandfather, also named Benjamin Harrison, was a signer of the Declaration of Independence, one of the 56 brave men who boldly pledged "our lives, our fortunes and our sacred honor."

As one of the signers, the great-grandfather of our 23rd president risked a British hangman's noose. Perhaps it was his willingness to sacrifice everything in the noble cause of liberty that allowed him to produce such a remarkable group of offspring.

In addition to his great-grandson and presidential namesake, the Declaration's signer also fathered a son, William Henry Harrison, the 9th president of the United States. By signing the Declaration, the great-grandfather risked everything to give birth to a great nation. His great-grandson, as a soldier in the Union army, risked everything to restore that same nation.

Proverbs 13:22 says, "A good man leaveth an inheritance to his children's children."

As president of the United States, Benjamin Harrison would lead the nation, a country created by the actions of Benjamin Harrison, his great-grandfather.

America's history is His story!

February 25

"Sir, we are not weak, if we make a proper use of the means which the God of nature hath placed in our power. Three millions of people, armed in the Holy cause of liberty, and in such a country as that which we possess, are invincible by any force which our enemy can send against us." –Patrick Henry

Of all our Founding Fathers, more than anyone else, it could be said that Patrick Henry was truly the spark that lighted liberty's torch.

Henry's flaming oratory in St. John's Church, where he gave his most famous speech, inspired everyone who heard it.

Not only were Patrick Henry's words a source of inspiration, they were also prophetic. The Continental Army did make good use of the means the God of nature had placed in their hands.

The British troops were used to fighting their battles in long lines and precise formations. Moreover, their training and tactics made them the most highly-trained and formidable army in the world.

However, the Continental Army often didn't fight the British on their own terms. As a veteran of the French and Indian War, General Washington learned some tactics and lessons from the Indians. It was there he also learned the British patterns of warfare.

Although his army actually won few battles, Washington always retreated to fight again another day. Using the terrain, the general sometimes employed guerilla tactics against the British. More importantly, Washington never allowed his army to be captured.

Patrick Henry was right. The people of America, armed in the Holy cause of liberty, were truly invincible by any force the enemy could send against them.

America's history is His story!

February 26

"The Christian religion is the religion of our country. From it are derived our prevalent notions of the character of God, the great moral governor of the universe. On its doctrines are founded the peculiarities of our free institutions." –William McGuffey

America's History is His Story:

In 1836, McGuffey authored and published the first edition of *McGuffey's Reader*, a textbook used in schoolhouses all across America. The books were filled with all manner of moral principles, character lessons, and religious teachings.

Millions of schoolchildren learned to read and write from his texts. Since their first publication, over 100 million copies of the books have been sold.

Prior to McGuffey's books, schoolchildren were often instructed from the pages of Scripture. In fact, some of our early Founders were critical of any textbook that took the traditional place of the Word of God in childhood education.

For almost 43 years, there was little distinguishable change in McGuffey's books. Sadly, the 1879 editions of *McGuffey's Readers* were scrubbed of much of their openly religious content. Without William McGuffey's approval or consent, the books that bore his name were changed to gain a much more secular appeal.

Perhaps it's no coincidence that the more any remaining traces of religion have been purged from our public schools, the more our children's education has suffered and test scores have fallen.

A gifted educator, William McGuffey understood the critical link between education and the Word of God.

America's history is His story!

February 27

"There are myriads of people on this earth who believe in the divinity of Christ, people of the finest minds and the greatest learning. It is not a mark of intelligence to question divine things." –Edward Bok

Born in the Netherlands, Edward Bok, the Pulitzer-prize winning author, was the editor of the *Ladies' Home Journal*.

For the first 150 years of this country's history, it was rare to find anyone who questioned the origins of this earth or the existence of a Divine Creator. It was even rarer still to find someone of great intelligence who rejected the Genesis account of our beginnings.

However, as education gave way to philosophy and intelligence was replaced by vanity, it became acceptable to challenge the truth contained in Scripture.

Today, it is nearly a hallmark of faith that all life evolved from some lower form of being. Yet even the most zealous disciple of evolutionary theory cannot adequately explain where that first insignificant form of life had its origin.

Whenever confronted with this question, the so-called intellectual is soon reduced to babbling like a toddler, proving the finite mind of man simply isn't capable of explaining away the Divine.

The United States was formed by men of faith. Its liberty was preserved by numerous acts of faith. And if our nation falls, it will be because we rejected that faith.

America's history is His story!

February 28

"It is the duty of the clergy to accommodate their discourses to the times, to preach against such sins as are most prevalent, and recommend such virtues as are most wanted." –John Adams

Like many of the Founding Fathers, John Adams was a man of deep and abiding faith. In his letters to his wife, it's not uncommon for

Adams, who traveled much as an ambassador, to comment on the church he just attended or the sermon he heard there.

Oftentimes, American pastors are criticized for railing against what they recognize as the predominant sins of the times. Those in the government are attempting to silence their message by the threat of "hate crimes" legislation.

This has already happened in Canada, where it is illegal, for instance, to preach against the sin of sodomy. The pastor can be fined or face serious jail time for violating these ordinances. Understandably, it's had a chilling effect on the free exercise of religion in the land to our north.

President John Adams knew our nation's liberty would soon be snuffed out if our pastors and pulpits were in any way silenced.

The First Amendment made it very clear that government shouldn't intrude on the church, since the Constitution emphatically stated, "Congress shall make no law."

America will only remain free as long as its churches are not restricted from declaring the Gospel freely.

America's history is His story!

February 29

"Israel is a light unto the world. The hearts and history of our people are woven together. The Land of Israel is an ancient home, a sacred place of worship, and a solemn promise to the Jewish people that we will never again repeat history's darkest hour."

–President Donald Trump

Presidents Bill Clinton, George W. Bush, and Barack Obama all issued campaign promises to Israel that they would move our American embassy from Tel Aviv to Jerusalem. While the others merely paid lip service to those promises, President Trump became the first candidate to actually keep the pledge he made to Israel.

During his administration, Trump did much more for the people of Israel than simply moving our embassy. Trump also brokered several historic peace accords between Israel and their Arab neighbors, accomplishments that nobody in the media or Trump's recent presidential predecessors ever thought possible.

Israeli Prime Minister Benjamin Netanyahu even said, "I want to thank President Trump for all you have done and are doing for peace. You've made a real difference, achieving one breakthrough after another, bringing the UAE, Bahrain, Morocco, and Sudan into the circle of peace."

In the pages of Holy Writ, we learn that God places his blessing upon those nations that bless Israel. President Trump's administration made sure our nation was a strong and trusted ally. Let each one of us pray that America never again forsakes the people of Israel and that they never again face the evils of another Holocaust.

America's history is His story!

March 1

"I have lived, sir, a long time, and the longer I live, the more convincing proofs I see of this truth, that God governs in the affairs of men. If a sparrow cannot fall without his notice, can a nation rise without his aid?" –Benjamin Franklin

Ben Franklin was 82-years old when he spoke these words to the members of the original Constitutional Convention.

America's History is His Story:

Over and over again, the assembled body would come to an impasse. Based on the arguments and disputes that occurred, the wise, old gentleman realized that, perhaps they should turn to the Lord for daily guidance.

It was then the statesman and inventor wisely rose from his chair to speak those profound words.

Following his admonition, the creators of our wondrous Constitution followed Mr. Franklin's advice and began each day with prayer. The foundational document that they created, the document that defines our freedoms, and the document that still guides us today, the United States Constitution, is the product of prayer and Divine guidance.

It cannot be disputed the United States was founded on Judeo-Christian principles. It is tragic that our country has increasingly turned its back on them.

America's history is His story!

March 2

"Do not pray for easy lives. Pray to be stronger men! Do not pray for tasks equal to your powers. Pray for powers equal to your tasks."
–Phillip Brooks

A graduate of Harvard, Phillip Brooks was a prominent American writer and speaker. He is perhaps best known for writing the beloved Christmas song, *O Little Town of Bethlehem.*

From our earliest beginnings as a nation, Americans have labored to make an easier life for themselves and their loved ones. They often succeeded at these tasks because they were seldom afraid of confronting hardship.

Migrating to this country in tiny, wooden ships wasn't an easy means of travel. Declaring war against King George certainly wasn't a task for the weak of heart. And charging the hostile, machine gun fire on Omaha Beach wasn't a mission for the timid.

But America succeeded at them all.

Speaking at Rice University in 1962, President John F. Kennedy said, "We choose to go to the moon in this decade and do the other things, not because they are easy, but because they are hard."

No matter what the obstacle has been, Americans have always proven they were up to the challenge. Moreover, it should never be doubted that our willingness to confront hardships has been a product of our faith.

America's history is His story!

March 3

"That grand old Book of God still stands; and this old earth, the more its leaves are turned over and pondered, the more it will sustain and illustrate the Sacred Word." –James Dwight Dana

James Dana was a professor at Harvard and a noted geologist, who authored several books on the subject.

The more you study the comments made by this country's greatest professors, scientists, educators, authors, and religious leaders, the more convinced you become that something caustic has tainted the well of public education.

Over and over again, these men spoke of the authority of Scripture and the surety that we came into existence by the very breath of God.

Scientists used to be dedicated professionals, devoted only to using their minds in a search for the truth. Increasingly, their profession has now been compromised, to endorse any number of preconceived notions their evidence clearly doesn't support. And those who dare to challenge the dogma of the misinformed are now regarded as idiots or extremists.

Mr. Dana's extensive study of mineralogy and geology, and the books he authored, gave us all a much greater insight into the subject. Yet nothing yielded by his study and research challenged God's Divine account of creation. In fact, this editor-in-chief of *The American Journal of Science* believed further scientific discovery would only confirm the accuracy of Scripture.

As Dana so accurately noted, "That grand old Book of God still stands."

America's history is His story!

March 4

"There is nothing so absurd but if you repeat it often enough people will believe it." –William James

William James was an American philosopher and psychologist, who wrote a book called *The Meaning of Truth*. However, his development of the theory of pragmatism makes it abundantly clear he never truly discovered the meaning of anything meaningful.

James' quote also brings to mind the words of Joseph Goebbels, who was the propaganda minister of Hitler's Third Reich.

Goebbels said, "If you tell a lie big enough and keep repeating it, people will eventually come to believe it. The lie can be maintained only for such time as the State can shield people from the political, economic, and/or military consequences of the lie."

The big lie—it was this philosophy that led Hitler's Germany to blindly allow the slaughter of over six million Jews.

Unfortunately, in the past century, Americans have also allowed themselves to embrace other big lies, such as the theory of evolution, the belief in man-made climate change, a woman's "right" to choose, and the idea that government is justified in taking from one individual and giving those proceeds to another.

Goebbels also stated that "the truth is the greatest enemy of the State."

In John 8:32, the Lord told us that "the truth shall make you free."

By embracing truth, America won its freedom from the British Crown. And by rejecting the Big Lie, America stopped Hitler's slaughter of the Jewish people.

America's history is His story!

March 5

"The principles of the Bible are the groundwork of human freedom."
–Horace Greeley

Before times of war and great turmoil in America, God has often blessed our nation with a number of great revivals. These sweeping, spiritual transformations started in our churches and spread to our homes and communities like a wildfire.

The First Great Awakening occurred in the early to mid 1700s. Led by preachers such as John Wesley, George Whitefield, and Jonathan Edwards, this revival prepared the Colonists for the suffering and sacrifices of the American Revolution. It also gave us the spiritual courage to throw off the shackles of King George.

Approximately one hundred years later, America experienced the Second Great Awakening. This spiritual renewal was started by ministers such as Peter Cartwright, James Brainerd Taylor, and Charles G. Finney.

Not only did it sustain and repair our nation from the darkest days of the Civil War, it also acted as a catalyst to end the practice of slavery in America.

The Third Great Awakening covered approximately 30 years, from the late 1900s into the early part of the 20th Century. Led by men such as Dwight Moody and Billy Sunday, America would acquire the moral fortitude to face the hardships of World War I, the Great Depression, and World War II.

Before times of great national crisis, God has often brought Americans to bended knee, so that the hardships they faced wouldn't bring them to their knees.

America's history is His story!

March 6

"Young man, if God gives me four years more to rule this country, I believe it will become what it ought to be, what its Divine Author intended it to be, no longer one vast plantation for breeding human beings for the purpose of lust and bondage. But it will become a new Valley of Jehoshaphat, where all the nations of the earth will assemble together under one flag, worshipping a common God, and they will celebrate the resurrection of human freedom." –Abraham Lincoln

Not long after his re-election, President Lincoln spoke these words to a young state senator. However, an assassin's bullet would keep the president from his efforts to fully heal the nation from slavery, secession, and the Civil War.

Although there are often questions about Lincoln's faith, the evidence would lead one to believe that a nation at war drove the president to find peace with the Savior. Moreover, the death of his son, Willy, also brought him closer to the Lord.

Abraham Lincoln's bold and visionary speech is not language of an atheist. His words are certainly not the reflections of an agnostic. Nor are they the declaration of a man who is not intimately acquainted with the Bible.

From his writings, we can see Lincoln's pen was often immersed in the ink of Holy Scripture. His tongue was endued with the words of the Psalmist and Saint Matthew. Moreover, the president obviously followed the admonition of Saint Paul to the Philippians: "Let this mind be in you, which was also in Christ Jesus."

In words and in actions, Abraham Lincoln tried to follow the truths of Scripture. And like Moses led the children of Israel, the president also longed to bring America out of the wilderness.

America's history is his story!

March 7

"The church must take right ground in regards to politics. The time has come for Christians to vote for honest men, and take consistent ground in politics or the Lord will curse them." –Charles G. Finney

Charles G. Finney was a preacher and an evangelist, a man who played a significant role in America's Second Great Awakening.

America's History is His Story:

It wasn't uncommon in our nation's history for men to be both preachers and educators, to go from the church house to the school house and from the pulpit to the blackboard.

The more you study American history, the more obvious it becomes our American educational system once did something that is largely unheard of now, by embracing religious instructors.

Charles Finney wasn't only one of the most dynamic preachers in our nation's history; he was also one of the presidents of Ohio's Oberlin College.

Finney was also a pioneer, directing the institution to award the first college degrees in America to women and blacks. Moreover, under his leadership, Oberlin took an active role in the Underground Railroad.

Thanks to the contributions of our nation's preachers, Americans have enjoyed greater literacy and more freedom. Preachers once took the lead in politics and America is certainly a better country for their involvement.

America's history is His story!

March 8

"Peace is the goal of my life. I'd rather have lasting peace in the world than be president. I wish for peace, I work for peace, and I pray for peace continually." –Harry S. Truman

President Harry Truman was both a soldier and a statesman.

As the only American president to have experienced combat in World War I, the former artillery officer was intimately acquainted with death on the battlefield. Perhaps his experiences in warfare are what gave Truman his great desire for peace.

Following the death of President Franklin Roosevelt, Vice President Truman was given the oath of office as president. Not long after, he was first briefed on the Manhattan Project, involving the development and testing of the atomic bomb.

Modern day writers and historians are often critical of Truman's decision to drop the atomic bomb on Hiroshima and Nagasaki. Some of them might even suggest that Truman's decision to bomb Japan was in conflict with his stated desire for peace.

However, nobody can ever question the fact that those two atomic weapons led to the Japanese surrender in World War II.

In the days leading up to the bombings, American military personnel were preparing for a massive invasion of Japan. And had those plans ever been implemented, millions of Americans and Japanese would have been killed in the invasion.

Truman's fateful decision to drop the bomb ended the war; it saved lives. It also initiated a long and lasting peace with the people of Japan.

America's history is His story!

March 9

"The hand of Providence has been so conspicuous in all this that he must be worse than an infidel that lacks faith, and more than wicked that has not gratitude to acknowledge his obligations."
–George Washington

The preceding words were a communication that General Washington sent to Thomas Nelson in the midst of the Revolutionary War.

Washington was acknowledging the goodness of the Lord, for the many blessings God sent their way in their struggles against the British army.

At the time of this writing, Washington's troops had survived the brutal winter at Valley Forge. His men had successfully crossed the Delaware River and defeated the Hessians on Christmas day. Moreover, the nation of France had agreed to help the Colonists in their war with Britain.

Without these things, General Washington knew they would have been defeated. He was also wise enough to know the odds had consistently been against them, ever since Jefferson penned the Declaration. Only the hand of God sustained them.

Washington's habits of prayer and reliance on God are well documented. So was his gratitude for the blessings bestowed upon all those placed under Washington's leadership, as a landowner, as a general, and as America's first president.

America's history is his story!

March 10

"God grants liberty only to those who love it, and are always ready to guard and defend it." –Daniel Webster

As the battles continued to rage on the island of Iwo Jima, a Marine commander asked for a volunteer to take out several armed, Japanese pillboxes.

Stepping forward was a young Marine, named Hershel Woodrow Williams, volunteering for what he expected to be a suicide mission.

The Marine commander ordered four other Marines to arm themselves with Browning Automatic Rifles, in order to give some covering fire for young "Woody" Williams.

Strapping a 72-pound flame thrower to his tiny 5'6" frame, Williams also grabbed a 12-pound pole charge. These would be his only weapons against the determined Japanese soldiers, who would rather die than surrender.

Repeatedly braving hostile gunfire, and sometimes crawling on his hands and knees, Williams made a number of attacks on the Japanese positions. And approximately four hours later, the guns from the Japanese pillboxes had been silenced.

Unlike two of the Marine rifle men who had been ordered to cover him, Woody Williams survived the mission.

For his gallantry in battle, this young West Virginia Marine was awarded our nation's highest military citation, the Congressional Medal of Honor.

In times of crisis, America always produced brave souls in the cause of freedom.

America's history is His story!

March 11

"Whenever the pillars of Christianity shall be overthrown, our present republican forms of government, and all the blessing which flow from them, must fall with them." –Jedediah Morse

Trained for the ministry at Yale, Jedediah Morse was the father of Samuel Morse, the inventor of the Morse Code. However, Jedediah Morse also made his own mark on our country, in the field of education.

Morse realized there was a need for students in our country to know their geography. To meet that need, he authored the book *Geography Made Easy* in 1784. He later published other textbooks on the subject that were well-received.

With our new country beginning to take shape, Jedediah Morse, the educator, believed it was important to know the places from whence we came. The pastor in him also thought it was essential for us to know where we were going, on this earth as well as in the world to come.

To that end, Morse founded the *New England Tract Society* and *The American Bible Society*.

Often referred to as the "Father of American Geography," Morse knew our nation was built on the foundation of Christian principles.

The United States was founded on them. It thrived on them. It cannot survive without them.

America's history is His story!

March 12

"Only a virtuous people are capable of freedom. As nations become corrupt and vicious, they have more need of masters."

–Benjamin Franklin

When the great writer and inventor spoke these words, Franklin knew that virtue was indeed a rare quality in people and nations.

Virtuous people are not routinely enslaved by bad habits and poor choices. They are people who obey the law. They do the right things, even when nobody is around to witness their actions.

As any parent can tell you, a well-behaved child requires less supervision and discipline than an unruly child.

The same principles are equally true in respect to nations.

Virtuous people don't spend the majority of their time focused on their rights and their freedoms. Instead, the virtuous ones direct their attention to their responsibilities.

Law-abiding citizens don't require a lot of governmental policing. They aren't engaged in thefts or insurrection. And they aren't trying to kill their fellow man.

When our country was young, its citizens were a people of great religious fervor. Therefore, these people of high moral character longed to throw off the shackles of government intervention and interference.

Over two hundred years later, a seemingly-less virtuous people continually cry out for much more governmental oversight and assistance, forging their own bonds.

Virtue has always been the key that unlocks America's freedom.

America's history is His story!

March 13

"A patriot without religion in my estimation is as great a paradox as an honest man without the fear of God. Is it possible that he whom no moral obligations bind, can have any real good will towards men?"
—Abigail Adams

Some of history's richest treasures are contained in the writings of Abigail Adams, the wife of John Adams, America's second president.

In them, we are able to peer through a window into America's past. We may learn of their hardships and trials. These writings also allow us to enter into the minds of those engaged in this great struggle for freedom. We also learn about the sentiments that passed between this remarkable woman of the times and those she adored.

It's not surprising that Abigail couldn't picture a patriot without religion, because she certainly never saw an absence of those qualities in her own husband.

From his own words and writings, it is obvious that John Adams was both a patriot and a man of great faith.

Abigail's husband was also a man of deep principle.

Following the Boston Massacre, John Adams, believing so strongly in a person's right to a good defense, and at the risk of his reputation, agreed to defend several of the British soldiers involved in the killing.

Only a Christian nation like the United States could have produced men and women such as John and Abigail Adams

America's history is His story!

March 14

"I am glad to see so many of you out to hear preaching this Sabbath morning, and I would to God, that all the men of my command were true followers of Christ Jesus, the Lord. Soldiers, allow me to express, with your chaplain, the sincere desire of my heart, that we may meet at the right hand of the Great Judge in that day, which he has described to us." –Oliver Otis Howard

During the Civil War, General Oliver Howard was a Union officer. He was also the Superintendent of West Point.

After the war, the general founded Howard University as a place for former slaves to receive an education.

Throughout the wars in which America's been involved, there has always been a great number of its leaders who called upon God for guidance in their personal lives. Perhaps we should not find it strange that dynamic leaders of men are often themselves dedicated followers of the Lord.

Oliver Howard not only committed his life to freeing the slaves in the war; he also dedicated himself to preparing them for their new-found freedom, in the future lives they would choose to lead.

Without an education, these liberated slaves would find it extremely difficult to find a job or to make a living. The university that bears Howard's name helped to prepare them for a future without bondage.

General Howard is just one of the many men of faith, who loyally served his country in time of war and paved the way for others in time of peace.

America's history is His story!

March 15

"If the power of the Gospel is not felt throughout the length and breadth of the land, anarchy and misrule, degradation and misery, corruption and darkness will reign without mitigation or end."
–Daniel Webster

Whenever they are asked about the conditions of their country, Americans often criticize the current state of our nation.

Many of them blame the politicians in Washington. Others blame society and the deterioration of the family. Some blame the churches.

Maybe it can best be illustrated this way: Have you ever started to make a statement to a person in another room and quickly forgotten what you were going to say? It's happened to all of us.

However, you will often recall the thought if you immediately return to the place you were standing when the idea first came to your mind.

When it comes to this country, Americans instinctively realize that something is missing. They know things have changed, but they can't seem to put their finger on the cause of the transformation.

Perhaps if they will only return to the place where they first stood when the idea came to them, maybe they can remember what they've lost and forgotten.

America's History is His Story:

Our ideas about America came to us from a place and time when we once valued the Gospel. If we return to that place, maybe we can recall those ideals and actually recapture them. Perhaps we can restore the United States to the country we knew, if we only go back to where we lost ourselves.

America's history is His story!

March 16

"Men who see not God in our history have surely lost sight of the fact that, from the landing of the Mayflower to this hour, the great men whose names are indissolubly associated with the colonization, rise, and progress of the Republic have borne testimony to the vital truths of Christianity." –Henry Wilson

Wilson, who was both a United States Senator and Vice President of the United States under President Ulysses S. Grant, recognized that Christianity was the cornerstone of our country's ascendency.

Every American is a product of our godly American heritage. Despite the fact our history is replete with references to our Christian origins, there are still those who seek to deny that irrefutable truth.

Every day, these agnostics of truth have been remarkably blessed. They've gazed upon the resplendent orchard of liberty, which was planted by the seeds of faith. They have picked the fruits. They have tasted its sweetness. However, they apparently wish for nothing more than to set the orchard afire.

It is disturbing that those who have grown strong from the nourishment of this harvest seek to keep those delicacies from their offspring.

And although they routinely attempt to purge all references to the Lord and the Gospel from our history books, there are still those among us who have joined hands, forming a circle to protect the orchard.

America must defend it. We must cultivate it. And we must keep it strong and vibrant, so that our children and grandchildren can also taste of its fruits.

America's history is His story!

March 17

"God is going to reveal to us things He never revealed before if we put our hands in His. No books ever go into my laboratory. The thing I am to do and the way of doing it are revealed to me. I never have to grope for methods. The method is revealed to me the moment I am inspired to create something new. Without God to draw aside the curtain I would be helpless." –George Washington Carver

Born into slavery before its abolishment, George Washington Carver was an outstanding black scientist and inventor.

Carver is probably best known for his experiments into the usages of the peanut, to which he discovered hundreds. He is also credited with discovering dozens of usages for pecans, soybeans, and sweet potatoes.

It is clear that Carver was devoted to his work and his faith.

In these days, when scientists often scoff at the existence of God, it is refreshing to see a man who accomplished so much, by turning to the Lord for guidance.

Perhaps it is no coincidence that the name of George Washington Carver is known by school children across the nation, while many of today's scientists are nameless. It is also quite likely that Carver's phenomenal success is directly the product of his reliance on God.

Maybe there is a lesson to be learned here, for the untold number of skeptics in the scientific community. This great American inventor gained his fame and success because he was wise enough to humble himself before the Great Creator.

America's history is His story!

March 18

"The Founding Fathers believed devoutly that there was a God and that the unalienable rights of man were rooted—not in the state, not the legislature, nor in any other human power—but in God alone."

–Thomas C. Clark

Thomas C. Clark was an Associate Justice on the United States Supreme Court, appointed by President Harry S. Truman.

From the days of the first Colonists to modern times, Americans such as Thomas Clark have realized that rights are a sacred gift. They are handed down to us from the benevolent hand of Almighty God.

Therefore, it would follow, if rights are granted to us by the government, then they can also be taken from us by the hand of men. However, if they are granted to us from the Lord, they are clearly eternal. Moreover, these unchanging rights are also preserved by the hand of God.

It is certainly reasonable to assume that God's anger may be kindled against those who seek to take away that which He alone has given. Perhaps the Lord may also choose to raise His hand of chastisement upon those individuals or nations who deny their citizens those most sacred rights.

If America wants to continue enjoying its status as the guarantor of individual rights, then it needs to reaffirm its knowledge of their Author.

America's history is His story!

March 19

"Just fifty years ago this fall, in a large city by the seashore, nearly a thousand miles from here, a lady, whose husband was dead, took her little boy by the hand, and led him to the Sabbath school. For thirty years afterwards he was a scholar or a teacher of the Sabbath school, and he has never forgotten those instructions of youth. The lady who took her little boy to that Sunday school is now in a happier land, but the boy is still living." –Schuyler Colfax

The man who told this story was Schuyler Colfax, a United States Congressman and Vice President for President Grant.

If you were to read the rest of Colfax's touching story, you would learn that the lady who took the boy to Sunday School was his own mother and the boy she led was Schuyler Colfax.

You would also learn that the Vice President followed her steps, and brought his little boy, along with his son's mother to that same place, in order that his own son might benefit from the Christian teaching that made him the man he eventually turned out to be.

Stories like this were often repeated in the first two hundred years of our nation's founding. America has clearly been blessed with a legacy of Christian families, men and women, fathers and mothers who lovingly raised their children according to the wise and unchanging dictates of Scripture.

The United States ultimately became a great nation because it was a product of godly homes and inspiring churches, which provided it citizens with a priceless legacy of Christian love and example.

America's history is His story!

March 20

"As a token of Jesus Christ our Lord, and in honor of the Christian faith." –Christopher Columbus

The preceding words were Christopher Columbus' reason for having his men to erect a huge wooden cross. The man we credit for the discovery of America, the New World, planted a cross at the site of each place they stepped upon shore.

In short, America's discovery began with the cross.

Perhaps it is no coincidence that Americans are understandably, undeniably, and unstoppably drawn to the cross of Jesus Christ. It unites us.

Somebody recently claimed that the cross is almost a part of our DNA, giving us an incessant need to plant a cross wherever we go.

Americans worship them as a symbol. We wear the cross upon our necks as jewelry. We erect them on our hillsides and along our highways, for all the world to see. We install them over the graves of our departed loved ones. We often look to the cross for inspiration in times of great national tragedy. And we place them in great rows, silently standing in formation, to honor the deaths of our military fallen.

When discoverers came to his strange New World, the first structure erected on American soil was the cross of Christ. Is it any wonder Americans place so much value on this precious Christian symbol?

The cross of Jesus Christ stands in honor over our country in much the same way the Stars and Stripes flutters in the winds over our homes.

America's history is His story!

March 21

"I have sworn upon the altar of God eternal hostility against every form of tyranny over the mind of man." –Thomas Jefferson

Despite the fact Jefferson might have been one of the least religious of the Founders, he was still intimately acquainted with the words of Scripture.

He was fully cognizant about the inherently sinful nature of man. Jefferson also understood that any form of government they succeeded in establishing would eventually be subject to corruption among its leadership.

After just having dissolved their relationship with the British monarchy, Jefferson feared the creation of another government, one that would become just as powerful and just as threatening to individual rights as the one General Washington's troops defeated.

As the author of the Declaration of Independence, this penman of liberty was a man who had every right to sit back and take great pride in what he accomplished. However, it would appear that our third president was never fully comfortable with the government to which they had given birth.

He had seen the Colonists' suffering at the hands of King George. And despite the surrender of the British, Jefferson never fully lost his mistrust for the power a large and intrusive government might inflict upon the public.

To his final breath, Jefferson stood guard as a watchman upon the wall of liberty.

America's history is His story!

America's History is His Story:

March 22

"We have grasped the mystery of the atom and rejected the Sermon on the Mount. The world has achieved brilliance without conscience. Ours is a world of nuclear giants and ethical infants." –Omar Bradley

General Bradley was one of the great generals of World War II. He was promoted to five-star general and was chosen as Chairman of the Joint Chiefs of Staff.

In his comments, we can see the concern General Bradley had with a world that had achieved so much in science but had no use for God's own Word.

At the time the general made this statement, the United States and the Soviet Union were bitter enemies, with nuclear arsenals that easily could have wiped out most of our major cities. Perhaps the only thing that kept Communist Russia at bay was the threat of their mutually assured destruction.

On the Sermon on the Mount, Jesus said, "Blessed are the peacemakers."

That is the major difference between the old Soviet empire and the United States. America had no real interest in world domination by force.

Although America is less than perfect, ours has traditionally been a nation that helped others in need. We liberated those in oppression. And our actions opposed the evil slaughter of six million Jews in Europe.

Despite the fact America has often gone to war, our country has been blessed, unlike the old Soviet Union, because it primarily desires to be a peacemaker.

In fact, when Apollo 11 landed on the moon, Neil Armstrong and Buzz Aldrin left behind a plaque there that read, "We came in peace for all mankind."

America's history is His story!

March 23

"Tyranny, like hell, is not easily conquered; yet we have this consolation with us, that the harder the conflict, the more glorious the triumph. What we obtain too cheaply, we esteem too lightly. Heaven knows how to put a price upon its goods, and it would be strange indeed if so celestial an article as freedom should not be highly rated."

–Thomas Paine

General George Washington ordered that the words you have just heard were to be read aloud to the Continental Army at Valley Forge.

The men who heard them were freezing in the snow. Many of them didn't have shoes to wear, their frostbitten feet often leaving a crimson path wherever the soles of their feet had walked. Their ranks had been decimated by hunger and disease.

Their coats and uniforms were inadequate for the bitter, freezing conditions. Washington's troops used whatever they could find to stop the icy winds from blowing through their meager shelters.

Perhaps we will never know what made these brave soldiers endure those hardships in the cause of liberty.

No doubt some of them did it for their family and friends. Some were merely defending the land of their birth. It is also quite likely, a portion of them were looking deep into the future and seeing those yet unborn.

Perhaps these men made these sacrifices for the generations to come. Maybe their freezing bodies were warmed by the torch of liberty they carried, a torch their sacrifices passed to each of us. Let us remember them, from our warm, comfortable homes, and sitting around our abundant dinner tables. Let us pause for a moment to give thanks.

America's history is His story!

March 24

"I remember my mother's prayers and they have always followed me. They have clung to me all my life." –Abraham Lincoln

As someone who benefitted from her prayers, President Abraham Lincoln recognized the true worth of a godly mother.

What manner of woman was Lincoln's mother, Nancy Hanks Lincoln?

According to Lincoln, his mother was "the illegitimate daughter of Lucy Hanks and a well-bred farmer or planter." He also claimed she was quite intelligent.

As a young woman, growing up in deep poverty, Lincoln's mother was an attractive barmaid in a tavern frequented by the South Carolina statesman, John C. Calhoun, who some have suggested fathered her illegitimate child, Abraham.

But no matter the president's origins, we know that Nancy came to know the Lord and loved her son very much. She read to Abraham from the Bible and taught him his letters. Nancy recited Scripture as she worked and gave him a sense of the beauty and power of the English language. His mother even took her son to a church that abhorred the practice of slavery.

While dying at 34-years old from "milk sickness," Nancy called young Abraham into her room and told him of her love. She died soon thereafter, leaving behind a frightened nine-year old, who couldn't imagine a world that didn't have mother in it.

Despite her faults, Nancy Lincoln truly loved her son, training him to be the fine, young man, who would eventually grow up to be an outstanding leader of a great nation.

America's history is his story!

March 25

"In the language of the Holy Writ, there is a time for all things. There is a time to preach and a time to fight." –John Peter Muhlenberg

John Muhlenberg followed in the footsteps of his godly father, Henry Muhlenberg, as a faithful minister of the Gospel.

As the early battles of the American Revolution were raging in the Colonies, John preached a fiery sermon in his church from the third chapter of Ecclesiastes.

After Muhlenberg closed his message with the words about a time to fight, he stepped out from behind the pulpit. Saying nothing further, the minister thrust off his clerical robes. Underneath them was the uniform of the Continental Army.

Muhlenberg urged the men in his congregation to join him in the fight for America's freedom. A number of the men stopped to embrace their wives and children, before following their pastor out of the church to enlist in the conflict.

During times of war, America's pastors have often taken the lead, but never more so than during the fight for American Independence.

America's History is His Story:

The Colonists saw the struggle with the British as a spiritual conflict, a holy mission for the Lord. They approached the war for Independence with much the same fervor they committed to their faith. And their noble actions gave birth to a nation.

America's history is His story!

March 26

"Blandishments will not fascinate us, nor will threats of a "halter" intimidate. For, under God, we are determined that wheresover, whensoever, or howsoever we shall be called to make our exit, we will die free men." –Josiah Quincy

A number of years ago, particularly during the midst of the Vietnam War, it was popular for college-aged, young people to say, "Better red than dead!"

The phrase was often used to express their opposition to the war in Southeast Asia. Some of them foolishly believed the ultimate triumph of Communism was a better fate than risking their lives in a war.

However, as many of those who have escaped from Communist countries have already told us, mass murders and genocide are often the fates of those forced to live under tyrannical governments.

Our Founding Fathers wisely realized this fact over two hundred years ago.

There are fates in this world that are ultimately worse than death. The loss of one's freedom is definitely one of them.

Like the brave men and women in uniform, who risk their lives on a daily basis to preserve our freedom, these brave, Revolutionary War patriots risked their lives to give birth to our freedom.

Like our military personnel, these men were willing to freely die in order that we might all freely live.

America's history is His story!

March 27

"Without religion we may possibly retain the freedom of savages, bears, and wolves, but not the freedom of New England. If our religion were gone, our state of society would perish with it, and nothing would be left." –Timothy Dwight

Like most of Yale's first presidents, Timothy Dwight was also a preacher of the Gospel, a calling for which the university apparently has little regard today.

Sixty years ago, William F. Buckley, who had recently graduated from the university, wrote a book called *God and Man at Yale*.

In his book, Buckley attacked his alma mater for its embrace of liberalism and its hostility to matters of faith.

The book was groundbreaking for its time. Moreover, the principles and points contained in Buckley's work are as pertinent now as the day they were first penned.

For several years, Yale Law School tried to ban military recruiters from their job fairs, because of the military's "don't ask, don't tell" policy on homosexuality in the armed services. In addition, the university allows self-proclaimed Communists and anarchists on their faculty. They are also actively seeking to link religion and ecology in their studies.

Unfortunately, Timothy Dwight wouldn't be welcomed to speak at Yale University Church today, because God's Word says nothing about ecological justice.

America's History is His Story:

Perhaps Dwight was absolutely correct; without religion, it will be hard to retain the freedom of New England.

America's history is His story!

March 28

"The Bible goes equally to the cottage of the peasant, and the palace of the king. It is woven into literature, and colors the talk of the street. The bark of the merchant cannot sail without it; and no ship of war goes to the conflict but it is there. It enters men's closets; directs their conduct, and mingles in all the grief and cheerfulness of life."
–Theodore Parker

Perhaps nothing has influenced our country more than the Word of God.

For many of the early settlers and colonists, it was their first textbook. It was their entertainment and enlightenment. It taught them to read; it influenced their philosophies. It permeated their writings. It instructed them in the beauty and simple eloquence of the English language.

The Bible was the basis for our laws and systems of justice. It was the inspiration for the American Revolution. The principles of Scripture ended the practice of slavery.

The Scriptures have been carried on horseback and by airplane, from Atlantic to Pacific, from one end of this continent to the other.

The New Testament, carried in the pocket of a soldier, has been known to stop the bullet which would have ended his life. Its concepts gave young men in uniform the spiritual peace and courage to charge into the hostile fire of the enemy. It granted peace to those who stood around the grave of a fallen brother-in-arms.

The Word of God troubles the agnostic; it angers the atheist. It beckons us to the Savior. It gives us the way to life eternal.

The Bible has been our greatest gift, giving our country both the foundation and the structure in which we live.

America's history is His story!

March 29

"But all of us—at home, at war, wherever we may be—are within the reach of God's love and power. We all can pray. We all should pray. We should ask the fulfillment of God's will. We should ask for courage, wisdom, for the quietness of soul which comes along to them who place their lives in His hands." –Harry S. Truman

For most of our nation's history, our presidents routinely acknowledged their need for prayer and their dependence on God.

Those revelations were not earth-shattering or ground breaking at the time. In truth, they were generally accepted by every American.

It only made sense that any man who wanted to lead the greatest nation in the world wouldn't be so vain as to think he couldn't benefit from the Supreme guidance of the Almighty.

It was rare for anyone to believe that a president's reliance on God's wisdom did anything to weaken his authority or to demean his office. If General Washington needed to bow his knee in the snows of Valley Forge, then it certainly wouldn't be out of line for a president to bow his knee in the warmth and comfort of the Oval Office.

If humble prayer before God, on the part of our leadership, will give our nation victory over the British, the Japanese, and the Third Reich, then it will certainly lead us out of the problems that confront us today.

America's history is His story!

March 30

"What do I think of the Bible? It is the infallible Word of God, a light erected all along the shores of time to warn against the rocks and breakers, and to show the only way to the harbor of eternal rest."
—William Strong

In the 1800s, William Strong was an Associate Justice of the United States Supreme Court, a body that once placed great significance on the truth of God's Word.

As you walk up the steps of the building that houses the Supreme Court, if you raised your eyes, you would see some figures carved near the top of the building. Moses holding the Ten Commandments is the centerpiece of those carvings.

In addition, you will also find Moses with the Ten Commandments in the Rotunda of Congress

In fact, there are few places you could go in Washington D.C. where you wouldn't be confronted with pictures and symbols of our religious heritage and the exalted place that Scripture holds in our halls of government.

Unfortunately, many of those in government, who live and work among these symbols every day, are doing their best to deny their existence. Moreover, these same people are actively seeking to abolish all mention of God from the public square.

However, as long as these buildings, monuments, and institutions continue to stand in Washington, then it will be impossible for Americans to dismiss the truths they contain in granite and marble, that America is indeed a Christian nation.

America's history is His story!

March 31

"Can the liberties of a nation be thought secure when we have removed their only firm basis, a conviction in the minds of the people that these liberties are the gift of God, that they are not to be violated but with His wrath? Indeed I tremble for my country when I reflect that God is just; that his justice cannot sleep forever." –Thomas Jefferson

Increasingly in America, it has become commonplace to place the word "justice" behind every cause or issue.

The term criminal justice has been diminished and all but eliminated, thanks to the arrival of such terms as economic and social justice. To these causes, they have now added the terms ecological and environmental justice.

However, the ones using these words rarely give much thought to the justice of God or His Divine retribution.

For much of our nation's history, justice didn't require someone to take something that belonged to someone else. Justice didn't mean that you denied others those things that rightfully belonged to them. And justice was also blind, meaning it was never affected by the appearance or economic condition of those involved.

Our Just and Powerful God allowed His own Son to be born in a stable. And not one time in Scripture did God ever say that the wealthy innkeeper should have been required to provide better accommodations for the Lord.

Thomas Jefferson knew that a Merciful God wouldn't always withhold his justice. But this great penman of liberty also knew that justice was to be found in the pages of Scripture, not in the minds and theories of unjust men.

America's history is His story!

April 1

"Before God we are all equally wise—and equally foolish."
–Albert Einstein

On this day, often known as *April Fools' Day*, many Americans will seek to entertain themselves by deceiving or pulling good-natured pranks on their friends.

Dr. Albert Einstein, one of the most brilliant men to have ever become an American citizen, realized that God is certainly not impressed by man's earthly knowledge. In fact, the most intelligent thing about Einstein might possibly have been his confident belief in a Divine Creator.

Many of those in the scientific community openly question the existence of God and the Scriptural account of creation. Moreover, these so-called academics routinely praise themselves and applaud each other for their "intelligence."

Romans 1:22 says, "Professing themselves to be wise, they became fools."

Perhaps the most offensive April Fools' jokes ever played in this country are those perpetrated on a daily basis by godless, academic professors, imparting their earthly brand of wisdom to eager, impressionable, young minds.

As Einstein observed, those who think they are wise are only succeeding in fooling themselves. And it is the Lord who is laughing, because the joke is certainly on them.

America's history is His story!

April 2

"Never forget, Americans, that yours is a spiritual country. Yes, I know you're a practical people. Like others, I've marveled at your factories, your skyscrapers, and your arsenals. But underlying everything else is the fact that America began as a God-loving, God-fearing, God-worshipping people." –Carlos Pena Romulo

During World War II, Carlos Romulo served as an aide to General Douglas MacArthur on Corregidor. Rising to the rank of general, this prominent Filipino citizen would make his mark in both journalism and diplomacy, winning a Pulitzer and working at the United Nations.

Although he wasn't a citizen of the United States, Romulo wisely recognized the greatness of America. His observations about our country are remarkably similar to those made by Alexis de Tocqueville.

As in Alexis de Tocqueville's, *Democracy in America*, the Philippine general saw what so many Americans routinely overlook. Because we've been a God-loving people, the Lord chose to bless us with factories, skyscrapers, and mighty arsenals.

Perhaps it's not a coincidence that, as our country's love for the Lord has waned, an increasing number of our factories have fallen silent. American workers have been facing unemployment and families are struggling to make ends meet.

If American industry and its great cities are to once again bloom as before, then we must first return to our roots as a God-fearing people.

America's history is His story!

April 3

"He was a foe without hate, a friend without treachery, a soldier without cruelty, and a victim without murmuring. He was a public officer

without vices, a private citizen without wrong, a neighbor without reproach, a Christian without hypocrisy, and a man without guile. He was a Caesar without his ambition, a Frederick without his tyranny, a Napoleon without his selfishness, and a Washington without his reward." –Benjamin Hill

An outstanding Southern orator and politician known for his eloquence, Benjamin Hill spoke these words about Confederate General Robert E. Lee.

The more you study the life of the general, the more you realize the truth of Hill's remarkable tribute.

In these days of short-sighted history teachers and even shorter attention spans, General Lee is often portrayed as little more than a bigot and a racist, simply because he led the Confederate forces. However, if that is all you *think* you know of the man, then you certainly lack much more than a cursory knowledge of history.

Only a Christian nation like the United States of America could have produced a man such as Robert E. Lee, who was both a general and a gentleman, patriot and pariah.

As the son of famed Revolutionary War general, Henry "Light Horse Harry" Lee, it's not surprising that, from his childhood, Robert was immersed in warfare and baptized in the struggle for Independence.

Lee was a man of great contradictions. The general was loved by his men and feared by his opponents. He was a brilliant military strategist, while still a gentle man of quiet faith. The general was a great lover of country, but ultimately rejected by his nation.

Just thank God our nation has given birth to such men.

America's history is His story!

April 4

"While I can make no claim for having introduced the term "rugged individualism," I should be proud to have invented it. It has been used by American leaders for over a half-century in eulogy of those God-fearing men and women of honesty whose stamina and character and fearless assertion of rights led them to make their own way in life."
–Herbert Hoover

As President Hoover observed, American men and women once gladly embraced the term of "rugged individualists."

It was a quality that drove us to be explorers and pioneers, innovators and trailblazers. Like Moses led the children of Israel out of the wilderness in search of the Promised Land, our country has produced men who have boldly led us forward.

It appears our country has lost something as a nation when we quit reaching for the stars. Our abandonment of the manned space program has robbed us of our manhood. It has taken the quality of "rugged individualism" and turned it inward.

America no longer confidently looks to the heavens. Instead, we all too often hang our heads in shame, while our leaders bow before the world.

When we took our first steps on the moon, Americans of all colors and all faiths swelled with pride at our accomplishment. As we gathered around our television sets, watching NASA's brightest minds struggle to bring the damaged Apollo 13 home, a country united in prayer for their safe return. Moreover, all Americans felt a sense of loss when the Challenger fell from the sky.

Proverbs 29:18 tells us, "Where there is no vision, the people perish." We would be wise to remember that.

America's history is His story!

America's History is His Story:

April 5

"I shall allow no man to belittle my soul by making me hate him."
–Booker T. Washington

Born into slavery on this day in 1856, fathered by an unknown white man, Booker Taliaferro chose his step-father's last name to be his own. Booker T. Washington was to become one of the finest minds our country ever produced.

Following the Civil War, his family moved to West Virginia, where Washington worked in the coal mines. Encouraged to further his education, he worked his way through college, and was later named to head up Tuskegee Institute, an academic institution which was primarily a vocational school.

Washington thought that former slaves, many of them poor and illiterate, could only fully realize the blessings of liberty if they learned a trade or went into industry. He believed this was the logical path to many black Americans gaining acceptance in the days following Reconstruction.

This opinion often placed him at odds with others, the more vocal black leaders of his time, who felt it was a needless compromise. They believed education and confrontation were the only ways to winning full civil rights for former slaves.

The debates regarding these two approaches would rage on for another fifty years, long after their proponents were dead and buried.

As a former slave, Booker T. Washington cared greatly about black Americans and did everything in his power to gain them all the rights and privileges of citizenship.

America's history is His story!

April 6

"Now more than ever before, the people are responsible for the character of their Congress. If that body be ignorant, reckless, and corrupt, it is because the people tolerate ignorance, recklessness, and corruption. If it be intelligent, brave, and pure, it is because the people demand these high qualities to represent them in the national legislature." –James Garfield

If you hadn't just heard the name of the man who made this statement, you might believe those words had just been spoken by somebody in Washington today.

Before being elected to the presidency of the United States, James Garfield was an exceptional teacher and president at Ohio's Hiram College. His term of office ended with an assassin's bullet, only four months after he was inaugurated.

And as you can see, Garfield's words about Congress are as true today as when they were first spoken.

In America, it is critical that each citizen takes some responsibility for those he elects to represent him. Those we send to Washington, to walk the halls of Congress, should clearly reflect our values and seek to uphold them.

Our Founders believed that Congressmen should be people of good moral character, pillars in their communities, and often men of faith.

While it's true that America's restoration is dependent on our homes and churches, not on politics; it's equally true that politicians can make that job harder for all of us, by the laws they pass.

Americans shouldn't be surprised to witness poor behavior from their politicians as long as they demand nothing exceptional from themselves.

America's history is His story!

America's History is His Story:

April 7

"I am sure that never was a people, who had more reason to acknowledge a Divine interposition in their affairs, than those of the United States; and I should be pained to believe that they have forgotten that agency, which was so often manifested during our Revolution, or that they failed to consider the omnipotence of that God who is alone able to protect them." –George Washington

When General Washington retreated from New York, he saw his army decimated from an original force of 30,000 to a measly 3,000 troops. At that time, you can be certain the general had doubts about the Continental Army's chances of success.

However, as you all know, Washington would eventually preside over the surrender of Lord Cornwallis at Yorktown, as the British band played *The World Turned Upside Down.*

Perhaps it was pride that led to the British defeat, and humility that led to the Colonists' victory.

Britain, a land that routinely calls its leaders "lords," was defeated by the one true Lord and Savior. Moreover, it is hard to argue that it was the prayers and petitions offered up to God by General Washington and the Colonists, that allowed him to gain the ultimate triumph.

George Washington was right; America owes its prosperity, freedom, and success to nothing other than the mercies of our gracious Heavenly Father.

As important as our military is to each one of us, it has been God who has often gone before us in battle. History has proven that a nation or an army, marshaled by the Lord, is utterly incapable of defeat.

America's history is His story!

April 8

"A democracy—that is a government of all the people, by all the people, for all the people; of course, a government of the principles of eternal justice, the unchanging law of God; for shortness' sake I will call it the idea of freedom." –Theodore Parker

When Abraham Lincoln used the words "that government of the people, by the people, for the people" in his Gettysburg Address, many historians believe he borrowed the phrase from Theodore Parker's writings in 1850.

Perhaps Parker and Lincoln both borrowed the phrase from John Wycliffe, who was an English theologian, preacher, and translator in the 1300s. He was also one of the first men to translate the Bible into the English language.

Wycliffe wrote these words: "The Bible is for the government of the people, by the people, and for the people."

It matters not where the words originated. What does matter are the principles these men so eloquently espoused.

Our American form of government, and the Word of God upon which it was clearly based, have traditionally been a government of the people, by the people, and for the people.

Studying our nation's history, you are immediately confronted with the fact that the principles and ideals of our nation's greatest statesmen have been built upon the ideas and writings of others. In addition, you will also observe that nearly all of these great men's words and actions can be traced back to the pages of Holy Scripture.

America's history is His story!

April 9

"The rights of the colonists as Christians may be best understood by reading and carefully studying the institution of The Great Law Giver and Head of the Christian Church, which are found clearly written and promulgated in the New Testament." –Samuel Adams

Samuel Adams is often known as the "Father of the American Revolution." He not only signed the Declaration of Independence; he labored for the first Continental Congress. In addition, Adams is the Founding Father often credited with being the catalyst of the Boston Tea Party.

Adams understood that rights are not granted by governments; they are gifts from the Lord. Rights are not enumerated; they are endowed from on High. Rights are not temporal; they are eternal.

Sam Adams' writings, circulated to the communities on horseback, often inspired the faith and will of the colonists to boldly resist the British monarchy.

So feared was he by the British government, the troops which marched to Lexington and Concord not only wanted to capture the Colonists' supplies of powder and armaments; it was also their intention to arrest Samuel Adams.

Perhaps more than any single individual, Samuel Adams, a man of deep and abiding Christian faith, became the heart, the soul, the pen, and the voice of the American Revolution.

America's history is His story!

April 10

"It's not the honor you take with you but the heritage you leave behind." –Branch Rickey

In 1947, Brooklyn Dodgers' president Branch Rickey signed Jackie Robinson to a Major League Baseball contract, breaking the color barrier and making Robinson the first black player in big league baseball.

Despite the fact that Rickey was a brilliant man and a great innovator in the game of baseball, he was also a man of great faith, who helped found and fund the Fellowship of Christian Athletes.

As a baseball coach at Ohio Wesleyan, Rickey once saw his black catcher break down into tears, after the player was refused accommodations in a whites-only hotel.

The incident broke Rickey's heart.

Although he couldn't alter the views of society as a whole, Rickey committed himself to doing what he could for black Americans. The signing of Jackie Robinson to break the color barrier in baseball wasn't undertaken simply because it was good business; Rickey saw the situation as a moral injustice he could rectify for all mankind.

Although Jackie Robinson faced some opposition from players and fans alike, his attitude and success on the field earned him the approval of baseball fans everywhere. Therefore, it could arguably be stated that no man in America did more to advance the Civil Rights movement in America than the actions of Branch Rickey.

America's history is His story!

April 11

"It is impossible to build sound constitutional doctrine upon a mistaken understanding of Constitutional history. The establishment clause has been expressly freighted with Jefferson's misleading metaphor for nearly forty years. There is simply no historical foundation for the proposition that the framers intended to build a wall of separation. The recent court decisions are in no way based on either the language or intent of the framers." –William Rehnquist

America's History is His Story:

"A wall of separation of church and state"—Thomas Jefferson's words have become the most misunderstood and misused writings from any of our Founders.

Despite the opinions of many uninformed Americans, these words are not found in the Constitution. Nor are they anywhere to be found in the Declaration of Independence.

The former Chief Justice of the United States Supreme Court, William Rehnquist was absolutely correct in his understanding of Jefferson's statement.

In Jefferson's letter to the Danbury Baptists, he was attempting to explain that this invisible "wall" was only to separate the church from the federal government. At no time did Jefferson believe that religion should be separated from all civil government. Nor did he believe religion should be completely removed from the public square.

As President of the United States, Jefferson attended the church services that were held in the House of Representatives; he didn't try to abolish them.

Does that sound like a man who wanted to erect a wall between church and state?

While it's true that Jefferson was quite likely one of the least religious of all our Founding Fathers, he definitely wasn't hostile to matters of faith.

America's history is His story!

April 12

"In no Book is there so good English, so pure and so elegant, and by teaching all the same they will speak alike, and the Bible will justly remain the standard of language as well as of faith." –Fisher Ames

Perhaps no book was more important to the founding of our country than the King James Version of the Bible.

The early colonists were known for saying, "Virginia knew no king but King James."

In 1782, Robert Aitken published a King James Version of Scripture, the first English language Bible to be printed in America. In fact, it was the only Bible ever authorized by the United States Congress.

Obviously in fear of what faith might mean to the Revolution, England refused to allow the importation of Bibles to the colonists.

In response to Britain's action, the Continental Congress took action to see that these Bibles were widely available to the colonies.

Aitken's version of the King James was small enough to fit in a soldier's pocket. And years later, the man was even commended by President George Washington for making the Bible available for every American.

Moreover, it was the ascension of King James that ended the reign of King George.

The King James Version of the Bible remains the most published book in human history. And since nobody owns a copyright to this edition of Scripture, its Divine Author has allowed it to be freely shared with all mankind.

America's history is His story!

April 13

"The very men who, in the pride of their investigations into the secrets of the internal world, turn a look of scorn upon the Christian system of belief, are not aware how much of the peace and order of society, how much the happiness of households, and the purest of those who are the dearest to them, are owing to the influence of that religion extending beyond their sphere." –William Cullen Bryant

America's History is His Story:

There are people all over America who have devoted their lives to proving the supposed inaccuracy of Scripture. These people want all religious symbols removed from our city squares and public buildings. They demand that any references to God be stricken from our Pledge of Allegiance or removed from our currency.

These individuals are routinely bitter and hateful to others, and scornful of anyone who dares to challenge their assertions or the veracity of their scientific theories. They are continually at war, viciously engaging a God they claim doesn't truly exist.

But ultimately, it is the Lord's gentle mercy that allows these academics to continually display their pride and ignorance to the world in the name of science.

In the heavens, God merely laughs. So, should you.

II Corinthians 10:12 says, "For we dare not make ourselves of the number or compare ourselves with some that commend themselves; but they measuring themselves by themselves, and comparing themselves among themselves, are not wise."

It is God who has blessed our land with liberty. It is God who keeps us free and allows us to worship without penalty. And it is God who graces our homes with the tender devotion of a mother's love or the beautiful simplicity of a child's affection.

We are all the beneficiaries of God's love, even those who question His existence.

America's history is His story!

April 14

"He said he wanted to visit the Holy Land and see those places hallowed by the footprints of the Savior. He was saying there was no city he so much desired to see as Jerusalem. And with the words half spoken

on his tongue, the bullet of the assassin entered his brain, and the soul of the great and good president was carried by the angels to the New Jerusalem above" –Mary Todd Lincoln

In the preceding words, Mary Todd Lincoln described the last words and wishes of her husband, Abraham Lincoln, who was assassinated on this date by John Wilkes Booth.

Five days earlier, General Robert E. Lee surrendered to General Ulysses S. Grant at Appomattox. The Civil War, a bitter conflict that divided a nation and stooped the shoulders of the president, was virtually at its end.

In his final words upon this earth, Lincoln talked about touring the land where the Savior had walked.

The man who just presided over the bloodiest conflict in our nation's history wished to see the land where Christ shed his blood. This president, who fought to restore the Union, longed to see the place where Christ died, in order to restore the soul of all mankind. This humble man, who freed other men from bondage, desired to see the place where Christ would free men from the bondage of sin.

In the end, Abraham Lincoln gave his life for a cause that was much greater than himself. The president died to make men free.

That is what Americans have always done. It is the foundation upon which our country was built. And it is a reflection of what the Lord did for each one of us.

America's history is His story!

April 15

"There is perhaps no one of our natural passions so hard to subdue as pride. Disguise it, struggle with it, beat it down, stifle it, mortify it as much as one pleases, it is still alive and will every now and then peep

out and show itself. Even if I could conceive that I had completely overcome it, I should probably be proud of my humility."

—Benjamin Franklin

The year was 1912. President William Howard Taft was in the Oval Office. It was a time of great national arrogance, leading up to a bloody World War, which would take place in little more than two years.

Britain's White Star Line manufactured a ship named *Titanic*, of which it was said, "Even God couldn't sink the *Titanic*."

You all know the story.

As the luxury liner steamed towards New York, it failed to carry enough lifeboats for the 2,200 passengers. The "unsinkable" *Titanic* struck an iceberg and eventually sank, killing approximately 1,500 passengers, including one of America's wealthiest citizens.

There is much to be learned from this story.

The United States became a great nation as a result of our dependence on God. However, if our country ever arrogantly dismisses the Lord or no longer believes it needs His guidance, then the icebergs of this life will be our fate as well.

Immense wealth and military power are not enough to preserve our freedom, in much the same way they weren't enough for Britain to keep America from gaining ours.

If our nation is to stay afloat, and not suffer the same fate as the *Titanic*, then it is essential we return to our Godly American heritage.

America's history is His story!

April 16

"It is foolish and wrong to mourn the men who died. Rather we should thank God that such men lived." —George S. Patton

As a child growing up in Britain during World War II, Cyril Richard Rescorla came to admire the America soldiers who were stationed there. Eventually moving to New York, he enlisted in the United States Army.

In 1965, Rick Rescorla was a platoon leader in Vietnam. The Britturned-American survived some of the most brutal fighting of the war, in the Battle of la Drang, immortalized in Joe Galloway's book, *We Were Soldiers Once...and Young.*

Years later, Rick became the director of security for Morgan Stanley, which was located in the World Trade Center.

Before the Trade Center car bombing of 1993, Rick tried to alert the Port Authority to the dangers of a terrorist attack on the Trade Center.

Despite their complaints, Rick Rescorla made sure the employees performed evacuation drills, in preparation for the attack he feared would eventually come.

On September 11, 2001, Rescorla's preparations proved to be critical, when the airliners crashed into the North and South Towers. Due to this one man's dedicated efforts, and the good-natured songs and encouragements he spoke into a bullhorn, all but six of Morgan Stanley's 2,700 people were spared from certain death.

True to his nature as a leader, Rick returned to the structure to save others. And although his remains were never found, we should thank God that such men lived.

America's history is His story!

April 17

"I do not question that the great austerity of manners that is observable in the United States arises, in the first instance, from religious faith. Its influence over the mind of woman is supreme, and women are the

protectors of morals. There is certainly no country in the world where the tie of marriage is more respected than in America or where conjugal happiness is more highly or worthily appreciated."

–Alexis de Tocqueville

Alexis de Tocqueville correctly determined the causes of America's greatness. As the Frenchman observed, America has always been blessed with strong, courageous, and decent women.

Like a mighty army they came to these shores and barren wildernesses. And with their arrival, they brought morality and civilization to a rugged land.

These women sailed over turbulent seas, on tiny wooden ships. They rode or walked alongside the wagon trains, headed west, towards distant mountains. They bounced along in carriages and stage coaches, going places women had never been.

They fed and protected their families, sometimes alone, when the husband was hunting for game or trapping for fur. These strong but feminine women occasionally worked alongside their husbands, trying to plant crops in the tough prairie soil. They reloaded the rifles, for their husbands and brothers to fight those who meant them harm.

They remained behind, prayerfully striving to keep their families together, while their men fought brutal wars across the sea. All the while, the brave and resourceful women of this country endured poverty, hardship, sacrifice, fear, and loneliness.

American women raised flowers in desolation, they bore children in agony and heartbreak, and they brought beauty and sweetness to a barren land.

America's history is His story!

April 18

"Men cross the ocean and encounter the fatigues, dangers of a journey to the other side of the earth, that they may walk through the streets of Jerusalem where our Savior trod, or look out from the hill of Zion, or wander amid sacred places. These scenes bring to their minds the story of the past in a way that thrills their nerves." –Horatio Seymour

In the Japanese language, *kami* means "god" and *kaze* means "winds." Therefore, the word *kamikaze* is loosely translated "god winds."

In the 1200s, a commander led his mighty army across the Sea of Japan, with the intention of conquering Japan. Before they reached land, the *kamikaze*, or the god winds, overwhelmed the ships and drowned the invaders.

For that reason, the Empire of Japan believed they were invincible to attack.

On this date in 1942, in retaliation for their attack on Pearl Harbor, Lt. Colonel Jimmy Doolittle led a daring air raid on the Japanese mainland.

Fearing they were spotted by the Japanese, Doolittle's Raiders were forced to leave the *U.S.S Hornet* early. The fuel supplies of the heavy bombers, already strained by the distance, would be insufficient to safely land in China.

Leading a force of sixteen B-25 bombers off the deck of the carrier, something never before attempted in aviation, Doolittle's men lifted off on their suicide mission.

But this time, the *kamikaze* did nothing to help the Japanese. However, the Lord of Heaven held up the wings of the American bombers.

The Raiders completed the bombing mission in Japan. A number of them were killed and captured, and Col. Jimmy Doolittle was awarded the Medal of Honor.

America's history is His story!

April 19

"By the rude bridge that arched the flood, their flag to April's breezes unfurled, here once the embattled farmers stood, and fired the shot heard round the world." –Ralph Waldo Emerson

The Battle of Concord Bridge was fought on this date in 1775, because the British army was attempting to capture the militia's supply of powder and armaments, stored at the city of Concord.

That was the point of Paul Revere's famous ride, and that of William Dawes, to warn the colonists that the British regulars were coming to disarm them.

When the Minutemen lined the bridge, it was solely for the purpose to stop the British from denying the Colonists the means to defend themselves. Moreover, it must be stated, the Colonists never took up arms against their government, not until King George tried to forcefully disarm them.

It was for this reason the Founders placed the Second Amendment in the Bill of Rights. James Madison knew that the American people had just cast off a tyrannical government, that couldn't successfully impose its will on the people unless they were forcibly disarmed.

However, the Second Amendment didn't grant Americans the right to bear arms; it simply denied the government the authority to take away those rights.

After all, rights come from the Lord, not from governments.

America's history is His story!

April 20

"Man derives his greatest happiness not by that which he does for himself, but by what he accomplishes for others. This is a sad world at best—a world of sorrow, of suffering, of injustice, and falsification; men stab those whom they hate with the stiletto of slander, but it is for the followers of our Lord to improve it, and to make it more as Christ would have it." –Schuyler Colfax

There is not a country in the history of the world that has been more generous or more giving than the United States of America.

Although Americans have often been blessed with great wealth, many of those who experienced the greatest bounty in this land have also chosen to share a portion of that wealth with others.

Perhaps it is our Christian heritage that has ingrained the need for sharing into the minds and hearts of the American people. It has become a part of our national character.

America's great philanthropists didn't choose to give to others because they were forced to do so by the government. In fact, it has been the actions of the government, their never-ceasing demand for excessive taxes, which has been largely responsible for harming the American spirit of giving.

Our Founders envisioned a nation where the American people would willingly share with those in need; however, they never intended for this generosity to be mandated by the government. It was to come through our homes and churches, people giving of their abundance to those who lacked.

In the book of Acts, the Apostle Peter said, "But such as I have give I thee."

America's History is His Story:

It is that spirit that made America the benevolent country it has become.

America's history is His story!

April 21

"We have this day restored the Sovereign to Whom all men ought to be obedient. He reigns in heaven and from the rising to the setting of the sun, let His kingdom come." –Samuel Adams

After the final signatures were placed upon the Declaration of Independence, these words were spoken by Samuel Adams, who became "The Soul of the American Revolution."

Although he knew these men hadn't actually restored the Lord to His throne, Adams believed the tyrannical demands of King George had made it nearly impossible for the Colonists to devote their worship to anything other than the British Crown.

If the Founders succeeded in their efforts, Adams assumed another kingdom would replace the one they vanquished, one that recognized only the Lord as its Master.

The nation they conceived that July day was a matchless Republic, founded on liberty and the principles of God's Word.

America was bathed in prayer. It was tempered in battle. It was forged in sacrifice. And it was purchased with blood.

America's history is His story!

April 22

"I want to tell you how happy and impressed I have been at the remarkable progress made by the new State of Israel." –Harry S. Truman

In fulfillment of Bible prophesy, Israel officially became a nation in May, 1948.

The United States and the Jewish people have been inseparably linked throughout our nation's history.

Moses gave us the Ten Commandments, written by the finger of God, which have been the basis for much of American law. His leadership of the Hebrews out of Egypt, through the wilderness, was an inspiration for our country's westward movement. And our country embraced that same God of Heaven, who led them out of bondage.

And when it came to establishing a great seal and motto for the United States, the design was to be selected by Thomas Jefferson, Benjamin Franklin, and John Adams.

Franklin's early suggestion was: "Moses lifting up his wand, and dividing the Red Sea, and Pharaoh in his chariot overwhelmed by the waters. This motto: Rebellion to tyrants is obedience to God."

Jefferson suggested: "The children of Israel in the wilderness, led by a cloud by day, and a pillar of fire by night."

There is no denying the fact that our nation's Founders were greatly influenced by the Word of God and His chosen people, the Children of Israel. Throughout our nation's history, they have been our inspiration and our example.

America's history is His story!

April 23

"The Constitution is a mere thing of wax in the hands of the judiciary, which they may twist and shape into any form they please."

–Thomas Jefferson

Thomas Jefferson wasn't only a patriot; he also may have been a prophet.

His remarks about how the judiciary might misuse the Constitution have proven to be true time and time again.

For the past forty years, some of those who have been selected for the land's highest court have abused their powers in much the same way Jefferson suggested.

Repeatedly, a number of recent Supreme Court rulings have violated every principle of our Founders. These rogues in black robes have deliberately ignored the limitations of power that were clearly expressed in the document. Moreover, they have instituted judicial edicts that clearly have no basis in Constitutional law.

Like the Word of God, the Constitution is ageless.

The Constitution doesn't need to be rewritten or changed. It doesn't need to be updated. It just needs to be followed and respected.

In much the same way that the Bible is a light unto our pathway, the Constitution is the torch that lights the path of liberty.

America's history is His story!

April 24

"The energy, the faith, the devotion which we bring to this endeavor will light our country and all who serve it—and the glow from that fire can truly light the world." –John F. Kennedy

During the American Revolution, an eighty-year old farmer came to his country's aid, when he believed liberty was under assault.

After the Battles of Lexington and Concord, the British regulars were in full retreat, losing all sense of order and running for their lives. Their short-lived victory was all but forgotten, as the enraged Colonists picked them off one-by-one from the trees.

Samuel Whittemore was toiling in his fields when he learned the British were sending reinforcements to aid in the retreat.

Sticking a pair of dueling pistols and a sword in his belt, grabbing his powder and shot, and arming himself with a musket, the old farmer chose to make his stand beside a stone wall.

As the British approached, he stood to his feet and dropped one of the regulars with his musket. Then he pulled his pistols and fired both of them at the nearby troops, killing two more. After discharging his guns, Samuel was forced to use his sword.

Quickly overpowering the lone patriot, the British troops shot Whittemore and bayoneted the old man thirteen times, leaving him for dead.

Apparently, Samuel Whittemore was as hard to kill as the cause of liberty he willingly offered his life to protect. Whittemore died at the ripe, old age of 98, a free citizen in a young and promising Republic.

America's history is His story!

April 25

"I do not doubt that our country will finally come through safe and undivided. But do not misunderstand me...I do not rely on the patriotism of our people...the bravery and devotion of the boys in blue...or the loyalty and skill of our generals...But the God of our fathers, Who raised up this country to be the refuge and asylum of the oppressed and downtrodden of all nations, will not let it perish now. I may not live to see it. I do not expect to see it, but God will bring us through safe."

–Abraham Lincoln

Whenever you think of great American statesmen, Abraham Lincoln would have to be near the top of your list.

Throughout our nation's history, and in the pages of God's Word, it seems that God often prepares and equips a man to lead His people through whatever challenges they must face.

America's History is His Story:

It is obvious from his statements and his writings that the Civil War made a great transformation in the life of President Lincoln.

The war brought Lincoln to his knees. It made him seek out the guidance and assurance of Almighty God. And the Scriptures obviously brought him comfort in the war's eventual outcome.

And like Moses in Scripture, who wasn't permitted to enter the Promised Land, President Lincoln clearly didn't believe he would live to see the States united.

However, before he died, God did allow Moses to climb the mountain and see that land from afar. And Lincoln lived long enough to see the war end, God also giving him a brief glance of what his labors had won.

As these two choice servants of God looked out over the free and beautiful land stretched out before them, you can be certain it brought a smile to their faces.

America's history is His story!

April 26

"Build me a son, O Lord, who will be strong enough to know when he is weak, brave enough to face himself when he is afraid, one who will be proud and unbending in honest defeat, and humble and gentle in victory." –Gen. Douglas MacArthur

In these words, General Douglas MacArthur described the qualities that he believed would make for the perfect son.

Please allow me to tell you about one born with these qualities.

This son has often been the toughest kid on the block, so he was rarely forced to prove his strength. But when he was attacked, this son would fight like nobody in history.

However, after the fight was over, this son often stooped down to offer a hand to his enemy, lifting him from the ground.

This son has often been afraid in the midst of a skirmish, but he cast aside his fear as he ran headlong into the teeth of the enemy.

As a youngster, he was often beaten and humbled. Yet he knew his cause was just and proudly refused to be defeated. And when he won the eventual triumph, this son was humble and gracious to those he conquered.

All of these qualities can be found in the land we know as America.

Despite its vast armies, America prayed for God's strength. When our nation feared losing the Revolution, it found its soul. When America won the war, it befriended those it had defeated. And when America was strongest, it tried to be a peacemaker.

The son that General MacArthur desired was in essence the nation that he served.

America's history is His story!

April 27

"If religious books are not widely circulated among the masses in this country, I do not know what is going to become of us as a nation. If truth be not diffused, then error will be." –Daniel Webster

Increasingly in America, the seeds of error have taken root and we are now reaping a bitter harvest.

Due to our woeful educational system, Americans no longer have any idea what is actually in the Constitution. Many of them even foolishly believe the phrase, "separation of church and state," is found in the blueprint of our Republic. These words are also not to be found in the Declaration of Independence.

America's History is His Story:

Another error that has been repeatedly spoon-fed to the American people is the theory of evolution and man-made, global climate change.

Skeptics of global warming and evolution are considered to be little more than kooks and crackpots. However, nobody ever gives us a credible explanation of why we're supposed to believe the scientific evidence of people who deliberately tampered with the results in order to obtain their predetermined results.

Americans landed on the moon at a time in our nation's history when the Apollo astronauts were reading God's Scriptural account of creation in Genesis, live from space. Now, we routinely scoff at God's Word and don't have the technological ability to successfully plug an oil leak for nearly three months.

Does it really look like man is truly evolving?

America's history is His story!

April 28

"There never has been a period of history, in which the common law did not recognize Christianity as lying at its foundation."

–Joseph Story

Today, there is no shortage of people who wish to deny our undeniable history and tradition. Like an ever-growing fungus, they have infected our elementary and secondary schools and institutions of higher learning.

These enemies of the truth seek to remove all traces of Christianity from our science books, history books, and law books.

If America continues down the path we are currently traveling, then it won't be long before Mr. Story's statement is no longer true.

Christianity is our nation's foundation, its basis, its bedrock, its groundwork, its underpinning, and the cornerstone of our society. In fact, the English vocabulary is wholly inadequate to describe the importance that Christianity has made in this country.

You can no more remove Christianity from our history than you can remove the contributions of George Washington or Samuel Adams.

The faith of our fathers formulated our viewpoints, it guided our decisions, it altered our paths, and it lighted our way.

Throughout our nation's remarkable journey, Christianity has been both the vehicle and the roadmap for the United States.

America's history is His story!

April 29

"When I left the house of bondage, I left everything behind. I wanted to keep nothing of Egypt on me, and so I went to the Lord and asked Him to give me a new name...I set up my banner, and then I sing, and then folks always comes up 'round me, and then...I tells them about Jesus." –Sojourner Truth

Sojourner Truth was the self-chosen name of former slave, Isabella Baumfree, who escaped with her infant daughter, Sophia.

While living in the home of Isaac and Maria Van Wagener, Isabella came to learn the truth of God's Word. In fact, the woman decided to change her last name to "Truth."

After trying to reclaim and relocate some of the children she was forced to leave behind, the woman became greatly active in the abolitionist movement and gaining women the right to vote.

Like many abolitionists of that time, it was the Word of God that transformed her life and became her passion.

In the case of Truth, and other lesser-known American sojourners, the Scriptures often transformed their minds and souls, ushering the love of God into their hearts, and altering our nation's path.

Without the influence of the Bible, then America, unlike other nations, wouldn't have acknowledged our national disgrace of slavery, nor had the courage to abolish it.

The Founders wrote a Constitution that not only gives us direction about how we should be governed; it also effectively gave us the means to correct the errors of the past.

Like the Bible, it offers us a pathway to truth and redemption.

America's history is His story!

April 30

"Let us look forward to the time when we can take the flag of our country and nail it below the Cross, and there let it wave as it waved in the olden times, and let us gather around it and inscribe for our motto: "Liberty and Union, one and inseparable, now and forever," and exclaim, Christ first, our country next." –Andrew Johnson

Becoming President of the United States upon the assassination of Abraham Lincoln, Andrew Johnson was forced to oversee the Reconstruction of the South. It was certainly a daunting task for any man to step into the shoes of Abraham Lincoln.

Regarded by many historians as a poor president, Johnson was smart enough to acknowledge America's union of citizenship and Christianity.

Some of the greatest Americans in our nation's history have also been some of its greatest Christians.

Perhaps it is a Christian's obedience to God that also demands his willing submission to the laws of our land. The Christian's calling to serve the Lord likewise prepares him for faithful service to his country.

Maybe this condition is simply another quality inherent to our American culture, the inseparable connection between the flag and the Cross.

Americans naturally respond to these symbols.

Therefore, it is only appropriate that those who sacrifice their lives in the service of our flag are often buried under the symbol of the cross.

America's history is His story!

May 1

"The spirit of man is more important than mere physical strength, and the spiritual fiber of a nation than its wealth." –Dwight D. Eisenhower

On this day in 1931, New York's Empire State Building was dedicated. The tallest structure in the world at the time, the building's construction was completed in a little over thirteen months.

In the early part of the Twentieth Century, America was dominated by a robust spirit that made monumental tasks seem rather commonplace.

Today, there are those who routinely question America's place in this world. They deny our history. They challenge the facts of our moral upbringing.

In this climate of doubt and denial, America has seemingly lost its spirit. And with that loss, our country has often lost the ability to master the challenges that hindered lesser nations.

In the smoking ashes and twisted debris at Ground Zero, America temporarily realized its dependence on Almighty God. Our nation returned to our churches. Americans also looked to their pulpits for answers.

The answers for those things that trouble us as a nation can still be found in our faith. They are also still spelled out for us in the Holy Scriptures.

We have only to reclaim them.

America's history is His story!

May 2

"Fellow citizens! God reigns, and the government at Washington still lives." –James A. Garfield

Upon learning that President Abraham Lincoln had been assassinated, James Garfield would speak these words to a gathering in New York.

Approximately sixteen years later, President James Garfield would also succumb to an assassin's bullet.

In times of great national tragedy or deep personal loss, Americans have always turned to the Lord for strength, comfort, and direction. They also have every right to look to their leaders for wise, calm, and principled leadership.

As a man of faith, James Garfield understood that the future of our nation was not dependent on any one man. And despite the fact that President Lincoln appeared to be an instrument to achieve God's purpose, the perpetuation of America's future is solely dependent on the Lord.

Isaiah 9:6 says, "For unto us a child is born, unto us a son is given: and the government shall be upon His shoulder: and His name shall be called Wonderful, Counsellor, The mighty God, The everlasting Father, The Prince of Peace."

Although America's great moral leaders are extremely rare, the God we serve is always there to direct our paths into the future.

America's history is His story!

May 3

"Can he be a patriot who, by openly vicious conduct, is undermining the very bonds of society?" –Abrigail Adams

Benedict Arnold—perhaps there has never been another name in history that has ever become so synonymous with treason and treachery against one's own government.

He was also once a fine general in the Revolutionary cause.

While serving in the Continental Army, Benedict Arnold and Ethan Allen were largely responsible for the taking of Fort Ticonderoga. His daring actions at the Battle of Saratoga rallied the American troops to a victory.

However, Arnold seemed to be less concerned in acquiring liberty for the Colonies than he was in his desired military promotions and his dreams of personal enrichment.

Unlike the settlement at Jamestown, the venture at Roanoke was lost to history because it was strictly a financial enterprise. Perhaps the heroic actions of General Arnold weren't rewarded, as well, because they were simply undertaken to advance one man's dreams of personal glory.

Had Arnold been true to the loyalty that George Washington placed in him, it's likely the general would now be embraced as one of our nation's glorious heroes.

In the cause of liberty, the fifty-six brave signers of the Declaration of Independence willingly pledged their lives, their fortunes, and their sacred honor.

In the end, Benedict Arnold was much too selfish to offer the same things.

America's history is His story!

May 4

"It is the will of heaven that the two countries should be sundered forever. It may be the will of heaven that America shall suffer calamities still more wasting and distresses more dreadful. If this is to be the case, it will have this good effect, at least: it will inspire us with many virtues which we have not, and correct many errors, follies and vices, which threaten to disturb, dishonor, and destroy us. The furnace of affliction produces refinements in states, as well as individuals." – John Adams

As John Adams wrote these words to his wife, Abigail, after the Continental Congress approved the Declaration of Independence, I am sure he was both fearful and excited.

In signing this document, Adams knew there would be many labor pains yet to be experienced in the birth of the American Republic. The Declaration was only the beginning of sorrows.

Knowing that the British commanded the most powerful military force in the world, Adams had no misconceptions about the hardships that awaited the Colonists.

America would experience many challenges on the road to freedom.

The flickering candle of liberty was nearly extinguished by the harsh, chilly winds of Valley Forge. Benedict Arnold nearly sold out his country and his countrymen for *his* thirty pieces of silver. And the battle was nearly lost, had General Washington not wisely chosen to evacuate his troops from Long Island, across the East River.

As Adams penned this letter to his wife, maybe he was thinking of Romans 8:28, which states, "And we know that all things work together for good to them that love God, to them who are the called according to His purpose."

America's history is His story!

May 5

"There is an unbroken history of official acknowledgement by all three branches of government of the role of religion in American life. The Constitution does not require a complete separation of church and state. It affirmatively mandates accommodation, not merely tolerance, of all religions and forbids hostility towards all." – Warren Burger

This Chief Justice of the Supreme Court knew there could be no legitimate denial that our American form of government is strongly based on the Word of God.

Isaiah 33:22 says, "For the Lord is our judge, the Lord is our lawgiver, the Lord is our king; He will save us."

In this verse, it mentions judge, lawgiver, and king, from which America derives its three unique branches of government. The judicial, legislative, and executive branches clearly have their origins in this text from Scripture.

The judicial branch consists of the judges, who determine if the legislation we passed is Constitutional. The legislative branch is made up of the lawgivers, who write the laws we are all required to observe. The executive branch is the president, who would quite often act as a king, if he were not restrained by the other branches of government.

Do you perhaps need further proof that the Scriptures greatly influenced our system of government?

The first Ten Amendments to the United States Constitution are known as the Bill of Rights. Have you ever wondered why only ten were chosen? If God was satisfied with giving His people Ten Commandments, written by his hand on stone tablets, then that same number was also sufficient for the Framers of our Constitution's Bill of Rights.

America's history is His story!

May 6

"There is no country in the world where the Christian religion retains a greater influence over the souls of men than in America, and there can be no greater proof of its utility and of its conformity to human nature than that its influence is powerfully felt over the most enlightened and free nation of the earth." – Alexis de Tocqueville

The term "American exceptionalism" comes from the writings of Alexis de Tocqueville, where he suggested that there was something exceptional in the character of the United States.

De Tocqueville was absolutely correct.

America was exceptional in its founding. America was exceptional in its faith. Moreover, America was exceptional in its families.

Today, however, there are those among us who say that America isn't an exceptional nation. These critics apparently hate their own country and fail to study their own history.

Our Founders tried to create a Republic, different from anything the world had ever seen. The things that made us exceptional were the qualities that made us unique.

In trying to win the love of our critics, America is quickly losing its soul.

Greatness is rarely to be found in uniformity.

The more we *succeed* in becoming more like the rest of the world, the less exceptional we become. When we allow the continued slaughter of the unborn, we are no longer exceptional. When we surrender our sovereignty, we are no longer exceptional.

America has been an exceptional nation in its past and it could be so once again.

America's history is His story!

May 7

"In this day of calamity, to trust altogether to the justice of our cause, without our utmost exertion, would be tempting Providence."
— Jonathan Trumbull

On this day in 1945, the Germans surrendered and signed an unconditional treaty that ended America's war in Europe.

It took the United States a number of years before we entered the war, but once our nation finally engaged the enemy, we gave it our all to see the Nazis and Japanese defeated.

World War II wasn't just won on the ground, air, and seas. It was also won in our factories. Working like never before, American workers raced to manufacture thousands of planes, tanks, and jeeps that would take us across Europe and throughout the Pacific.

America's History is His Story:

The war was also won at home. Rationing of sugar, tires, gasoline, and other commodities were commonplace for the time.

World War II was felt in every home and street corner. It was experienced in every hamlet and community. If you weren't engaged in some facet of the war effort yourself, then it was certain you knew somebody who was.

Moreover, any careful study of World War II will reveal the ever-present blessing of God in much the same way the Lord interceded for America in the Revolutionary War.

The end of the war was greeted with smiles and laughter, reunions and homecomings, celebrations and ticker tape parades.

It also brought many Americans to their knees, in heartfelt prayers of thanks.

America's history is His story!

May 8

"Thank God! War will now be ended, and peace, independence, and happiness bless our country." – Mary Washington

Mary Washington, the mother of George Washington, lived to see the Colonists win the American Revolution. She also lived long enough to learn that her son had been elected the first President of the United States.

We can only imagine the pride Mrs. Washington must have felt for the child we know as the "Father of our Country."

None of us will ever know the impact a mother's prayer had on General Washington and how it affected his contributions to the Revolutionary cause.

Mothers have been praying for their sons in warfare as long as there have been wars and sons. It has often been recorded that the last words uttered by the lips of a fearful, dying soldier is a cry to mother.

Perhaps there is nothing in this world that comes closer to matching the love of God for His children than the devotion and concern of a Godly mother for her child.

Each one of us should be thankful for the young man that Mary Washington raised to adulthood. We should also give thanks for the profound influences in his life.

While we often comment on the strength, grace, and impeccable character of President Washington, you can be assured that young George learned those traits from the lessons instilled in him by a Godly, loving mother.

America's history is His story!

May 9

"While just government protects all in their religious rights, true religion affords to government its surest support." – George Washington

President Washington clearly understood that, in America, true religion and good government were inseparable.

In fact, the two are so closely entwined, our system of government will eventually fall unless it continues to be supported by the pillars of religious faith.

For proof of this, you needn't look any further than the current budgetary crisis in Washington.

In the parable of the talents, the Lord made it plain that he expected us to be good stewards of those things He has given us. However, those in our government no longer feel the need to be good stewards of the money we have entrusted to them.

Instead, many of those in Washington are seeking to take more and more from our paychecks. Failing to respect those persons they supposedly claim to serve, they often ridicule the outrage expressed by the public. And with each successive tax increase, Americans lose more and more of their freedom, while the mountain of governmental debt continues to grow and grow.

The Lord also teaches us in II Corinthians 3:17, "Where the spirit of the Lord is, there is liberty."

If our politicians truly come to know the One who gives us liberty, then our nation will be freed from our budgetary woes and the massive taxation that enslaves us all.

America's history is His story!

May 10

"The true Christian is the true citizen, lofty of purpose, resolute in endeavor, ready for a hero's deeds, but never looking down on his task because it is cast in the day of small things." –Theodore Roosevelt

On this date in 1869, the workers of the Union Pacific and the Central Pacific Railroad met in Promontory, Utah, for the completion of the Transcontinental Railroad.

The Transcontinental Railroad was the dream and passion of Theodore Judah, who spent years lobbying Congress for its construction.

Known by some as "Crazy Judah," for his devotion to the project, the young engineer and son of a preacher scouted and mapped out a proposed route for the railroad over the Sierra Nevada Mountains.

Judah would live to see President Lincoln sign the Pacific Railroad Act into law, which authorized the Transcontinental Railroad's construction. He obtained the financing for the project. However, Judah died before its construction.

This venture was probably the greatest feat of engineering ever attempted in America at the time.

Before the final spike was driven, Rev. Todd led in prayer, asking God's blessing upon their work.

At 2:47 PM, the final spike was driven to complete the construction, as iron rails finally spanned the entire continent. As the spike was driven into place, a telegraph signal was sent to Washington, notifying them of its official completion.

In America, East and West became one.

America's history is His story!

May 11

"Every freedom-loving man has two fatherlands; his own and America. Today, America is the hope of every enslaved man, because it is the last bastion of freedom in the world. Only America has the power and spiritual resources to stand as a barrier between militant Communism and the people of the world." – Richard Wurmbrand

Persecuted for his faith, the late Richard Wurmbrand spent over a decade in a Romanian prison. This former Lutheran minister knew what it was to suffer under godless Communism.

As a result of his experiences, Wurmbrand saw America as the last, best hope for people in bondage.

While many here are clamoring for more socialistic policies from their government, the tortured souls of oppressed states everywhere are

America's History is His Story:

praying that America will resist the calls to willingly surrender our freedom.

Without America's bright beacon of freedom to light the way, then the globe would be forever plunged into a vast and eerie darkness of physical and spiritual servitude.

As a prisoner in a Communist regime, Rev. Richard Wurmbrand was forced to confront the worst evils that one man can impose on one another. The man had witnessed the false and empty promises of Communism. Moreover, it was this knowledge that brought him to the realization that liberty wouldn't survive without the United Sates.

Embracing our country as their own, the Romanian minister and his wife chose to spend their final years in America, the hope of every enslaved man.

America's history is His story!

May 12

"If the next centennial does not find us a great nation, it will be because those who represent the enterprise, the culture, and the morality of the nation do not aid in controlling the political forces." – James Garfield

Despite the fact he was a politician, President Garfield recognized that political forces were the biggest threat to prolonging our country's greatness.

That is precisely the reason our Founding Fathers wanted religion to influence our government.

A man's faith should alter his political views. Sadly, however, we see too many politicians whose faith is altered by their politics.

Perhaps that is why Washington is currently in such a mess. There are a surplus of politicians and a deficit of statesmen.

A statesman is a politician who actually practices the tenets of his faith, instead of someone who merely talks about it to gain votes every election.

It is dishonest for someone, who claims to be morally opposed to a certain act, to cast his vote in favor of allowing it to continue. Those two views are simply inconsistent and incompatible with one another.

That is why our nation was so exceptional at its inception. The people who founded our nation believed that their actions might lead to their imprisonment or execution; however, they still were willing to risk that fate for generations yet to come.

America is struggling right now because our enterprise, our culture, and our morality have failed to demand the very best from Washington.

America's history is His story!

May 13

"It appears that the unerring hand of Providence shielded my men from the shower of balls, bombs, and rockets, when every ball and bomb from our guns carried with them a mission of death."

– Andrew Jackson

In the War of 1812, the United States was forced to defeat the British for the second time in less than forty years.

General Andrew Jackson, who was destined to become President of the United States, defeated British forces in the Battle of New Orleans.

Although the news of a peace treaty being signed to end the war wouldn't arrive until the battle was concluded, the assistance of Almighty God arrived just in time.

The general had expected the British to sail into New Orleans with a vastly superior fleet of soldiers.

In the preceding words, Jackson acknowledged his belief that the Lord miraculously intervened in this battle, sheltered them from harm, and ultimately delivered to them the victory over their enemies.

The battle would make Jackson famous with his countrymen and pave his way to the White House. Yet the general was smart enough to realize the battle was the Lord's.

In his letter to the Secretary of War, General Jackson said, "Heaven, to be sure, has interposed most wonderfully in our behalf, and I am filled with gratitude, when I look back to what we have escaped."

America's history is His story!

May 14

"A Christian is just as much under the obligation to obey God's will in the most secular of his daily business as he is in his closet or at the communion table. He has no right to separate his life into two realms, and acknowledge different moral codes in each." –Archibald Hodge

Much too often, Americans are guilty of trying to separate the secular from the sacred. They try to have one set of behavior for Sunday morning and another for Monday. They treat their Christianity like a suit of clothes, putting them on or taking them off, according to where they are at the time.

However, the men who founded this country rarely drew those distinctions. Their brand of Christianity was an all-week affair.

It influenced their writings. It affected their actions. It led them to stubbornly challenge a mighty empire.

The decisions they made and the Declaration they signed gave them no other options. There were no days off. If the Founders were to survive, then they would need the intercession and protection of Almighty God.

Perhaps there is nothing like the threat of a hangman's noose to focus one's attention on the condition of his eternal soul.

The Founders wore their faith on a daily basis and it allowed each of us to enjoy our freedom on a daily basis as well.

America's history is His story!

May 15

"Who but a Washington, inspired by Heaven, could have conceived the surprise move upon the enemy at Princeton, that Christmas even when Washington and his army crossed the Delaware? Who but the Ruler of the winds could have delayed the British reinforcements by three months of contrary ocean winds at a critical point of the war? Or what but a Providential miracle at the last minute detected the treacherous scheme of traitor Benedict Arnold, which would have delivered the American army, including George Washington himself, into the hands of the enemy? The United States are under peculiar obligations to become a holy people unto the Lord our God." – Ezra Stiles

Ezra Stiles, a preacher and a president at Yale, was fondly acquainted with both Benjamin Franklin and Thomas Jefferson. He was also a staunch supporter of the American revolutionary cause.

Contained in the preceding words is one of the most clear and compelling accounts of the Lord's intercession in the American Revolution.

Today's revisionist historians are continually trying to erase the truth of our nation's history. They seek to discredit the quotes of our

Founders. These destroyers of young minds seek to deny the faith of our Founding Fathers. They never miss an opportunity to try to undermine the vision, greatness, and remarkable foresight of these brave and noble men.

But who will you choose to believe?

Do you wish to accept the word of those who blindly deny America's history or the words and writings of those who actually gave birth to it?

Despite the best efforts of the revisionists, the evidence of our nation's religious underpinnings is overwhelming.

America is a Christian nation.

America's history is His story!

May 16

"I have just finished the Bible; I make it a point to read it through every cruise. It is certainly a wonderful Book, a most wonderful book. From boyhood I have taken a deep interest in Christianizing the heathen and in imparting knowledge of God's revealed truth everywhere."

– Matthew C. Perry

Commodore Matthew Perry was the brother of Captain Oliver Hazard Perry, who defeated British naval forces in the Battle of Lake Erie, during the War of 1812.

Perry successfully negotiated a treaty with Japan, which opened them up for trade and the restocking of coal on American steamships.

This naval commander made it a point to read through the Scriptures on every cruise. The Bible guided him through this life in much the same way his navigational tools helped him plot the course of his ship.

Not only did the Word of God make him a better person; perhaps it also made the Commodore a better leader to his crew.

Like those who guided our nation in America's first war with Britain, Perry willingly chose to make the Word of God his navigational tool through the seas of life.

"The Bible is no mere book," Napoleon once said, "but a living creature, with a power that conquers all that oppose it."

As somebody who traveled around the world and was exposed to many other books, Perry could have chosen many books. However, the Commodore selected the Holy Scriptures as his one indispensible source of reading material.

Like it helped Commodore Perry, perhaps the Bible would also aid you in navigating the turbulent seas in your own life.

America's history is His story!

May 17

"The purposes of God, working through the ages, were, perhaps, more clearly revealed to him than any other. He was the greatest man of his time, especially approved of God for the work He gave him to do."
– William McKinley

President William McKinley spoke these words about the late president Abraham Lincoln. Strangely enough, President McKinley, like Lincoln, would also be gunned down by an assassin, not long after his reelection.

It is only recently that Americans have begun to hold little regard for the heroes and giants of our country's history. Much of that indifference can be attributed to revisionist historians, who seek to remove any religious references from the ungodly textbooks they write.

Is it any wonder our young people are no longer inspired by the true heroes of our American history?

Unfortunately, many of these present-day historians are not only seeking to deny the influence that faith played on these great men; they are also attempting to diminish their deeds and character. Meanwhile, these same individuals deliberately ignore and minimize the faults of our current leaders, thereby lowering the bars to greatness.

However, morals and character still matter. If today's leaders wish to have the adoration once reserved for our Founding Fathers, then they must first exhibit the selfless qualities that made these historical figures unique and worthy of our respect.

In order to earn the elevated status of Lincoln, Washington, or Jefferson, then our political leaders must finally start leaving the nation in better shape than they found it.

America's history is His story!

May 18

"Nor is this spiritual and moral disease to be healed by a better education, a few external, transient thoughts. It requires the hand of the great Physician, the Lord Jesus Christ."– John Armstrong

Despite the cries of some in Washington, all of America's woes cannot be cured by increasing educational funding. It is irrational to think every social and moral problem can be cured by more education.

That wasn't true at our country's founding; it certainly isn't true now.

Arguably, a Godless educational system has done more lasting harm to this country than anything else.

If the Lord has no place in our schools, then there is no higher moral authority to Whom students must answer. If there is no God in the classroom, then there can be no absolutes, no guaranteed standard of truth. If God is banned from our classrooms, then there is no motivation for students to behave like anything other than an animal.

"Education without God," C.S. Lewis observed, "only makes man a more clever devil."

Is it any wonder young people bring guns to school and kill their fellow students?

Without God in the schools, education becomes shallow. Instruction is empty. Learning holds no truth. Moreover, the teaching does absolutely nothing to lift up society.

If America truly desires to once again chase away the intellectual darkness of its classrooms, then it must once again allow the Light of the World to walk its halls.

America's history is His story!

May 19

"But I am confident that the Almighty has His plans, and will work them out; and, whether we see it or not, they will be the best for us."
—Abraham Lincoln

Invited by his parents to join them at Ford's Theater, Robert Todd Lincoln turned down their request. A few hours later, he would be awakened with the news his father, Abraham Lincoln had been assassinated by John Wilkes Booth.

In 1881, as President James Garfield's Secretary of War, Robert was with him, when the president was struck down by an assassin's bullet.

America's History is His Story:

At the invitation of President William McKinley in 1901, Robert Lincoln was also present when McKinley was killed by the gun of another assassin.

As a result of these events—except for the dedication of the Lincoln Memorial—Robert declined all future presidential invitations.

It's quite likely the deaths of these other presidents caused him to revisit the nightmare of his father's assassination. Lincoln never got over the notion his presence at the theater might have somehow prevented Booth from accomplishing his mission.

But despite the great tragedy that touched the life and family of Robert Todd Lincoln, you cannot find one instance where he advocated the disarmament of private citizens. Moreover, he took no actions that might lead to limiting their freedoms.

Robert knew his father died in the pursuit of liberty and the restoration of the Union. Perhaps Abraham Lincoln's compelling influence on his son made Robert Lincoln unwilling to do anything to undermine his father's great deeds and noble sacrifice.

America's history is His story!

May 20

"All must admit that the reception of the teachings of Christ results in the purest patriotism, in the most scrupulous fidelity to public trust, and in the best type of citizenship." –Grover Cleveland

On this day in history, Jimmy Stewart was born in Indiana, Pennsylvania.

Although most of you will simply know the man as a well-known Hollywood actor, Stewart was also a great American patriot.

Raised in a deeply religious home, Stewart came from a family with a rich heritage of military service. His grandfathers saw combat in the

Civil War and his father served in the Spanish-American War and World War I.

Standing at 6'3", Stewart was much too skinny to make the weight requirements for enlistment. The actor promptly went home and gorged himself on all kinds of fattening foods before returning. This time, the actor barely made the weight specifications and entered the Army Air Corps.

After earning his pilot's license many years before, Jimmy wanted to fly bombers in Europe. His military commanders had no interest in sending a high-profile actor to die in the skies over Germany, but Stewart was insistent on flying heavy bombers overseas.

His stateside commanders finally relented, after seeing the actor's desire to get into the war led him to foot the bill for some of his training hours, out of his own pocket.

At the controls of a B-24, Captain James Stewart flew 20 hazardous bombing missions over Europe. Jimmy Stewart, the Hollywood actor, could have chosen the safe and easy way in World War II, but he was willing to risk his life for the country he loved.

America's history is His story!

May 21

"As a patriot, he had me serve my country with all I had, even with my life if need be; as the daughter of an accepted Mason, he had me seek and comfort the afflicted everywhere, and as a Christian, he charged me to honor God and love all kind." –Clara Barton

In the preceding words, Clara Barton described the death-bed admonition she received from her dying father, a veteran of the French and Indian War.

America's History is His Story:

Sometimes referred to as "The Angel of the Battlefield," Clara Barton served in the Civil War, treating the wounded or giving comfort to the dying. Her duties often took her to the front lines, where she was nearly killed by a bullet that took the life of a soldier Clara was helping to stand.

"What could I do but go with them, or work for them and my country?" she stated. "The patriot blood of my father was warm in my veins."

One distinguished general of the time called Barton "the greatest humanitarian the world has ever known."

In 1865, President Abraham Lincoln gave Clara the responsibility to locate the remains or determine the status of missing Union soldiers for their families. Later, working with Dorence Atwater, Clara was able to place markers on the burial sites of many of the dead Union prisoners confined at Andersonville.

Today, we remember Clara Barton.

For it was on this date in history, Clara founded the American Red Cross, an organization primarily known for its peacetime services, as much as it was for its aid to soldiers in times of war.

America's history is His story!

May 22

"To be forced to believe only one conclusion, that everything in the universe happened by chance, would violate the very objectivity of science itself. What random process could produce the brains of a man or the system of the human eye?" – Werhner von Braun

For much too long now, the American public has been subjected to the idea that evolution is the only truly scientific explanation for our earthly origins. This attitude has only been reinforced by our country's educational system.

Children are routinely indoctrinated with these teachings from their first days in elementary school. Unabated, the brainwashing continues throughout their junior and senior high school years. Then, this theory of evolution is even further perpetuated in our institutions of higher learning.

Those who bravely challenge these notions are quickly shouted down by the scholars and scientists, joined by the sheep who blindly follow them.

As someone who stared into the heavens at an early age, von Braun, this giant of the NASA space program, understood the perfection and wonder of the human eye couldn't have existed without the touch of a divine Creator.

Werner von Braun was not alone in that opinion.

"To suppose that the eye with all its inimitable contrivances for adjusting the focus to different distances, for admitting different amounts of light, and for the correction of spherical and chromatic aberration, could have been formed by natural selection, seems, I confess, absurd in the highest degree."

The man who spoke those words was none other than Charles Darwin.

America's history is His story!

May 23

"I do not believe human society, including not merely a few persons in any state, but whole masses of men, ever have attained, or ever can attain, a high state of intelligence, virtue, security, liberty, or happiness without the Holy Scriptures." –William Henry Seward

America's History is His Story:

Perhaps the best proof of those words was Seward's own life.

Maybe it was his devotion to the Word of God that transformed William Henry Seward, the former vice-president of the American Bible Society, into such a man of extraordinary character, intelligence, and vision.

As Secretary of State in the Lincoln administration, Seward was a man who saw deep into America's future, realizing the wisdom, profit, and importance of acquiring Alaska and eventually, Hawaii for the United States of America.

When Seward negotiated the purchase of Alaska from Russia, he was widely ridiculed. His detractors called it "Seward's Folly."

In addition, perhaps it was only God's protection that ultimately spared his life.

On the night of Lincoln's assassination, part of the conspiracy also involved an attempt on the life of William Henry Seward, scarring him for the rest of his life.

Lewis Powell, one of Booth's conspirators, entered Seward's home and repeatedly stabbed the Secretary of State and wounded his sons, who would all recover.

The scars of the assassination attempt weren't the only thing that remained from Seward's years as Secretary of State. Years later, when asked about his greatest achievement in the office, Seward replied, "The purchase of Alaska, but it will take the people of the United States a generation before they realize it."

America's history is His story!

May 24

"If it be the pleasure of Heaven that my country shall require the poor offering of my life, the victim shall be ready at the appointed hour of

sacrifice, come when that hour may. But while I do live, let me have a country, a free country." –John Adams

In short, John Adams said that he was willing to die to purchase his country's freedom. Although his life was spared and Adams would be elected as one of those who would lead this young Republic, many of his countrymen made the ultimate sacrifice in the cause of liberty.

Although Adams' death wasn't required to purchase our liberty, it's important for you to realize that he certainly made sacrifices for the cause. And he was willing to die.

On his trips abroad to represent the Colonies and trying to enlist the support of the French, Adams was forced to leave his wife and home. His ship was repeatedly pursued, but eluded several ships of the British navy.

On one occasion, while sailing on the *Boston*, they encountered the British ship, *Martha*, returning from England. The American sailors armed themselves for battle. Standing among them, with a gun at the ready, was John Adams.

Citing his orders from the Continental Congress to get Adams safely to France, Commodore Tucker finally persuaded the future president to go below deck with his son, John Quincy Adams.

This signer of the Declaration, John Adams, wasn't merely an intellectual, or a philosopher of freedom. When the time came to take up arms in the fight for liberty, Adams was also prepared to draw blood or to shed his own.

America's history is His story!

May 25

"It being among my first wishes to see some plan adopted by which slavery in this country may be abolished by law." –George Washington

America's History is His Story:

Recently, the South Carolina NAACP hosted a rally at the Columbia statehouse to honor the late Martin Luther King.

At the rally site, there is a statue of George Washington, which the organizers chose to hide behind a three-sided wooden box. This was done for the stated purpose that they "didn't want to offend anyone."

It is absolutely shameful that anyone who dares to call themselves an American would be offended by a statue of the great George Washington!

If it weren't for the contributions of General Washington, then Black Americans wouldn't have a country where they were free to hold a public rally. If it weren't for this statesman's wise and principled leadership at the Convention, then we wouldn't have a Constitution that could eventually recognize the rights and freedoms of Americans must be equally applied to every race.

Today, black citizens living in the African continent still find themselves laboring under slavery. They are routinely killed by pestilence, famine, or hostile and corrupt governmental regimes that indiscriminately kill anyone they choose.

Black Americans living in the United States enjoy a freedom unmatched by any other country in the world. Moreover, it was one of the Lord's choicest servants, George Washington, who helped to secure those rights for each and every one of us.

America's history is His story!

May 26

"Humanism is not new. It is, in fact, man's second oldest faith. Its promise was whispered in the first days of the Creation under the Tree of the Knowledge of Good and Evil: 'Ye shall be as gods.'"

–Whittaker Chambers

As a former Communist agent who defected to America, Whittaker Chambers was intimately familiar with the utter destruction humanism does to a nation or to the never-dying soul of mankind.

Every wrong and evil of society can be traced to humanism, a worship of the mind and a deification of self. It is faithless and empty, a religion of the fool.

Our Founders understood the truths of Scripture, that man is inherently sinful. Man is not evolving; he is devolving. Mankind is getting worse, not better. Humanism loudly disputes that claim.

A number of years ago, there was a popular bumper sticker, posted on an untold number of cars that proclaimed, "No Fear."

Of course, the slogan appealed to the macho tendencies of thousands of young men. Teenagers were often drawn to the slogan as well. But those two words—No Fear—are perhaps the greatest definition of humanism that was ever written.

There are certainly things in this world a reasonable person *ought* to fear.

There can be no true bravery without the presence of fear. Children will not learn obedience to parents without fear of the consequences. Moreover, it is fear of the Lord that often brings us to Him or inspires us to walk a straight and righteous path.

It was the fear of Godless tyranny that inspired brave men to form a great nation.

America's history is His story!

May 27

"You would be convinced that natural liberty is a gift of the beneficent Creator, to the whole human race, and that civil liberty is founded in

that, and cannot be wrestled from any people, without the most manifest violation of justice." –John Adams

Increasingly, our country has been subjected to presidents who question the idea of "American exceptionalism." They challenge the indisputable facts of our Godly American heritage. And they routinely travel around the globe, bowing to foreign dictators, and apologizing for all the supposed *evils* of America.

However, it needs to be stated that if a president doesn't believe our nation is exceptional—if he doesn't believe we have been extraordinarily blessed by God—then he needs to immediately resign from his office and find himself an honest line of work.

Better still, perhaps that occupant of the Oval Office should simply catch a plane, to whatever nation he thinks is better, and petition them for citizenship.

Nobody is suggesting the United States doesn't have any faults. And it may be true that we owe some apologies for actions that have occasionally taken place in our nation's past.

However, those humble apologies should only be directed towards the God of Heaven, not to man.

America certainly doesn't owe the world an apology for anything. And it is inappropriate for our leaders to ever bow to them. The strength, freedom, and wealth we have enjoyed for over two hundred years has been given to us by the hands of Almighty God, because our country willingly bowed our knee to Him at our inception.

America's history is His story!

May 28

"Charlestown is laid in ashes. The battle began upon our entrenchments upon Bunker's Hill, Saturday morning about three o'clock, and

has not ceased yet. And it is now three o'clock Sabbath afternoon. It is expected they will come out over the Neck tonight, and a dreadful battle must ensue. Almighty God, cover the heads of our country men, and be a shield to our dear friends." –Abigail Adams

From the rocky summit of Penn's Hill, Abigail Adams and her seven-year old son, John Quincy Adams, watched the battle taking place in the distance. Sadly, one of their closest friends, Dr. Joseph Warren was killed in the fighting.

In this letter, Abigail reveals one of the great truths of warfare: it is not only the men who sacrifice.

Whenever America has gone to war, it is the wives and mothers who often have to carry the load on the home front.

With these battles of the war for American Independence taking place within walking distance of her residence, Abigail Adams had to be prepared to flee her home at a moment's notice, to get her children to safety.

And as the wife of one of the Declaration's signers, Abigail Adams and her children were likely to be taken hostage or killed.

"Fly to the woods with our children," John Adams wrote, knowing the dangers his family might face from an approaching British army.

During the midst of a brutal war on our own soil, Abigail Adams often faced these dangers alone. Remarkably, she selfishly clung to her faith and raised a brilliant and accomplished son who, like his father, would one day lead this great, young nation.

America's history is His story!

May 29

"My endeavors to quell the rebellion of the heart have been sincere and have been assisted with the blessing from above. As I advance in life, its evils multiply, and the instances of mortality become more

America's History is His Story:

frequent and approach nearer to myself. The greater is the need for fortitude to encounter the woes that flesh is heir to, and of religion to support the pains for which there is no other remedy."

– John Quincy Adams

Recently, a troubled and evil individual opened fire on a young, Arizona Congresswoman, and all those who gathered around her for a meeting.

Whenever one of these horrible acts occur, Americans futilely spend their time trying to understand the actions that would drive a man to try to assassinate a governmental leader. Instead, they should be happy they don't.

A person who could fully comprehend the actions of an obviously evil or insane individual wouldn't be someone you would want to have around you. Insane or evil deeds can only be adequately explained by a diseased mind.

Despite the claims to the contrary, evil does exist in this world.

Americans should take some comfort in the fact these actions still shock and outrage us. That tells us they aren't commonplace and they aren't indicative of America.

We can also gain comfort in knowing we live in a country, where evil isn't allowed to triumph or overwhelm us for long.

Before this crazed young man could reload, he was tackled by those in the crowd. In the midst of evil, brave and good Americans selflessly risked their lives to stop the carnage. They make us proud. Ultimately, it is *that* quality we should seek to understand and emulate.

America's history is His story!

May 30

"In this age of space flight, when we use the modern tools of science to advance into new regions of human activity, the Bible, this grandiose,

stirring history of the gradual revelation and unfolding of the moral law, remains in every way an up-to-date Book." –Wernher von Braun

In 1968, the crew of Apollo 8 became the first humans to ever conduct a lunar orbit or visibly observe the far side of the Moon.

There were a lot of tense moments, and plenty of uncertainty, at the loss of communications, as the capsule passed behind the dark side of the moon. And successfully leaving lunar orbit was another fear overcome by the men of Apollo 8.

As the crew confronted the challenges of space, America was also facing many obstacles at home in 1968. The country endured the assassinations of Martin Luther King in Memphis, followed by Robert Kennedy's murder in Los Angeles. There were violent, anti-war protests on colleges all across the nation.

The crew, led by Commander Frank Borman, along with Jim Lovell and Bill Anders, in a nationally-televised Christmas Eve broadcast, read aloud the first 10 verses from the Book of Genesis, in which the Scriptures stated God's divine act of creation.

But in the midst of turmoil, for one brief, shining moment, three American astronauts wisely acknowledged our God and Creator, the One who controls our destiny.

As we have seen many times in our nation's history, Americans often touched the skies whenever our scientists and explorers looked beyond themselves.

The crew of Apollo 8 reminded us how we might find calm in the midst of insanity. And even in turbulent times, America could discover the Prince of Peace.

America's history is His story!

May 31

"The Americans combine the notions of Christianity and of liberty so intimately in their minds, that it is impossible to make them conceive one without the other." –Alexis de Tocqueville

Like many of those in America, John Hancock had little regard for the arrogance of British rule. As one of the wealthiest men in the Colonies, Hancock often employed his vast fortune in support of the cause of American Independence.

The British regarded him as little more than a smuggler.

When Hancock's sloop, *Liberty*, came into Boston with a huge load of wine, the British officials ignored their habitual leniency on tax charges and seized his ship.

As the *Romney*, a British man-of-war, tried to tow the *Liberty* away, a number of the Colonists objected to the move. Passions soon ignited and British retaliatory gunfire was threatened. As the *Romney* towed Hancock's sloop out of the harbor, the enraged Colonists threw rocks at the custom-house officials, broke their windows, and set fire to one of their pleasure boats.

The events of that day led to a great town hall assembly, called by the "Sons of Liberty." Speaking on behalf of the Colonists were the firebrands, Samuel Adams and James Otis. The British loyalist called their speeches "the most violent, insolent, abusive, and treasonable declaration that perhaps ever was delivered."

America has a rich and noble history of anger in the cause of freedom. As modern-day Sons of Liberty, we shouldn't let *Liberty* be snatched away from us without a fight as well.

America's history is His Story!

June 1

"The heart is sometimes so embittered that nothing but Divine love can sweeten it, so enraged that devotion can only becalm it, and so broken down that it takes all the forces of heavenly hope to raise it. In short, the religion of Jesus Christ is the only sure and controlling power over sin." – Francis Marion

The man known as the "Swamp Fox" gained great notoriety for his swift and daring, surprise attacks on the British.

General Marion's words reveal a heart that was heavy with grief and a soul deeply stricken with bitterness. They also bring to light a person who allowed the love of God to gently wash over him, ultimately forgiving those responsible for the loss he suffered.

The British never succeeded in their desire to take the Swamp Fox as a prisoner. But like many of those who fought in the American Revolution, Marion didn't escape the war unscathed. The currency of blood is often required in war.

The Swamp Fox's nephew, Gabriel Marion, was captured by the Redcoats. Upon learning the young man's identity, Gabriel was promptly executed.

Perhaps Marion was thinking of the cruel death of his nephew when he talked about the Lord's ability to lift a soul. Maybe it was this love of God, born in his heart, a love that might also explain Marion's refusal to mistreat those he had taken prisoner.

Francis Marion gave up his nephew in much the same way that God offered up His only begotten Son.

The blessings of liberty were purchased for us by men like Francis Marion, a man who recognized our liberty from sin was purchased by the Lord.

America's history is His story!

America's History is His Story:

June 2

"I prayed to God and asked him for a lot of things, and He delivered throughout the entire time." –Scott O'Grady

On this day in 1995, a United States Air Force pilot was shot down by the Serbs. His F-16 ripped in two by a surface-to-air missile, Captain Scott O'Grady ejected from his plane over northern Bosnia.

For the next six days, Capt. O'Grady, desperate to avoid capture, would employ every ounce of survival and evasion training he ever learned. Sleeping during the day and moving at night, Scott survived on grass and insects, drinking the water he caught in Ziploc bags or wrung out of his wet, woolen socks.

In between these activities, O'Grady fervently prayed.

Fearful that contacting his base too early might lead to his capture, the captain didn't attempt any communications until day four. Radioing for help, the voice on the other end was one known to him.

When the heavily armed helicopters came to rescue him, O'Grady ran to meet them. The young pilot was wet, cold, hungry, and severely dehydrated. The Marines quickly helped him aboard and cautiously scanned the area for hostile troops.

Although they were later fired upon, the Marines in the rescue helicopters assured O'Grady he was in good hands. Those brave Marines didn't know how right they were.

Thanks to the help of his military training, the dedication of those who determined to rescue him, and the grace of the Lord above, Capt. Scott O'Grady safely made it home.

America's history is His story!

June 3

"We have staked the whole future of American civilization, not upon the power of government, far from it. We have staked the future of all of our political institutions upon the capacity of mankind for self-government, upon the capacity of each and all of us to govern ourselves, to sustain ourselves according to the Ten Commandments of God."
—James Madison

In much the same way that Thomas Jefferson penned the Declaration of Independence, James Madison, the 4th president of the United States, was responsible for writing the Constitution.

Madison realized the government they were creating was truly unique and special. In order for this unprecedented experiment in liberty to survive, it would require the contributions of a good and moral population.

Freedom is a sacred trust from God. In addition, rights without responsibilities always lead to anarchy.

James Madison instinctively knew the Ten Commandments were a good prescription for morality. Those who sought to follow God's laws and implement those values in their personal lives would naturally be lifted to a higher plane of behavior.

If the Ten Commandments were good enough for the author of our Constitution, then perhaps we should also make every effort to live them in our daily lives, as well.

America's history is His story!

June 4

"Freedom is a need of the soul and nothing else. It is in striving toward God that the soul strives continually after a condition of freedom. God

America's History is His Story:

alone is the inciter and guarantor of freedom. He is the only guarantor."–Whittaker Chambers

As American citizens, we often take the freedoms and rights we've known in America for granted. Elsewhere around the world, citizens, suffering under Communist governments, long to savor the sweet benefits of liberty.

On this day in 1989, thousands of young protestors, in the cause of democracy, lined the streets in Beijing's Tiananmen Square.

The Chinese government, desiring to end the protests, instructed the military to crush these demonstrations. Armed with military tanks, Chinese soldiers were ordered to disperse the protestors at all costs.

We've all seen the picture of the young male, Chinese demonstrator, standing alone in front of a tank. His desire to taste the freedoms we currently enjoy, led him to place his life at risk in the pursuit of liberty.

There can be no question that the young man's final breaths on this earth were his courageous yearnings to breathe the air of freedom.

In the carnage to follow, hundreds of Chinese citizens were killed and many more were arrested.

Following the Boston Massacre, the Colonists wisely turned their prayers to the Lord; it's tragic that the massacre of Tiananmen Square didn't do the same.

America's history is His story!

June 5

"I place economy among the first and most important virtues, and public debt as the greatest of dangers to be feared. To preserve our independence, we must not let our rulers load us with perpetual debt. If we

run into such debts, we must be taxed in our meat and drink, in our necessities and in our comforts, in our labor and our amusements. If we can prevent the government from wasting the labor of the people, under the pretense of caring for them, they will be happy."

–Thomas Jefferson

On this date in history, we recognize the births of both Adam Smith and John Maynard Keynes, two of the world's most well-known economists. These two men, born 160 years apart, are clearly separated by a lot more than just the years.

Born in 1723, Adam Smith's theories on capitalism and free markets were adopted by the Founding Fathers. Like Smith, they believed that individuals would produce things and create wealth if the government would simply stay out of their way.

John Maynard Keynes, born in 1883, brought our world the idea that government must sometimes interfere in the free market system, manipulating the system with government spending and borrowing, supposedly in the effort to stimulate the economy.

Increasingly, America has foolishly abandoned the sound economic principles of Adam Smith for the sirens' call of John Maynard Keynes' economic policy.

Moreover, the economic theories of Keynes are leading our nation and the world into a downward spiral, pulling us under an ever-growing vortex of red ink.

Adam Smith's principles ruled America for most of our history, making us the great economic power in the world. John Keynes' theories became prominent in the 1930s and beyond, making our country the world's largest debtor.

One was embraced by the Founders, the other by Marxists. The choice is clear.

America's history is His story!

America's History is His Story:

June 6

"There comes a time when you've used your brains, your training, your technical skills, and the die is cast and the events are in the hands of God, and there you have to leave them." –Dwight D. Eisenhower

On this day in 1944, General Eisenhower gave the command to launch Operation Overlord, more commonly known as D-Day.

As the first rays of dawn broke over the English Channel, the seas were lined with thousands of warships and troop transports.

Freedom was coming to Europe.

When the ramps first dropped on the landing crafts, the German machine gun fire obliterated the bodies of the young, American lead troops. But more troops were coming. There would be many more, eventually overwhelming the massive number of German troops, concrete bunkers, and heavy armaments of Hitler's formidable Atlantic Wall.

The spray of machine gun fire filled the air. The cries of the wounded and dying could be heard along the seashore. The briny seas ran crimson on June Sixth, as the tides washed away the soldiers' blood from the sandy beaches.

That evening, as the sun was setting over the bloody beaches of Normandy, over 9,000 Allied troops had been killed or wounded. Over 100,000 more had landed successfully and were starting their assault on Europe.

As they have always done in battle, American troops refused to back down from the guns and mortars of the enemy. And as they have always done, American troops willingly offered up their lives to bring liberty to the oppressed.

America's history is His story!

June 7

"Timid men prefer the calm of despotism to the tempestuous sea of Liberty." –Thomas Jefferson

America, a land started by rugged individualists, has always been a tough country for the timid. There is a good reason why our nation is known as the "land of the free and the home of the brave."

In America, life is not certain. Success is not guaranteed. Responsibility is required. And failure always remains a possibility.

Freedom is messy. And it is occasionally dangerous.

When our Founders established this nation, they knew a free people couldn't be protected from every evil in society.

Ben Franklin said, "Any society that would give up a little liberty to gain a little security will deserve neither and lose both."

A government large enough to prevent every danger will quickly become a government large enough to become one.

In a free society, individual acts of random violence can never be fully prevented. Our Founders placed the responsibility for one's own protection solely in the hands of the individual. No doubt that is the reason why the Second Amendment was included in the Bill of Rights.

However, we are not totally defenseless. Our protection also rests in the hands of the Lord, upon whom the Founders also rested their trust.

America's history is His story!

June 8

"In my tent last night, after a fatiguing day's service, I remembered that I had failed to send you my contribution for our colored Sunday

America's History is His Story:

School. Enclosed you will find my check for that object, which please acknowledge at your earliest convenience."

–Gen. Thomas "Stonewall" Jackson

The preceding words of Confederate General Thomas "Stonewall" Jackson were written to his pastor.

The life of this remarkable man is certainly a study in contradictions.

Although he commanded soldiers for the Confederacy, Jackson was opposed to the institution of slavery. Although he was strict with his subordinates, Stonewall was gracious and charitable in his personal dealings. Although Jackson could be relentless on the battlefield, he was a devout Christian, generously giving his money to educate black school children.

Much of what is said and written about Stonewall Jackson today is misinformed and critical. Most of the hatred for the general is generally confined to those individuals who spend the most time lecturing American about the need for "tolerance." Moreover, little of the condemnation for General Jackson has any basis in historical fact.

When it was still considered a crime to educate slaves, Thomas Jackson dared to teach a young, black friend how to write. Stonewall continued this practice as an adult, giving of his personal funds to educate slaves in the South.

While black Americans were still subjected to slavery, Jackson's deep sense of faith inspired him to educate and evangelize all those who came under his influence.

America's history is His story!

June 9

"The choice before us is plain: Christ or chaos, conviction or compromise, discipline or disintegration. I am rather tired of hearing about our rights and privileges as American citizens. The time is come—it is now—when we ought to hear about the duties and responsibilities of our citizenship. America's future depends upon her accepting and demonstrating God's government." –Peter Marshall

As Chaplain of the United States Senate, this Presbyterian minister spoke these words not long after the end of World War II.

However, these words are as timeless now as when they were first spoken. It is normal for Americans to clamor for their rights and to complain about their responsibilities.

Our ever-growing national debt is the product of a people focused only on their rights and not their responsibilities. Our political leaders routinely win their elections by appealing to their voters' desires and not their duties.

When our Founders signed the Declaration of Independence, not only were they acknowledging their rights; they were also accepting their responsibilities as citizens.

For some of these signers, their willingness to fulfill their duties cost them their lives, their families, or their possessions. In some cases, it cost them all three.

Whenever we provide for our own families, without looking to the government, then we are choosing the responsibilities of citizenship. When we cast our votes for those who will be faithful guardians of taxpayer funds, instead of playing Santa Claus with other people's money, then we are fulfilling our duties.

America's History is His Story:

America was founded by selfless men, who lifted others to higher purposes. Our country will return to greatness when each one of us demands less and devotes more.

America's history is His story!

June 10

"Europe is in flames, withering in a fire set by Hitler. All over that continent men and women and children are dying. Soon we too will be involved. And what am I doing? I'm sitting in the bull pen, telling jokes to the relief pitchers." –Moe Berg

Born the poor child of Jewish parents, Moe Berg was a Major League baseball player, known more for his great intellect than he was for his catching abilities.

Upon learning that Berg spoke seven languages, a teammate replied, "Yeah, I know, and he can't hit in any of them."

Selected to a touring All-Star team, that included the likes of Babe Ruth, Lou Gehrig, and Jimmie Foxx, the light-hitting Berg joined them in Japan. While the team was playing elsewhere, Berg made his way to the top of a Tokyo hospital and filmed the city, its coastline, and their munitions facilities with a 16-mm movie camera.

It has been speculated that Jimmy Doolittle used the footage Berg brought back to America in the planning of his bombing raid of Tokyo.

In addition to his undistinguished major league career, Berg became an agent of the United States government, serving in the Office of Strategic Services (OSS), a forerunner to the CIA. In that role, Berg investigated a German scientist, Werner Heisenberg, involved with that country's World War II atomic bomb development. Berg even plotted the man's possible assassination, which was never carried out.

America has always produced unique and talented individuals. Like many of those, this poor-hitting Major League catcher gave his talents to the country he loved.

America's history is His story!

June 11

"Consenting to slavery is a sacrilegious breach of trust, as offensive in the sight of God as it is derogatory from our own honor or interest of happiness." –John Adams

Lost among the stories of the American Revolution are the noble contributions of black Americans to the cause.

The first Colonists to fall in the fight for liberty were men of bondage.

At the Boston Massacre, British muskets killed five men in the crowd. The first life taken in the attack was Crispus Attucks, a runaway slave.

Courageously standing among the Lexington Minutemen, that April morning, was a slave named Prince Estabrook. After the "shot heard round the world" was fired, Estabrook's body was to be found among those brave but fallen patriots.

Although slavery didn't end with General Washington's victory at Yorktown, America's triumph would eventually lead to freedom for those of every color.

The deaths of Crispus Attucks and the wounding of Prince Estabrook were no less important to the Revolution than the loss of any white soldiers in the Continental Army.

Five Colonists were slain on that Boston street and eight Minutemen were killed on Lexington Green. As those men shed their final life's blood for the Revolution, it was impossible to segregate the blood stains of slaves from those of their free, white comrades. Moreover, it was that blood that germinated the precious seeds of liberty.

It is certainly not an exaggeration to say that Almighty God gave birth to a great nation because a black soldier willingly shed his red blood on Lexington Green.

America's history is His story!

June 12

"Go home and tell your master he has sent you on a fool's errand and broken the peace of our Sabbath. What, do you think we were born in the woods, to be frightened by owls?"–Sarah Tarrant

Upon learning the colonists were preparing cannons for battle, British General Thomas Gage sent Colonel Alexander Leslie to Salem to capture their armaments.

Being familiar with the tenets of their faith, the British hoped to use their knowledge of the Colonists' religious practices against them. Thinking many of them would be sitting in the church pews, instead of manning their guns on this Lord's Day, Gage figured he might catch the Colonists off-guard.

He guessed wrong.

Alerted to their mission, a hearty band of armed militia challenged the Redcoats. The militia halted their advance long enough for the Colonists to hide their heavy arms.

After failing in their mission to seize the powder and weapons, the 240 British troops retreated back through the town. In response to their actions, an enraged Sarah Tarrant shouted those words at the troops under Leslie's command.

Angered by her comment, one of the British troops aimed his musket at her.

"Fire, if you have the courage," Sarah Tarrant said, "but I doubt it." Sarah Tarrant was right about the soldier.

Although America's struggle for Independence couldn't have been won without the efforts of brave men, it also required the defiant courage and righteous indignation of Colonial women like Sarah Tarrant.

America's history is His story!

June 13

"Besides, sir, we shall not fight our battles alone. There is a just God who presides over the destiny of nations; and who will raise up friends to fight our battles for us." –Patrick Henry

Patrick Henry was absolutely correct; God would certainly raise up friends to help us in our war against the British throne.

During America's greatest time of need, the French came to our aid.

Patrick Henry wisely recognized a just God would raise up friends for America. However, in much the same way that France aided our Revolutionary cause, the United States has often come to the aid of other nations in need.

In a sense, the United States of America has become the friend and ally, to other nations, that God raised up for us during those dark days of the Revolution.

France, the nation that graciously came to our need, has also been on the receiving end of America's benevolence during times of war.

When France was in need during World War I, the George M. Cohan song, *Over There*, proudly told the world the Yanks were coming to her aid. When France was invaded by the Nazis in World War II, the United States once again came to the rescue.

Today, the nation of France is home to eleven military cemeteries, containing the bodies of thousands of brave Americans. These honored dead gave their lives, paying in full any remaining debt to the French.

America's history is His story!

June 14

"But I am filled with amazement, when I am told, that, in this enlightened age and in the heart of the Christian world, there are persons who can witness this daily manifestation of the power and wisdom of the Creator, and yet say in their hearts, 'There is no God.' "

–Edward Everett

When you look at the nighttime sky, what do you think about?

When former astronaut, Alan Bean stared at the heavens, he often thought about the silver flight pin that he left on the surface of the moon in 1969.

Since there is no moisture or atmosphere to degrade the object on the lunar surface, the pin will still be as shiny as the day he left it behind.

Another thing unaltered on the moon's surface are the footprints the astronaut left behind, since there is no wind or rain to erase them.

As the fourth man to walk on the moon, Alan Bean not only left a silver pin and his footprints on the moon's surface; he also left a great legacy of space exploration.

Each one of us should look to the heavens and reflect on what heritage our passing will bestow on our homes, communities, and country. Will those who come along behind us find we have left behind a shining legacy, something that won't mildew, rust, or corrupt? Are the footprints you leave behind ones that others would do well to follow?

Will your passing through this life be one of faith and love for country? Will your footprints inspire others to emulate those same qualities you value? Will you build the bridges across the chasms, making the pathway easier for those who follow you?

What will you leave behind for America?

America's history is His story!

June 15

"A sense of duty pursues us ever. It is omnipresent, like the Deity. If we take to ourselves the wings of the morning, and dwell in the uttermost parts of the sea, duty performed or duty violated is still with us, for our happiness or our misery. If we say the darkness shall cover us, in the darkness as in the light our obligations are yet with us."

– Daniel Webster

Although many of you will know Ted Williams, the great ballplayer for the Boston Red Sox, you may not know he was also a great military pilot. Serving in both World War II and Korea, Williams bravely served his country as a Marine pilot.

While flying bombing missions in Korea, Williams occasionally served as the wingman for future NASA astronaut, John Glenn. Once, when his plane was badly damaged, Williams was forced to make a dangerous belly–landing of his flaming aircraft.

This Hall of Famer's service to America not only limited his baseball career; it could have easily taken his life.

Williams, one of the game's premier hitters, was the last man in Major League baseball to hit .400. However, it's quite likely some of the game's other formidable records might have fallen, had Williams not lost nearly five years of his baseball career in service to his country.

Baseball was blessed to have witnessed the career of this remarkable athlete. More importantly, America has been blessed to have produced many brave and selfless military people, just like Ted Williams, who willingly put their nation's security before their own comforts and careers.

America's history is His story!

June 16

"Oh God, let this horrible war come quickly to an end that we may all return home and engage in the only work that is worthwhile, and that is the salvation of men." –Gen. Thomas "Stonewall" Jackson

During World War I, Alvin C. York was a poor, young man from the mountains of Tennessee. Believing his Bible taught him to be a "conscientious objector," York was drafted into the service, while many of those around him chose to enlist.

After several discussions about the Scriptures with his commanding officer, this superb marksman with no stomach for killing finally consented to serve in the infantry.

While in France, the young man from Tennessee saw his unit pinned down by hostile, German machine gun fire.

Moving across the terrain, he worked his way behind the German guns. York then proceeded to fire at them, picking them off one-by-one. When several of the enemy charged him with bayonets, York pulled his pistol and shot them from back to front, like he often killed flocks of wild turkeys back home.

Seeing they were no match for the determined American marksman, 132 German soldiers surrendered.

"I am a witness to the fact that God did help me out of that hard battle," York replied, "for the bushes were shot up all around me and I never got a scratch."

As a result of his extraordinary valor in combat, Alvin York, who once questioned the morality of killing in battle, was presented with the military's highest award, the Congressional Medal of Honor.

America's history is His story!

June 17

"If we abide by the principles taught in the Bible, our country will go on prospering and to prosper; but if we and our posterity neglect its instructions and authority, no man can tell how sudden a catastrophe may overwhelm us and bury all our glory in profound obscurity."
–Daniel Webster

Perhaps Daniel Webster was on to something. His words are eerily prophetic.

You don't have to look around your world too long to see that much of America currently has no use for the Bible or its principles. Another look will reveal to you that our country is no longer prospering as we have done in the past.

National unemployment is at record levels. Prices for consumer items are increasing dramatically. Our national debt has grown to a level that is certainly unsustainable.

And all of these things have coincided with a country that no longer appears to value God's Word.

It's entirely possible that America's greatest days are behind her, unless, of course, many of us return the Lord to His place before us.

America's establishment and its unparalleled rise to greatness were not built on hubris and humanism. Our nation enjoyed its remarkable success because of our reliance on the Lord and our willingness to follow His principles.

Our country has experienced at least one great, spiritual awakening in every century of its existence. It could happen once again in America, if we would only turn to the One who gave us life.

America's history is His story!

June 18

"The Almighty implanted in us these inextinguishable feelings for good and wise purposes. They are the guardians of His image in our heart. They distinguish us from the herd of common animals." –Thomas Paine

The United Nations recently warned us that overpopulation is a serious threat to our existence. However, one of the greatest threats to America's survival is contained in the brand of scientific counsel we continue to receive from that organization.

You should not find it surprising that the United Nations' solution to this problem involves more international funding for "family planning," a term that could be more accurately translated, "forced abortions."

America was founded on the first principle that all human life is sacred.

Whenever someone fails to place the proper value on human life, then it will not be long before he will feel no restraints to slaughter human beings like livestock.

It happened in Germany, when Hitler killed six million Jews in the Holocaust. Untold millions were slaughtered in China under the regime of Chairman Mao. And Stalin also murdered millions of his own citizens in Russia.

The United Nations did absolutely nothing to stop these ungodly human purges.

Unfortunately, the United States also joined this mass slaughter of the innocent, when the Supreme Court legalized abortion in 1973.

Abortion has taken the place of slavery as America's greatest sin, a transgression for which we need to bow before the Supreme Judge, not the Supreme Court.

America's history is His story!

June 19

"The Americans will always do the right thing...after they've exhausted all the alternatives." –Winston Churchill

Long before America chose to enter into World War II, Winston Churchill, the British Prime Minister, was strongly urging our involvement in the battle against Adolph Hitler's invasion of Europe.

Although he made a joke in his marvelously-stodgy sense of British humor, the words Churchill spoke said volumes about our nation.

Although Britain had been successful in preventing the Nazis' advance into their country, the wise Prime Minister knew they needed the help of America to fully defeat the powers of the Axis.

Perhaps our nation has made some mistakes, but Churchill was right. America *has* always done the right thing.

Although the United States was hesitant to get into World War II, nobody can question our nation's commitment, once war was officially declared. And despite the fact that slavery was legal at our nation's founding, our country eventually went to war with itself and freed the slaves.

America's History is His Story:

Our nation's commitment to doing the right thing is an integral part of our national character and a byproduct of our godly American heritage.

America's history is His story!

June 20

"This is a world of compensation; and he who would be no slave must consent to have no slave. Those who deny freedom to others deserve it not for themselves, and under a just God, cannot long retain it."

–Abraham Lincoln

This is a proud day for the citizens of West Virginia, which was founded on this date in 1863.

The origins of West Virginia are truly unique, for it was the only state that actually seceded from secessionist states. Created during the Civil War, its establishment effectively ended the practice of slavery within its borders, while Virginia willingly chose to maintain slavery and fight for the Confederate cause.

In a sense, the circumstances behind West Virginia's founding have some significant things in common with the events surrounding our nation's establishment. Not only was there a huge debate in regards to the issue of slavery, the residents of western Virginia were also outraged about what they believed to be unfair representation.

In much the same way that Gen. Washington led our nation through the Revolution and oversaw the creation of our foundational document, Abraham Lincoln, another great American president, also shepherded the process of West Virginia's complicated road to statehood.

Although the state of West Virginia and its people are often unfairly maligned on television or in the media, the origins of this state are uniquely American, and its citizens reflect their strong sense of pride in the motto: "Mountaineers are always free."

America's history is His story!

June 21

"The Bible is God's chart for you to steer by, to keep you from the bottom of the sea, and to show you where the harbor is, and how to reach it without running on the rocks and bars." –Henry Ward Beecher

During World War II, the *USS Indianapolis* set sail, with a cargo in her hold that would ultimately end our war with Japan. Unknown to most of the crew, the ship transported the bomb that would soon be dropped on Hiroshima.

Not long after delivering her deadly cargo, the *Indianapolis* was torpedoed by the Japanese. The ship sank in less than fifteen minutes, becoming a tomb for about 300 men.

Approximately 900 more were stranded in the shark-infested waters. Clinging to debris or anything else that would float—and often clinging to each other—the men waited for help that was much too long in coming.

For the next four days, hypothermia, dehydration, hunger, and shark attacks would greatly deplete their numbers.

One of the survivors believed his faith in the Lord kept him going throughout the ordeal. The young serviceman often prayed and quoted Scripture to his friend, who also survived their time in the deadly waters.

The same faith in God that gave this young serviceman the courage and strength to survive has often been embraced by Americans in times of war. This same faith has been the inspiration for our founding. It has been our refuge in times of crisis. It has often been our harbor in troubled waters.

God has always been there for our nation and for those who keep it free.

America's history is His story!

June 22

"The Hebrews have done more to civilize men than any other nation."
–John Adams

It is impossible to fully understand the establishment and expansion of the United States without a cursory knowledge of Moses and how he led the children of Israel out of Egypt into the Promised Land.

In Deuteronomy 4:9, Moses warned them to remember the things they had seen and to teach them to "thy sons, and thy sons' sons."

It was good advice for the children of Israel then; it is still good advice for America today.

Many of the problems in our country can be explained by a people who fail to adequately understand and value their history. Unfortunately, much of our history is being written and taught by people who hold nothing but contempt for the principles that made our country great.

Moses knew it was important that those, who experienced the parting of the Red Sea or saw manna fall from Heaven, would pass those experiences along to their children and grandchildren.

It is also critical that young people in the United States need to be taught and reminded of the miracles that Americans have seen and experienced. Unfortunately, many of those who write our history books are desperately seeking to remove those truths from our history. But their attempts to rewrite our history cannot change the facts...

America's history is His story!

June 23

"I heard a fine example today, namely, that His Excellency General George Washington rode around among his army yesterday and admonished each and every one to fear God, to put away the wickedness that has set in and become so general, and to practice the Christian virtues." –Henry Muhlenberg

No doubt many of you have seen the painting of Gen. George Washington kneeling in prayer, next to his horse in the snows of Valley Forge.

Over the years, there has been much speculation about whether it actually happened as how it is depicted. One can only wonder about the motives of those who seek to deny the event's credibility. Perhaps now, the questions can finally be put to rest.

Living close to the military encampments of Valley Forge was a British loyalist, a Quaker by the name of Isaac Potts, whose home was requisitioned by the general for his personal headquarters.

One day, while Potts was out on the road, he heard the sound of a man's voice coming from the woods. Curious as to its source, he decided to investigate. Tying his horse to a tree, Potts made his way through the wintry forest, eventually coming upon the general, knelt in prayer.

Although he remained there long enough to listen to a portion of Washington's prayer, Potts did nothing to disturb the general's petition before the Lord.

"Such a prayer I never heard from the lips of man," Potts related.

Apparently, the humble prayer of Gen. Washington made such an impression on the man, Isaac Potts was converted to the noble, American cause.

America's history is His story!

June 24

"Nay, men are so far from musing of their sins, that they disdain this practice, and scoff at it. What say they, if all were of your mind; what should become of us?" –Thomas Hooker

When discussing our Founding Fathers, one individual whose name has been generally lost to us is that of Thomas Hooker.

Forced to flee two different countries in Europe because of persecution over his religious teachings, Hooker crossed the Atlantic in search of religious freedom. Initially arriving in Boston, the minister soon raised the ire of the Puritans in Massachusetts.

Refusing to be silenced here in America, Hooker and his band of followers started a settlement in Hartford. As a result of his writings and ministry, he soon became a dominant leader among in New England.

In fact, it was one of his sermons, before the General Court of Connecticut, that inspired the writing of *Fundamental Orders of Connecticut*, the constitution upon which the colony of Connecticut would be governed.

As a result of its clear proclamation of such a unique set of democratic principles, the other colonies would use that ground-breaking document as the pattern for their own constitutions. Moreover, the

United States Constitution owes much more of its content to Connecticut's governing document than any other constitution.

Thomas Hooker was a man of great honor, bravery, and faith. It was this faith, and the desire to practice it freely, that brought Hooker to America. And it was this faith that inspired the ideals that became the governing principles of our everyday life.

America's history is His story!

June 25

"Humility and knowledge in poor clothes excel pride and ignorance in costly attire." –William Penn

On this date in 1876, Gen. George Custer and his 7th Cavalry were annihilated by Sioux and Cheyenne Indians, at the Battle of the Little Bighorn.

Unfortunately, that is the extent of what most people know about George Armstrong Custer.

Although his prideful actions at Little Bighorn may have ultimately led to his death, Gen. Custer was also a great soldier and officer in the Union Army.

During the Civil War, his daring and aggressive attacks on the enemy led him to quickly climb the ranks of leadership. On no less than two occasions, Custer had horses shot out from under him, but came away unscathed.

It was his actions at Gettysburg that often win him the most praise, helping to lead the troops who stopped Jeb Stuart's assault on the rear of the Union Army.

Despite his vanity and flamboyant manner of dress, Custer's gallantry in battle earned him the praise of Gen. Philip Sheridan, who presented Custer and his wife with the table, upon which Lee signed his surrender at Appomattox.

While the man may be deserving of ridicule for his actions at Little Bighorn, Gen. Custer's great service to the Union army is deserving of every American's respect. For without the contribution of men such as Custer, and many like him, our nation might not have known an end to the scourge of slavery.

America's history is His story!

June 26

"Religion begat prosperity, and the daughter devoured the mother."
–Cotton Mather

All around the country, we are seeing governors and state legislatures dealing with state budgets that are deeply in the red. Unfortunately, these state budgets also reflect the massive federal debt that the United States is currently facing.

In any careful reading of the Scriptures, you will soon discover that there are two ways in which God judges a nation for its transgressions. The Lord punishes them through famine and military conquest.

It is certainly not an exaggeration for anyone to suggest that America's current economic woes could be construed in Biblical terms as a "famine."

Men of faith founded this nation. Moreover, it was conceived in the principles of Scripture. And by adhering to those principles, God blessed our nation financially.

However, now that our nation is denying its religious origins, and many are trying to remove all semblances of faith from the public square, we have seen America's financial situation become grave. Does anyone see a connection?

Although our military has always been powerful enough through the years to protect our citizens, that reality could eventually be compromised by our present economic situation.

Perhaps it is time that Americans saw that we cannot enjoy economic prosperity without an acknowledgement of the Almighty God who made those gifts possible.

America's history is His story!

June 27

"True Godliness doesn't turn men out of the world, but enables them to live better in it, and excites their endeavors to mend it."
—William Penn

America has always been blessed with an abundance of godly men and women, people whose faith in the Lord inspired them to seek to become better citizens in their homes and communities.

Like the Scriptural story of the Good Samaritan, Christians in America have historically come to the aid of their fellow citizens in need. These generous souls give their money, they donate their time, and they do whatever they can to lift up all of those around them.

Although Christians often claim that their citizenship resides in Heaven, they spend their lives, doing whatever they can to bring a little taste of Heaven to their earthly communities.

It is no surprise that some of our nation's best citizens are often those who put their faith in God. They are cut from the same cloth as those who founded our nation.

America's History is His Story:

When the Colonies were in crisis, it was Christians who joined the militias. They took up arms for the Revolutionary cause. They circulated the news. Godly people warned of imminent attacks from the British. They left their pulpits to fight. They willingly offered their lives.

The godly Christian and the good citizen are wholly inseparable. The bloody footprints they left at Valley Forge are still being followed by many Americans today.

America's history is His story!

June 28

"It is believed that no army in the world's history ever had in it so much of a genuine, devout piety, so much of active work for Christ, as the Army of Northern Virginia, under the command of our noble Christian leader." –John William Jones

In the midst of a brutal Civil War, Gen. Robert E. Lee's army experienced a spiritual awakening unlike anything that ever happened in history. That is the story related to us by John William Jones, a Chaplain under the Confederate general.

While it's true that God often punishes a country for its national sins, the events of the Civil War were a noble attempt by America to right the wrongs of its past.

Although a great portion of those who were fighting for the Confederacy were trying to protect the rights of slaveholders, many of them were not.

Like Gen. Lee, who opposed slavery, some of those clad in gray uniforms saw the battle as a struggle to defend their states, a war to protect their homes and families.

Although the South would eventually lose the war, and with the death of Abraham Lincoln, a man whose life would have guaranteed a much more conciliatory Reconstruction period, the sweeping spiritual changes in the ranks of the former Confederate soldiers made it possible for the Union to more quickly heal itself from those bitter wounds of a great and terrible war.

In much the same way that a spiritual awakening prepared America for the Revolution, another spiritual awakening prepared America to survive a bloody Civil War and its aftermath.

America's history is His story!

June 29

"It is in scientific honesty that I endorse the presentation of alternative theories for the origin of the universe, life, and man in the science classroom. It would be an error to overlook the possibility that the universe was planned rather than happening by chance." –Wernher von Braun

According to one on his colleagues at NASA, Wernher von Braun was called "the greatest rocket scientist in history."

However, if Wernher von Braun were alive in America today, he would be endlessly ridiculed by an arrogant scientific community for his opinions and speculation that the universe and the existence of mankind didn't happen by a random act of chance.

But von Braun wouldn't be alone in that line of thinking.

His ideas about a Divine Creator have been shared by some of the greatest scientific minds in history, men such as Louis Pasteur, Francis Bacon, George Washington Carver, Michael Faraday, Blaise Pascal, and Sir Isaac Newton.

Moreover, this is by no means an exhaustive list of the scientists who challenged the questionable principles of evolutionary thought.

"Microscopic beings must come into the world from parents similar to themselves," Pasteur observed. "There is something in the depths of our souls which tells us that the world may be more than a mere combination of events."

If the scientists of today wish to rise to the levels of Louis Pasteur and Wernher von Braun, perhaps they should once again examine the godly foundational principles that made these men great.

America's history is His story!

June 30

"Yesterday, we fought a great battle and gained a great victory for which all the glory is due to God alone. My preservation was entirely due, as was the glorious victory, to our God, to whom be all the honor, grace, and glory." –Gen. Thomas "Stonewall" Jackson

The previous words were part of a letter that Gen. Stonewall Jackson sent to his wife, following the Confederate victory at Manassas.

Addressing her as "My Precious Pet," the general humbly took no credit for the battle's outcome.

During the midst of battle, it wasn't unusual to see Gen. Jackson astride his horse, looking heavenward, with his lips offering up a quiet prayer. And while he was engaged in prayer, Jackson was oblivious to the bullets that might be flying all around him.

A man of unquestioned faith, Jackson believed he was invincible, as long as he was in the center of God's will. And strangely enough, it wouldn't be the bullets of the enemy that would take the life of Robert E. Lee's most capable general.

At Chancellorsville, Stonewall Jackson was accidentally shot by his own troops, an incident that would lead to the amputation of his left arm. Developing pneumonia, he would die eight days later.

In regards to the incident, Gen. Robert E. Lee later stated, "He has lost his left arm and I have lost my right."

Perhaps the South's greatest tactician, Stonewall's presence at Gettysburg might have greatly altered the course of the Civil War. But the Lord had other plans for him.

America's history is His story!

July 1

"I am determined to sustain myself as long as possible and die like a soldier who never forgets what is due to his own honor and that of his country. Victory or Death." –William Barrett Travis

It is impossible to hear the word "Alamo," without thinking of qualities such as courage, honor, duty, and sacrifice.

For 13 days in a small, Catholic mission, approximately 189 men stood against the might of the Mexican army, no less than 2500 troops, led by Santa Anna.

Stationed inside that meager, Texas garrison with William Barrett Travis, were Davy Crockett and Jim Bowie, a pair of larger-than-life figures, whose legends have only grown as a result of their involvement.

The actual story of the Alamo is every bit as amazing as the myths that have grown up around it. Nobody knows for certain precisely how these men finally died, whether they were killed in battle or executed. However, we do know this about them:

Against vastly superior odds, those Texas defenders knew there was little chance for their survival. They also understood reinforcements were not ultimately coming to their aid. Despite those facts, those brave men chose to stay and fight.

In fact, when Santa Anna asked for their surrender, Travis responded to their message with only a hostile cannon blast.

Davy Crockett, Jim Bowie, Colonel Travis, and the other men of the Alamo willingly chose to give their lives for a cause they believed in. That kind of sacrifice is something the men of this country have done since we first landed on Plymouth Rock.

America's history is His story!

July 2

"He never felt so near his Master as he did when in a storm, knowing that on his skill depended the safety of so many lives."

–David G. Farragut

In April of 1942, American soldiers were ordered to participate in a highly-classified mission called *Exercise Tiger*, which was a critical practice run for the invasion of the Normandy beaches on D-Day.

Just off the shore of Devon, England, several LSTs (Landing Ship Tanks) were rehearsing their eventual troop landings. Unknown to the participants, those military vessels were discovered and viciously stalked by a number of deadly, German E-boats.

To make the exercises more realistic, the military and naval personnel used live artillery fire, seeking to simulate the actual conditions under which the GIs would storm the beaches.

During the ensuing battle and the bitter fog of war at Slapton Sands, over 600 Americans were killed by the Germans. Another 300

Americans perished on the beaches or in those chilly waters, the tragic victims of "friendly fire."

What started off as a training exercise became one of the most ill-fated incidents in the annals of American military history.

With the setting of the sun, it appeared the Germans had won a great victory over the Americans at Slapton Sands. However, the military exercises that cost 946 brave Americans their lives would prove to save the lives of many others, and eventually bring down the final curtain on Hitler's Third Reich.

America's history is his story!

July 3

"I feel no anxiety at the large armament designed against us. The remarkable interposition of heaven in our favor cannot be too gratefully acknowledged. He who fed the Israelites in the wilderness, who clothes the lilies of the field, and who feeds the young ravens when they cry, will not forsake a people engaged in so right a cause, if we remember His loving kindness." –Abigail Adams

Stamped on the papers of the officers who were sent to North Africa in World War II were the words "To Gib," which was short for "To Gibraltar."

Reversing the order of the letters "To Gib" created the word, "Bigot," which became the codename used to describe those rare, few officers who knew and planned the classified details of *Operation Overlord*, more commonly known as D-Day.

Fearful that that the Nazis would torture anyone who had knowledge of the secret Allied invasion plans, these American military officers, the Bigots, weren't permitted to serve in any capacity, if it was believed there was a likelihood of them being captured.

In the aftermath of the Germans' surprise attack on *Exercise Tiger*, the top-secret mission in which American practiced the beach landings for Normandy, ten "Bigots" were listed as missing in action.

Unless all these men could be accounted for, *Operation Overlord* would have to be scrapped. After a frantic and determined search, the remains of all ten of these "Bigots" were located and/or identified.

The secrets of the "Bigots" were safe from the Nazis and the D-Day invasions would go on as planned.

Therefore, it can be accurately stated that "Bigots" won World War II.

America's history is His story!

July 4

"I am apt to believe that it will be celebrated by succeeding generations as the great anniversary festival. It ought to be commemorated, as the day of deliverance, by solemn acts of devotion to God Almighty. It ought to be solemnized with pomp and parade, with shows, games, sports, guns, bells, bonfires, and illuminations, from one end of this continent to the other, from this time forward and forever."

–John Adams

The preceding words of John Adams were his nearly-prophetic vision of how our Declaration of Independence should be celebrated by future generations.

It is remarkable how close this Founder and eventual president came to actually describing our current Independence Day celebrations all over America.

Since this was so important to them, it's the least we can do to remember their courage and sacrifice to give birth to our glorious nation.

However, if there is one thing largely missing from the current celebrations of July Fourth, it is, as Adams described, the "solemn acts of devotion to God Almighty."

Americans already have the parades and picnics. Our country engages in the fun and fireworks. Speeches are made and Old Glory is on display for everyone to see.

However, all too often, lost in the hustle and bustle, Americans forget to stop and bow their heads, and say a simple word of thanks to the Lord, for graciously giving us this great nation.

Americans have been extremely blessed to have the privilege to be born and to live in this country, and to call ourselves citizens.

So, on this special day, please take at least a few brief moments to remember and thank the Lord who gave us this wonderful country we call home.

America's history is His story!

July 5

"What a cruel thing is war: to separate and destroy families and friends, and mar the purest joys and happiness God has granted us in this world; to fill our hearts with hatred instead of love for our neighbors, and to devastate the fair face of this beautiful world."
–Robert E. Lee

Born in Athens, Ohio, in 1959, architect and designer Maya Lin is the daughter of Chinese parents, who fled the country to escape the rule of the cruel Communist dictator, Mao-Tse-tung.

America's History is His Story:

Selected to design the Vietnam Veterans Memorial, the 21 year old undergrad's innovative design was initially the subject of bitter mocking and ridicule. However, with over 2.5 million visitors coming to the site each year, the "Wall" has become one the most popular and poignant memorials in Washington.

People come to remember their families and loved ones, the stark casualties of war. They come to reminisce over their fallen brothers-in-arms. In many cases, they simply come, to remember those who died and to silently pay tribute.

The V-shaped, polished, black granite wall lists the names of over 58,000 Americans killed or missing in Vietnam.

As a person stands before the Wall and stares upon its face, he can see a reflection of himself, one more precious life for which those brave Americans shed their blood.

Perhaps you should also see this memorial as the product of young Chinese immigrants, who saw America as a harbor of freedom, a place where they could live and worship freely, in a special land, of God's own precious design.

America's history is His story!

July 6

"Familiarity with that great story of redemption, when God raised up the slave-born Moses to deliver His chosen people from bondage, and with that sublimer story where our Savior died a cruel death that all men, without distinction of race, might be saved, makes slavery impossible." –Charles Sumner

As an unemployed Prussian military general, looking for work in France, Baron von Steuben would cross paths with Benjamin Franklin, who introduced the Prussian to Gen. George Washington by means of a letter.

When he came to Valley Forge, Baron von Steuben, volunteering to work without pay for a time, could speak only German and French. However, Washington's aide-de-camp, Alexander Hamilton, was able to communicate with him in French, and translate the Prussian's orders into English.

During those dark days at Valley Forge, von Steuben drilled the troops in Washington's army. He instilled in them strict codes of discipline. He improved their health, by teaching them more effective means of camp sanitation. Moreover, he schooled them in the benefits of the bayonet as a deadly offensive weapon, training that would ultimately lead to the Colonials' victory in the Battle of Stony Point.

This sad and discouraged army, which retreated to Valley Forge in shame, would emerge from those bitter, snowy quarters with new life, passion, and finally, victory.

Perhaps the answer to Washington's prayers had come in the person of Prussian general, Baron von Steuben, who transformed Washington's Continental Army into a disciplined fighting force, who would ultimately defeat the might of the British troops.

America's history is His story!

July 7

"The fundamental source of all your errors, sophisms, and false reasoning, is a total ignorance of the natural rights of mankind. Were you once to become acquainted with these, you could never entertain a thought, that all men are not, by nature, entitled to a parity of privileges." –Alexander Hamilton

When Alexander Hamilton used the phrase "the natural rights of mankind," he was referring to the same principles referenced by Thomas Jefferson in the Declaration of Independence as, "the laws of Nature and of Nature's God."

"Natural law" or "God's law" is a principle that certain rights are universal. They are granted to every person by God and these sacred rights cannot be taken away by earthly courts, legislative edicts, or the overwhelming force of arms.

Our Founding Fathers determined that the principles of "natural law" were so precious to them, they would boldly take up arms to restore them.

In the Declaration of Independence, Jefferson aptly and succinctly defined these laws as "life, liberty, and the pursuit of happiness."

In Jeremiah 33:25, they are called "the ordinances of heaven and earth." Moses and the Apostle Paul wrote of them. In the Sermon on the Mount, Jesus spoke of them

A wise and logical God created the universe and established a certain order in it. God has decreed that man and nature are inextricably bound by those same laws.

Moreover, these laws aren't simply reserved for the citizens of the United States; they belong to all mankind. America was just the first nation to openly declare them and to wisely build its Constitution around their abiding principles.

America's history is His story!

July 8

"In giving freedom to the slave, we assure freedom to the free, honorable alike in what we give and what we preserve. We shall nobly save, or meanly lose, the last, best hope of earth. Other means may succeed;

this could not fail. The way is plain, peaceful, generous, just—a way which, if followed, the world will forever applaud and God must forever bless." –Abraham Lincoln

The men of the Alamo weren't the only Americans to defend a compound against vastly superior odds. Such was also the case in the Battle of Groton Heights, in Connecticut, during the American Revolution.

Their ranks already depleted in battle, approximately 185 men, black and white, led by Colonel William Ledyard, retreated to Fort Griswold, trying to defend it against the treachery of the notorious American turncoat, Benedict Arnold.

With their ammunition nearly gone, the American patriots were forced to fight the 1,700 British soldiers with bayonets, roughly fashioned spears, and their guns as clubs.

Freed by his master, Col. Ledyard, the slave, Jordan Freeman, refused to leave the man he faithfully served. In fact, he vowed to remain behind to fight alongside him.

Since many freed slaves often chose their last name, history doesn't reveal to us, if Freeman possibly chose his last name to reflect his newly-liberated status.

However, this *Freeman* chose to remain loyal to his friends and to the cause of liberty. In fact, it was Freeman who speared and killed Major Montgomery, who was leading the hundreds of British attackers furiously scrambling over the walls.

Like the Alamo, Fort Griswold was taken. Outraged at their casualties, the British cruelly executed the survivors, Jordan Freeman and his white fellow patriots.

America's history is His story!

America's History is His Story:

July 9

"Permit me, then, to recommend from the sincerity of my heart, ready at all times to bleed in my country's cause, a declaration of independence; and call upon the world, and the great God who governs it, to witness the necessity, propriety, and rectitude thereof."

–Gen. Nathaniel Greene

Jordan Freeman wasn't the only slave involved in the Battle of Groton Heights; also among them was a slave named Lambert Latham.

Unable to stand against the onslaught of 1,700 British soldiers, the 185 men in Colonel William Ledyard's army made their final stand inside the walls of Fort Griswold.

Bravely and boldly, the Americans fought them with guns, until their ammunition and powder was gone. Then they fought on, clubbing the enemy with the butts of their muskets and running them through with stakes. When the American flag was shot from its staff and fell in the dirt, it was Lambert Latham who picked it up and held it aloft.

Finally, the sheer numbers of the British soldiers overpowered the few brave men in the fort and the British officer asked the survivors who commanded the fort.

Colonel Ledyard stepped forward, handed over his sword, and said, "I did once; you do now."

The British officer coldly plunged Ledyard's sword into the American's body.

Outraged at the murder, Lambert Latham retaliated. Running forward, he thrust his bayonet into the body of the British officer, mortally wounding the man.

For his loyalty, Latham received 33 bayonets stabbings. This slave would fall on the same soil, dying beside his leader, shedding his final drop of blood for Independence.

America's history is His story!

July 10

"I was made for action. The Lord drove me, but I was ready. I have always been going at full speed, harnessed to the Chariot of Christ, whose wheels of fire have rolled onward, high and dreadful to His foes and glorious to His friends." –Lyman Beecher

Unlike any other nation in history, America has been a land for dreamers. This land has also been a place where those individuals can often see those dreams realized.

Like Joseph in Scripture, another young man named Joseph was also a dreamer.

Joe Boyd grew up with dreams of playing athletics. Moreover he saw those dreams coming to reality, as an All-American football player at Texas A&M. And in 1940, Boyd helped lead his team to an undefeated season and the national championship.

Drafted in the first round by the Washington Redskins, the potential NFL star was diagnosed with a damaged vertebra, a condition which could have easily left him paralyzed, had he chosen to remain in the game.

Like Joseph in Scripture, this disappointing detour in Boyd's life would eventually bring him to the place where he was destined to serve.

Joe Boyd would no longer line his mantel with shiny trophies and individual awards. Instead, the former football star would lay up for himself treasures in Heaven.

As a minister of the Gospel and a traveling tent evangelist, Joe Boyd would travel the country, going after the souls of men with the same zeal he brought to the gridiron.

And like Joseph in Scripture, Joseph Boyd, this Aggie Hall-of-Famer, would eventually find the place he belonged, proudly devoting the rest of his life to the Lord.

America's history is His story!

July 11

"Any history of this army which omits an account of the wonderful influence of religion upon it, which fails to tell how the courage, discipline, and morale was influenced by the humble piety and evangelical zeal of many of its officers and men, would be incomplete and unsatisfactory." –John William James

The preceding words were written by a Confederate chaplain in the Civil War; however, they are equally true about our troops and officers in World War II.

God's hand was clearly upon America during the war.

Following their surprise attack on Pearl Harbor, it appeared that nothing could stop the seemingly-invincible, Japanese navy's advance in the South Pacific. However, as a result of breaking the Japanese communication codes, our victory in the Battle of Midway would prove to be the turning point in the final outcome of the war.

Indecision on the part of Japanese leadership, and the inability to find our carriers, left the enemy unable to decide whether to arm their planes with bombs or torpedoes.

While the American torpedo planes inflicted very little damage on the enemy's fleet, their low-flying attacks kept the Japanese fighter planes engaged, leaving our heavy bombers unattended, as they attacked from the skies above.

Unlike the torpedo planes, which were destroyed by the Japanese, the American bomb pilots caught the enemy carriers with fueled planes and torpedoes on their decks. The resulting fires and explosions sent three Japanese carriers to the dark ocean floor.

These and many other facts should lead you to believe that, like our Revolution, our victory at Midway was due to the actions of brave men and Divine intercession.

America's history is His story!

July 12

"I have often wished that I was a more devout man than I am. Nevertheless, amid the greatest difficulties of my administration, when I could not see any other resort, I would place my whole reliance in God, knowing that all would go well, and that He would decide for the right." –Abraham Lincoln

Although there are many questions regarding the faith of President Abraham Lincoln, the preceding words are not the expressions of someone who is conflicted about the need to bend his knee and will in service to the Almighty.

Other than George Washington, it is likely that Abraham Lincoln may have been the greatest leader this nation ever produced.

In fact, Theodore Roosevelt, another president whose granite sculpture resides next to Lincoln's on Mount Rushmore, said this about the Great Emancipator:

"If ever there lived a president who, during his term of service, needed all the consolation and strength that he could draw from the

Unseen Power above him, it was President Lincoln, sad, patient, mighty Lincoln, who worked and suffered for the people and, when he had lived for them at good end, gave up his life. If there ever was a man who practically applied what was taught in our churches, it was Abraham Lincoln."

Teddy Roosevelt was absolutely correct.

Our sixteenth president faithfully devoted his life to restoring the Union. Then, when Lincoln succeeded in his goal, his life was cut short by an assassin's bullet.

Without question, the matchless life and presidency of Abraham Lincoln is one of God's greatest gifts to our nation.

America's history is His story!

July 13

"The soldier above all others prays for peace, for it is the soldier who must suffer and bear the deepest wounds and scars of war."
–Douglas MacArthur

During World War II, many of those in the Japanese army had been educated in American universities and could speak our language fluently. Therefore, that fact also increased the difficulty in trying to find a code that couldn't be broken by the enemy.

Philip Johnston, the son of a missionary to the Navajo Indians made a proposal to the Marines that they should use the complicated language of the Navajos as a coded means of battlefield communication.

Although our Armed Forces had previously tried to employ Indian code talkers during other wars, never was this idea used as effectively as it was with the Navajo Code Talkers in World War II.

These original thirty Navajos employed their unique language in the development of a code that was never broken by the Japanese Imperial Army.

During the first two days of the invasion of Iwo Jima, six Navajo code talkers worked around the clock, flawlessly sending and receiving over 800 messages.

In the latter part of the Nineteenth Century, some of those in the military had tried to wipe out the American Indian population. Almost sixty years later, American soldiers would rely upon their innovative, secret communications for their own safety in battle.

"Were it not for the Navajos," Major Howard M. Conner said, "the Marines would never have taken Iwo."

America's history is His story!

July 14

"The whole continent of North America appears to be destined by Divine Providence to be peopled by one nation, speaking one language, professing one general system of religious and political principles, and accustomed to one general tenor of social usages and customs."

–John Quincy Adams

In a letter to his father, former President John Adam, John Quincy Adams wrote the preceding words in 1811. The sentiments he expressed were certainly not a new idea.

The first settlers to the New World saw America as a land of destiny.

Ours was a place where they could freely practice the individual tenets of their faith and evangelize the inhabitants of this land. It was a land of hope, where those who had sometimes failed could seemingly start their lives anew. America was a unique place, a land without boundaries, where dreamers might see their dreams realized.

However, the ideas expressed by John Quincy Adams have only recently fallen out of favor by many of those in our society.

Recently, we've seen a United States president essentially make light of the concept of "American exceptionalism."

He was wrong.

Colleges and universities all over our country tell America's youth that they should be ashamed of their nation's past. They tell us that our Founders aren't to be admired, that our traditions aren't to be respected, and that our history isn't to be treasured.

Those professors are wrong as well.

Abraham Lincoln correctly called our nation "that last, best hope of earth."

America's history is His story!

July 15

"Great necessities call out great virtues. When a mind is raised, and animated by the scenes that engage the heart, then those qualities which would otherwise lay dormant, wake into life and form the character of the hero and the statesman." –Abigail Adams

The late Audie Murphy is perhaps best known as a Hollywood actor. However, as a poor, uneducated, young man from the Texas plains, he longed to join the military.

Like young David in Scripture, Audie Murphy was initially turned down by the Marines because he was too young and too small. But also like David, when those around him were threatened, the young man boldly confronted the enemy as well.

During a fight with German infantry in France, after most of the men in his unit were killed, Murphy desperately tried to protect those who remained. Singlehandedly, he fired his rifle at the advancing Nazi troops until he ran out of ammunition. Throwing down the empty weapon, this unlikely hero scrambled on top of a burning tank destroyer.

Ignoring the flames and a bullet wound to his leg, Murphy turned the disabled tank destroyer's .50 caliber machine gun on the Germans. For nearly an hour, the small Texas boy with the baby face mowed down the Nazi troops and stopped their advance.

For his actions in battle, Murphy was awarded the Medal of Honor and became the most decorated soldier of World War II.

During times of great necessity and danger to our country, God has always seen fit to raise up American heroes and statesman, men and women who would willingly risk their lives for freedom or to save the life of those around them.

America's history is His story!

July 16

"God cannot sustain this free and blessed country, which we love and pray for, unless the Church will take right ground. Politics are a part of a religion in such a country as this, and Christians must do their duty to their country as a part of their duty to God." –Charles G. Finney

Throughout our nation's history, Christianity and the Church have always been at the forefront of American liberty.

It was the founders of Jamestown, who established that colony—not strictly for financial gain, but for the purpose of evangelizing the lost souls around them.

America's History is His Story:

Those who first stepped upon the shores of Plymouth Rock came to this New World in the pursuit of religious freedom for themselves and their loved ones.

During the Revolution, it was the churches that trained, sheltered, and organized those who would fight for our liberty. It was the pastors who often took up arms for the Revolutionary cause. Moreover, they inspired the members of their congregation to join them in the fight.

It can also be firmly established that the abolishment of slavery was solely a product of the churches. The preachers and pulpits of America thundered against the immorality of its practice. The determined voices of faith refused to be stopped; they wouldn't to be silenced until Black Americans were finally emancipated.

Every American, who has tasted the fruits of freedom, owes a great debt to our nation's churches, which have continually nurtured the precious tree of liberty.

America's history is His story!

July 17

"I have carefully examined the evidences of the Christian religion, and if I was sitting as a juror upon its authenticity, I would unhesitatingly give my verdict in its favor. I can prove its truth as clearly as any proposition ever submitted to the mind of man." –Alexander Hamilton

During the 1960s, a sad, lonely, and pathetic woman named Madalyn Murray O'Hair, claiming to be an atheist, did everything in her power to remove Almighty God from the public square, the public schools, and from all public discourse.

Taking her mission of madness to the courts, O'Hair successfully and singlehandedly led the effort to remove prayer from our educational system.

O'Hair even hated God so much, she even attempted to sue NASA and the crew of Apollo Eight, for the reading of the Genesis account of Creation in a nationally-televised broadcast from space. Fortunately, the Court thought her case was as far out of their jurisdiction as O'Hair was out of her mind.

One woman—one sad, bitter woman—took a wrecking ball to the foundations of America's religious liberty, established at great risk by our Founders.

Our nation was founded to protect the rights of the individual; however, one person's individual liberties were never intended to supersede the rights of society as a whole. Nobody in America has the individual right to take away *your* rights.

Strangely enough, the woman who hated God enough to challenge His very existence would die a brutal death at the hands of one of her own disciples. In the end, O'Hair died a brutal death, but the God she hated still lives on today!

America's history is His story!

July 18

"The subject of becoming a herald of the cross has often seriously engaged my attention, and I regard it as the most noble of all professions. It is the profession of our divine Redeemer, and I should not be surprised were I to die upon a foreign field, clad in ministerial armor, fighting under the banner of Jesus. What could be more glorious?"

—Gen. Thomas "Stonewall" Jackson

America's History is His Story:

Influenced by the preaching of George Whitfield, Shubal Stearns traveled from the Northeast to Virginia, to preach the Word of God. Still searching for the proper garden to sow the precious seeds of his faith, he soon left Virginia, moving to Guilford County, North Carolina, where he founded the Sandy Creek Baptist Church.

In just a few short years, the Lord blessed Stearn's ministry in Sandy Creek, as the church grew from a congregation of 16 members to over 600.

Shubal Stearns wasn't just a preacher; he was also an evangelist, with a flaming message of repentance that compelled those in his congregations to be "born again."

As the church at Sandy Creek continued to grow, so did the pastor's influence. Shubal's life and ministry gave birth to over 40 Baptist churches and approximately 125 preachers of the Gospel, who claimed Stearns as their pastor or greatest influence.

Stearn's simple but profound message of the Gospel spread like wildfire, making inroads throughout the entire South. The pulpit at Sandy Creek wouldn't just change the South; it would also change the face of America, spiritually and politically.

Moreover, it is certainly not an exaggeration to credit Shubal Stearns with the promulgation of the Baptist faith in the South, an area which would later come to be known as the "Bible Belt."

America's history is His story!

July 19

"I am well aware of the toil and blood and treasure that it will cost to maintain this Declaration, and support and defend these States. Yet through all the gloom I can see the rays of ravishing light and glory. I can see that the end is worth more than all the means." –John Adams

Although the actions of our Founding Fathers were indeed revolutionary, the circumstances that gave birth to the United States were not the foolhardy actions of reckless men.

Our Founders were educated and reasoned individuals, men of great faith and purpose, who fully realized the dreadful consequences of their actions.

John Adams knew that the Declaration of Independence would be seen by the British Crown as a declaration of war. It was certain that good men would die, families would be uprooted, and precious lives would be forever changed.

The flames of American liberty and the winds that fanned them would consume everything in their path.

Adams also realized that, if they succeeded, the freedom their sacrifices might purchase would ultimately be a cause for celebration for many generations to come. Moreover, this great man clearly acknowledged that their victory, although costly, would be worth all the hardships they would have to endure.

Yet the one thing that never wavered in these wise and decent visionaries was the confidence that Almighty God was clearly supporting their cause. And they firmly placed their reliance on His divine Providence.

America's history is His story!

July 20

"That which the unaided intellect of man could not compass, the spirit of God has granted to human exertions, for God is wont to hear the prayers of His servants who love His precepts even to the performance of apparent impossibilities." –Christopher Columbus

America's History is His Story:

Twelve men! Only twelve men in human history have ever placed their foot upon the surface of the moon. Only a dozen human beings have ever experienced the weightlessness of their walk upon the lunar surface.

These men were all Americans.

On this date in history in 1969, Neil Armstrong took "one small step for man, one giant leap for mankind."

Anyone under the age of forty has no memory of NASA's Apollo program. They do not remember men walking on the moon.

America's young people have no recollection of a country that attempted great feats of discovery. They hold no first-hand knowledge of an America that routinely tried to accomplish the seemingly impossible.

The moon walks of Neil Armstrong and Buzz Aldrin are merely a distant memory to some of us. To others, they are an obscure fact in a history book, like the voyages of Drake or Magellan.

However, they showed us what America could accomplish when it still believed there was an all-powerful God, whose strong and merciful hand ultimately controlled the destinies of men and nations.

America's history is His story!

July 21

"If there be a destiny, it is of no avail for us unless we work with it. The ways of Providence will be of no advantage to us unless we proceed in the same direction." –Calvin Coolidge

After seeing a movie, *Code of the Secret Service* (1939), starring an actor named Ronald Reagan, young Jerry Parr chose the Secret Service for his future career.

On March 30, 1981, Jerry Parr was living his childhood dream. As the agent in charge of President Ronald Reagan's protection detail, Parr would be called upon to make one of the most critical decisions in the agency's long, storied history.

When the assassin, John Hinckley began firing at the president, Agent Parr shoved Reagan inside the presidential limousine. Normally, the situation would have called for the president's protection detail to quickly return to the White House.

Even though Parr still didn't know Reagan had been struck by one of the assassin's bullets, the agent wisely chose to direct the motorcade to George Washington University Hospital.

With Reagan suffering major blood loss from his wound, Parr's decision to direct them to the hospital was responsible for saving the president's life.

Although he'd simply done his job, Special Agent Jerry Parr couldn't escape the belief that his decision had been guided by the unseen hand of God. In fact, the incident affected his life to such a degree, he later became a minister of the Gospel.

Like President Reagan, who believed his life had been spared for a purpose, Agent Parr surrendered his life to the Lord, who had used him for a purpose, as well.

America's history is His story!

July 22

"The legacy we leave is not just in our possessions, but in the quality of our lives." –Billy Graham

Although we may sometimes reflect on the godly American heritage our Founders left for us, we often fail to recognize that the same qualities, the characteristics that made these men exceptional in our founding, were also reflected in their personal, daily lives.

Their legacy wasn't only in the conception of a great nation; many of them also fathered great offspring, children who would care as much about the principles of individual liberty as they did.

Such was the case of John Jay.

Not only was John Jay an ambassador and a state governor; he was also a member of the First and Second Continental Congresses. As one of the authors of the *Federalist Papers*, his ideas and principles were also influential in the writing of our Constitution.

In addition, along with John Adams and Benjamin Franklin, Jay negotiated the peace treaty that ended the American Revolution with Britain.

The principles of freedom to which John Jay devoted his life were also reflected in his son, William Jay.

Moreover, it could be said that the abolitionist writings of John Jay's son might have contributed to finishing the work his father and the other Founders started, bringing about a final end of bondage for all men—of every color—in America.

John Jay left our nation a remarkable legacy of life, liberty, faith, and family.

America's history is His story!

July 23

"The family is one of nature's masterpieces." –George Santayana

Sarah, sometimes known as "Sally," became the first-born child to Thomas and Nancy in 1807. Two years later, her mother would give birth to Sarah's younger brother.

Described by her cousin as "kind, tender, and good natured," Sarah was fiercely protective of her brother. They shared the same gray eyes and same sorrows of life.

Sarah loved her younger brother and helped him to learn his reading and math. She also made sure he was accepted among the school children, often inviting her brother to join Sarah and her friends at play. Sometimes she scolded him when he misbehaved.

When tragedy came to their home, Sarah and her nine-year old brother wept together and comforted each other over the illness that suddenly took the life of their young and precious mother. It forced Sarah to become both sister and mother to the boy.

Finally discovering some happiness in life with her new husband, Aaron Grigsby, Sarah was thrilled to learn she was expecting a child. However, the 20-year old woman would die during childbirth and her baby was stillborn.

Upon learning of his sister's death, her tall, lonely brother covered his face and wept bitterly into his hands. He would experience more suffering in the years to come.

Although she never lived to see how God chose to use him as president, perhaps young Sarah's love and prayers were responsible for molding her brother, Abraham Lincoln, into the remarkable man he would eventually become.

America's history is His story!

July 24

"Virtue alone is sufficient to make a man great, glorious, and happy."
–Benjamin Franklin

America's History is His Story:

Paul Harvey was a legend in the world of radio broadcasting. For seven decades, he worked in the business as the "most listened to man" in broadcasting.

In a business that is often characterized by outrageousness on the part of its hosts, Harvey was consistently conservative. Throughout his career, he was as American as a Norman Rockwell painting. On the air, Harvey often referred to his beloved wife, Lynne, calling her "Angel."

Harvey loved our country. He shared our values. On a daily basis, he came into our homes, reiterating the simple truths that a majority of the country held dear.

Perhaps best of all, Harvey is known for the unique way that he ended his broadcasts.

His daily news broadcast ended show with the words, "This is Paul Harvey…Good day." And his other radio program concluded with the phrase: "And now you know…the rest of the story."

In fact, to make you aware of the rest of *this* story, the closing tag lines of these daily reminders of our Godly American heritage were in no small way influenced by the way this radio legend closed his broadcasts.

The late Paul Harvey was a man devoted to his wife and family. He treasured our country and loved the freedoms God granted to each one of us in America.

America's history is His story!

July 25

"Sunday is nature's law as well as God's. No individual or nation habitually disregarding it has failed to fall upon disaster or grief."

–Daniel Webster

As a society, there are relatively few American youth who are intimately familiar with the term and application of "Blue Laws," which were once prevalent in this country.

Blue Laws were laws, usually of a religious origin, that limited the activities that a city or community would allow on Sunday.

Like many American laws, that had their basis in Scripture, Blue Laws were instituted to follow the Ten Commandments' admonition: "Remember the Sabbath Day, to keep it holy."

Since many considered Sunday as a time for worship, Blue Laws were instituted to limit commercial activity on that day. They often mandated the closing of shopping centers and drug stores. In addition, Blue Laws are often still in place in regards to alcohol, restricting the hours of its sale and purchase.

One of America's more successful restaurant chains was founded just a few short years ago. Its founder sought to make his company one that upholds traditional Christian values, such as closing its restaurants on Sundays.

While employing these Christian principles, this restaurant chain has seen substantial growth, while winning the praise of many in the religious community, and the scorn of those who oppose them.

Like our nation, this business has thrived by placing the Lord before its profits.

America's history is His story!

July 26

"When a man's will and pleasure is his only rule and guide, what safety can there be either for him or against him but in the point of a sword."
–James Otis

America's History is His Story:

As a result of their intimate knowledge of Scripture, our Founders realized that evil truly does exist in this present world. These wise men, who just threw off the shackles of a tyrannical government, also realized that sinful men couldn't be trusted with unlimited power, without being tempted to abuse the exercise of that authority.

For those two reasons, our Founders insisted upon including the Second Amendment into our Constitution.

The right to keep and bear arms is a uniquely American concept. The principle also has some strong foundation in Scripture, in both the Old *and* New Testaments.

In Luke 11:21, Jesus said, "When a strong man armed keepeth his palace, his goods are in peace."

Christ also stated in Luke 22:36, "And he that hath no sword, let him sell his garment and buy one."

One has only to thumb through the pages of human history to see the many instances of nations and people, who were not armed, often becoming the victims of genocide. Therefore, the right to keep and bear arms is wise. It is Constitutional. And the principle certainly has its basis in Scripture.

History teaches us that the torch of liberty only continues to shine brightly when the people have the means to readily defend it.

America's history is His story.

July 27

"Let our object be, our country, our whole country, and nothing but our country. And by the blessing of God, may that country itself become a vast and splendid monument, not of oppression and terror, but of wisdom, of peace, and of liberty, upon which the world will gaze with admiration forever." –Daniel Webster

One of the great tragedies of modern society is the unwillingness of politicians to unselfishly do those things they know to be right, simply because they are not popular with the American people.

However, during the American Revolution, Samuel Adams and Patrick Henry didn't commission a poll to determine if their actions were supported by a majority of the Colonists.

It must be stated that, during this time, there were still Loyalists in America, who largely supported the policies of King George.

Not everybody believed that we should throw off the bonds of the British Empire. Moreover, some of the Colonists believed the Founders should be hanged. And when those brave 56 men placed their signatures on that Declaration, they knew a hangman's noose might certainly be in their future.

The men who founded our country were not concerned about the next election; they were thinking about the next generation. They didn't agonize over their own comforts. Unselfishly, these men were simply devoting their efforts to making life better for generations yet unborn.

America's history is His story!

July 28

"The battle, sir, is not to the strong alone; it is to the vigilant, the active, the brave." –Patrick Henry

On the day President Reagan was shot, there were any number of brave Secret Service agents who stood ready to willingly place themselves between an assassin and the President of the United States.

The Secret Service doesn't just train for the moments they are needed; they train for the seconds. A split second of hesitancy or indecision could make the difference between life or death for our nation's Chief Executive.

Perhaps we will never know if Timothy McCarthy was alerted to the assassin by a warning in his earpiece, from seeing the gunman, or simply from hearing the sound of the first bullet. However, the young Secret Service agent quickly responded to the habits of his training.

Offering himself as a human shield in order to protect President Reagan, McCarthy jumped forward, squared his body, and took the assassin's bullet in his chest.

Man's desire for self-preservation tends to make the average person take cover during a shooting. Although McCarthy survived, these brave agents learn to ignore their basic instincts, and to place the life of another individual above that of themselves.

America has always been blessed with the Tim McCarthys, men willing to sacrifice themselves to save the life of another. It's what makes America special.

America's history is His story!

July 29

"It is difficult to make a man miserable while he feels he is worthy of himself and claims kindred to the great God who made him."
–Abraham Lincoln

Ely S. Parker was a Seneca Indian, who grew up the son of a Baptist minister, on a reservation in Indian Falls, New York.

His father placed great value on education, making sure Ely was as well-prepared for life in the outside world as he was for life on the reservation. Therefore, his schooling would prepare him to be an engineer, a lawyer, and a tribal diplomat. After joining the military, he would eventually rise to the rank of Brevet Brigadier General. Later, he would be appointed by President Grant as the Commissioner of Indian Affairs.

During the Civil War, Parker became a military secretary to Gen. Ulysses Grant and wrote the final terms of surrender for the Confederate forces at Appomattox.

When Grant introduced the members of his staff to the Confederate officers, Gen. Robert E. Lee shook Ely Parker's hand and replied, "I am glad to see one real American here."

As Parker returned the General's handshake, he smiled politely and softly said, "We are all Americans."

Parker was correct.

The document that was signed at Appomattox—the document that Ely Parker penned—would guarantee each one of us could once again say, "We are all Americans."

America's history is His story!

July 30

"All I have seen has taught me to trust the Creator for all I have not seen." –Ralph Waldo Emerson

After the murder of his friend, John Tunstall, Billy the Kid went on a killing spree, acts of violence which would start off the deadly Lincoln County War in 1878. For the next few months, gun play and bloodshed would cover the New Mexico countryside.

In the midst of this carnage, one of the players in this true Old West drama would prove to be one of the finest Christian authors the country ever produced.

His name was Lew Wallace.

America's History is His Story:

Wallace had been one of Grant's generals in the Civil War. He saw action in the Battle of Shiloh. Moreover, he was later selected to serve on the military tribunal that tried the conspirators in the assassination of President Abraham Lincoln.

As governor of the New Mexico Territory, Wallace met with Billy the Kid and promised him amnesty in return for his testimony against some of those involved in the Lincoln County violence. However, when the Kid chose to kill again, the governor quickly rescinded his amnesty promise.

Despite the violence he saw in his professional life, Lew Wallace authored the country's best-selling novel of the 19th Century. Moreover, the book he penned was a story about how righteousness would always triumph over hatred and violence.

The book Wallace wrote was: *Ben-Hur: A Tale of Christ*.

America's history is His story!

July 31

"We have all been encouraged to feel in the guardianship and guidance of the Almighty Being, whose power regulates the destiny of nations."
—James Madison

During the American Revolution, some of the war's most bitter fighting took place around what we now know as New York City.

Despite Gen. Washington's leadership, the American forces were soundly defeated at Long Island. And had British General Howe chosen to push forward with his attacks, the war might have been over for the Colonial Army almost before it began.

As Gen. Washington was trapped on Long Island, with no apparent way to retreat across the East River, he issued a call for every sea-going vessel he could find.

Fortunately—or Providentially—Washington had a leader under his command by the name of John Glover, of Marblehead, Massachusetts.

A fisherman by trade, Glover had already come to the aid of Gen. Washington before, using his ship, *Hannah*, in the raiding of British supply vessels.

Right at the time Washington and America needed them the most, Glover arrived with his regiment of 1,000 able-bodied fishermen, men with the experience to evacuate the general's 8,000 troops across the turbulent waters of the East River.

The hostile winds that were blowing against their vessels soon subsided, giving way to a helpful wind at their backs. Their daring and time-consuming evacuation went on throughout the night. With the dawn, a heavy fog arose around their camp, making it impossible for the nearby British to identify or to thwart the general's miraculous escape.

Seemingly against all odds, Washington's army would be spared to fight again.

America's history is His story!

August 1

"The success of any great moral exercise does not depend upon numbers." –William Lloyd Garrison

America's History is His Story:

As the first winds of integration were starting to blow in this country, Jim Crow Laws made it hard for black athletes to make huge inroads in college sports in the South.

The Alabama Crimson Tide still hadn't granted a single scholarship to a black athlete. Against the wishes of George Wallace, his state's segregationist governor, Coach William Paul "Bear" Bryant knew it was time that Alabama, and other schools in the South, would have to make room for black athletes on their football squads.

Therefore, Bryant scheduled a 1970 opening-day football game with John McKay's team at Southern Cal, which had a large number of black athletes.

It has long been speculated, and never disproven, that Bear's strategy was to show Alabama fans the folly of universities failing to recruit the best athletes available, regardless of their race.

The plan worked.

In a score of 42-21, the USC Trojans soundly defeated Bryant's all-white squad of Crimson Tide players. Moreover, all six touchdowns against Alabama were scored by the black Trojan athletes.

The next year, Bryant's Alabama squad started its first black athlete, a change that would soon be followed in football programs all across the South.

One man named "Bear" helped to bring about the end of Jim Crow. America's history is His story!

August 2

"Duty is ours; results are God's." –John Quincy Adams

When the first American troops came charging down the ramps on Omaha Beach, the boats that transported them to the French Coast were designed and built in New Orleans by Andrew Jackson Higgins, the man who won the war.

Higgins was an industrialist and inventor, who initially made his fortune in the lumber industry. With the rise of hostilities in Europe, Higgins clearly predicted our future involvement in the war. Moreover, he also recognized a need for the Navy to employ thousands of small military vessels.

Fearing that the war effort would leave the country facing a steel shortage, he bought an entire year's mahogany crop from the Philippines.

After finally winning the contract from the military, the small wood and steel boats produced at his factory were critical to the war effort.

"Andrew Higgins is the man who won the war for us," Dwight D. Eisenhower said, in an interview after he became president. "If Higgins had not designed and built those LCVPs (Landing Craft, Vehicle and Personnel), we never could have landed over an open beach. The whole strategy of the war would have been different."

Although Andrew Higgins would see great profit from his design, the boats he produced saved untold American lives and allowed us to bring an end to the war sooner.

America's history is His story!

August 3

"The fate of unborn millions will now depend, under God, on the courage of this army. Our cruel and unrelenting enemy leaves us only the choice of brave resistance, or the most abject submission. We have, therefore to resolve to conquer or die." –George Washington

Relatively few citizens of this country know about the approximately 12,000 American prisoners, who died in squalor and disease off the shores of New York City.

These were the brutal and merciless conditions on the 12 British prison ships, which were anchored off Brooklyn's Wallabout Bay, during the American Revolution.

The British commanders had been ordered to put down the rebels, at all costs!

A number of the dead on these prison ships were American merchant seaman. Many of the others were privateers, essentially pirates. These were men who swore allegiance to the Colonies and robbed the British ships of treasure and armaments, which they used to support the American cause.

Captured by the British, and given the choice to join the British Navy or remain as captives, these brave and loyal Americans refused to take up arms against their own countrymen. For their refusal, they were tortured, starved, and neglected. These prisoners were forced to remain trapped in cold, dark, rat-infested, unsanitary conditions of human wastes, which quickly gave birth to disease and death. Upon their deaths, their remains were brutally thrown overboard or taken ashore, to be buried in shallow, forgotten graves.

More Americans died on these prison ships than were killed in the course of the war. These were our American patriots. These were the martyrs. These are the ones whose unselfish contributions to liberty made freedom possible for each one of us.

America's history is His story!

August 4

"In the supposed state of nature, all men are equally bound by the laws of nature, or to speak more properly, the laws of the Creator. They are

imprinted by the finger of God on the heart of man. Thou shall do no injury to thy neighbor, is the voice of nature and reason, and it is confirmed by written revelation." –Samuel Adams

Sadly, American history books fail to teach us about the horrors inflicted upon the Colonists by those commanders under British rule, whose actions inspired our rebellion.

One such man was William Cunningham, a native of Ireland, who sought to make his fortune in America from the labors of indentured servants. However, his treatment of those servants was so cruel, they were eventually freed by the courts of New York.

Vowing revenge against them, Cunningham would finally realize his chance, when the British took over New York, and Gen. Gage appointed him Provost Marshal.

As the man in charge of American prisoners, Cunningham would begin a reign of terror upon them, equaling anything that was done in Hitler's German prison camps.

On a nightly basis, Cunningham would remove five or six prisoners from their hold. Then he hanged them in the streets for his own entertainment. Moreover, the practice was only halted because the women of the neighborhood, all loyal British subjects, finally complained to Gen. Howe that their cries were disturbing their sleep.

William Cunningham was the man responsible for the deplorable conditions for American prisoners upon the British prison ships. Following the war, he was allowed to return to England, answering to nobody but the Lord for his crimes against humanity.

America's history is His Story!

August 5

"No people on earth have more cause to be thankful than ours, and this

America's History is His Story:

is said reverently, in no spirit of boastfulness in our own strength, but with the gratitude to the Giver of good who has blessed us."

–Theodore Roosevelt

During the midst of the Great Depression, a large and once prosperous, iron toy manufacturer in Kenton, Ohio, was struggling to survive. Riding to their rescue was Gene Autry, the singing cowboy, star of film, radio, and television.

The vice president of Kenton Hardware Company had an idea. He believed that an iron cap pistol, fashioned after Autry's pearl-handled six-shooter would be just the thing to save their business.

Autry not only willingly consented to their plans; he also sent the factory one of his guns to use for a model.

The small iron cap pistol, with a gun-metal finish, simulated pearl grips, and Autry's signature, would revitalize their business. By 1939, they had sold over two million of these toy six-guns in America and abroad. Additional employees were hired and the company was forced to work around the clock, just trying to keep up with the demand for the "toy that would save a town."

Already a hero to millions of children in America, Gene Autry also became the hero to the adults in a small manufacturing town in northwestern Ohio.

Back in the days before political correctness, our heroes were honest and straight shooting. They believed in God; they had values; and our children played with toy guns.

America's history is His story!

August 6

"You don't have to deserve your mother's love. You have to deserve your father's." –Robert Frost

As the son of a famous Civil War general, World War II Gen. Douglas MacArthur penned the following prayer about the kind of son he desired:

"Build me a son, O Lord, who will be strong enough to know when he is weak, and brave enough to face himself when he is afraid, one who will be proud and unbending in honest defeat, and humble and gentle in victory.

"Build me a son whose wishbone will not be where his backbone should be; a son who will know Thee, and that to know himself is the foundation stone of knowledge.

"Lead him I pray, not in the path of ease and comfort, but under the stress and spur of difficulties and challenge. Here let him learn to stand up in the storm; here let him learn compassion for those who fail.

"Build me a son whose heart will be clear, whose goal will be high, a son who will master himself before he seeks to master other men, one who will learn to laugh, yet never forget how to weep, one who will reach into the future, yet never forget the past.

"And after all these things are his, add, I pray, enough of a sense of humor, so that he may always be serious, yet never take himself too seriously. Give him humility, so that he may always remember the simplicity of true greatness, the open mind of true wisdom, the meekness of true strength.

"Then, I, his father, will dare to whisper, I have not lived in vain."

America's history is His story!

August 7

"The only gleam of hope, and I cannot overrate it, is from confidence in God. When I look upward, it calms my apprehensions for the future, and I seem to hear a voice saying: 'If I clothe the lilies of the field, shall

America's History is His Story:

I not also clothe you?' Here is my strong confidence, and I will wait patiently for the direction of Providence." —Samuel Morse

A number of years ago, there was a young woman in a major city, who, through no fault of her own, happened to be homeless. She survived on the food she scrounged daily, from garbage cans and public dumpsters. The woman slept on park benches or wherever she could find a warm and convenient place to lay her head.

Finally deciding she wasn't happy with her life's status, this brave and enterprising young woman took the steps she needed to change it.

As a result of her tenacity, dedication, and study, she was awarded a scholarship to one of the most prestigious universities in America.

This isn't to say that every homeless person in America could qualify for the great education she received; it does tell us, however, that America is still a country where a person can often realize their dreams of success and achievement.

Stories such as this are unheard of in other nations. Yet God has placed us in a land where, these types of incidents don't only occur, they are prevalent.

America's history is His story!

August 8

"Not only did our Savior consort with the seamen of Galilee, but there are many examples in history of noted naval heroes who exhibited the highest Christian virtues. I wish to be counted among this great company of believers in the divinity of Christ, and in the inspiration of all Scripture." —Stephen Luce

Like many of the great heroes of our American Revolution, John Glover willingly offered his life and fortune to purchase our liberty.

When America was in need, Glover employed the services of his schooner, *Hannah*, to seize supplies and armaments from the British. When Gen. Washington needed to retreat or to attack, and a large body of water stood between him and his objective, Glover met the general's needs with the boats and men to transport them.

Once, when Washington's forces were in danger of being surrounded, Glover's forces were ordered to defend the coastline, and slow the advance of the British army. He devised a successful plan, one that was extremely costly to the British in time and troops.

Like so many of the men under Washington's command, Gen. Glover's service to America was exemplary. Moreover, he also paid a great price for his involvement.

When Glover returned home, his wealth was largely gone. Hannah, his wife of 24 years, was suffering from an illness that would soon take her life. In addition, Glover's son, John, was captured by the British and lost at sea on the voyage to England.

Perhaps in these days when we are once again facing so many challenges to our freedom, God will continue to bless us with loyal American patriots such as John Glover.

America's history is His story!

August 9

"Whenever I hear anyone arguing for slavery, I feel a strong impulse to see it tried on him personally." –Abraham Lincoln

At the 1936 Olympics, held in Berlin, Adolph Hitler planned to display to the world, his belief that the people of Germany were indeed a Master Race.

America's History is His Story:

The Fuhrer's evil hatred of the Jews is certainly well-documented; however, his contempt for blacks in this country was equally as strong.

In Hitler's diseased mind, Jews and blacks were *inferior* peoples, subject to ill treatment and eventual destruction. Hitler was confident his belief in Aryan superiority would be tested in these games and proven to the world.

At the time, America's most promising hope for Olympic gold rested on the talented son of a share-cropper, a black sprinter by the name of Jesse Owens.

But Hitler was supremely confident in his superior Aryan athletes.

After fouling on two earlier attempts at the long jump, Owens risked a disqualification. Luz Long, a tall, blonde, blue-eyed German athlete, Hitler's brightest hope in the event, bravely and unselfishly gave his opponent some advice about how to time his leap.

The advice worked and Owens won Gold in the long jump.

On this day in history, with the red-and-black flag of the swastika flying all around him, Jesse Owens laid waste to Hitler's theory, by winning his fourth gold medal at the Berlin Olympics.

America's history is His story!

August 10

"The land we possess is the gift of Heaven to our fathers, and Divine Providence seems to have decreed it to our latest posterity."
–William Livingston

When the people of the world think of America, they often picture New York, our country's largest city and the home to our banking and financial centers.

When Islamic terrorists wanted to harm America on 9/11, they chose the city of New York. Hijacking our own airliners and using them as guided missiles, these Muslim extremists brought down the Twin Towers, which prominently marked the city's skyline for years.

Moreover, when the British came to America to permanently douse the fires of revolution among the Colonies, they came to New York City first. And they came in force!

In 1776, in the space of little over one month, over 500 British warships sailed into New York, bringing thousands of soldiers, supplies, and armaments. One observer described the scene as "all London afloat."

Greatly overmatched and completely out-gunned, Gen. Washington's forces were routed in New York and forced to retreat. Moreover, much of the city was soon set ablaze, perhaps in retaliation for the cruelty of the British invaders of New York.

During the entire course of the Revolution, British control over New York was never relinquished. Forced to evacuate the city following the war, one of the British ships fired a bitter, farewell cannon blast at the mocking American crowds on Staten Island.

America's history is His story!

August 11

"All of the ills which America suffers can be traced to the teaching of evolution." –William Jennings Bryan

Perhaps no truer words were ever spoken. William Jennings Bryan was absolutely correct about the destructive force evolution would turn out to be.

When man holds no more value than a beast or creeping thing, it is only reasonable to think he will soon behave like one. And if there is no Creator, then there is no one to whom we must answer for our transgressions.

Is it any wonder that young men in our inner cities have no inhibitions about pushing drugs and killing each other? And why are we surprised that teen pregnancies are prevalent in our society? There can be no respect for the moral authority of home or government, if there is no reverence for the One who granted power to those institutions.

One person has said "the goal of evolution is self-conquest."

In reality, nothing could be further from the truth. Deification of self is the ultimate goal of evolution. Lucifer was cast out of Heaven for trying to be like the Most High; evolution is mankind's attempt to bring the Most High down to his level.

Bertrand Russell said, "Since evolution became fashionable, the glorification of man has taken a new form."

Evolution attempts to elevate mankind; at the same time it devalues our society. Despite the claims of those who do not believe in God, America's greatness has always been realized when we placed our nation's reliance on our Creator.

America's history is His story!

August 12

"Let us, therefore, act like men, inspired with a resolution that nothing but the frowns of Heaven shall conquer us." –Gen. Nathaniel Greene

When most people hear the name Gen. MacArthur, they generally think of Douglas MacArthur, who guided our Pacific troops in World War II.

However, there is one other Gen. MacArthur you ought to know.

The father of Gen. Douglas MacArthur was Gen. Arthur MacArthur, who served with distinction in the Civil War.

In the Battle of Missionary Ridge, the 24th Wisconsin advanced against the Confederate troops and rifle pits. Meeting less-than-expected resistance, the troops realized they had advanced beyond their orders. Unwilling to retreat, they attacked.

During the battle, the soldier who carried the regimental flag fell in battle. Another soldier caught up the flag but was also killed in their assault. MacArthur grabbed the battered and fallen flag, hoisted it high, and shouted "On Wisconsin!" Carrying nothing but a pistol and the colors, the 18-year old First Lieutenant led the charge.

As the first one to reach the summit of Missionary Ridge, MacArthur planted the flag above them. Those in his unit quickly rallied to their colors and won an improbable victory for Gen. Grant and the Union cause.

For his gallantry in battle, MacArthur received the Medal of Honor, a citation later to be awarded to his son, many years later.

America's history is His story!

August 13

"I must soon follow him, and hope to meet him and those friends who have gone before me in the realms of bliss through the mediation of a dear Redeemer, Jesus Christ." –Andrew Jackson

Gen. Arthur MacArthur, the famed Civil War hero, always claimed that he wished he could have died at the head of his regiment.

America's History is His Story:

Almost fifty years after his heroics led his unit to victory at the Battle of Missionary Ridge, he was reunited with the remaining men of the 24th Wisconsin.

Although MacArthur was sickly and frail, he was asked to address the aged men with whom he'd served as young men. As he took his place on the stage, MacArthur stared at the tired, blood-stained, war-tattered flag that hung on the wall behind him. It was the flag he carried, leading his unit to victory.

MacArthur only spoke a few words before he collapsed onto the floor.

The first man to his side had been a surgeon with the 24th Wisconsin. After a careful examination, he told the assembled crowd that "the general is dying."

The men formed a circle around their dying comrade and recited the Lord's Prayer in unison, as the general went to be with those troops who earlier fell in battle.

One of the men removed the war-scarred battle flag and wrapped it around the fallen body of their friend and brother-at-arms.

Although it wasn't during the midst of battle, Arthur MacArthur finally got his wish. The general died at the head of his regiment.

America's history is His story!

August 14

"Government by kings was first introduced into the world by the heathens, from whom the children of Israel copied the custom."

–Thomas Paine

In 1770, the British government erected a massive, lead statue of King George III on Bowling Green, a small park which is located in present day, lower Manhattan.

The statue had King George, dressed in the style of a great, Roman conqueror, mounted on horseback.

As the hostilities between the Colonists and the British government increased, the statue naturally became the target of protestors, subjecting it to acts of vandalism and graffiti.

On July 9, 1776, the Declaration of Independence was read aloud to Washington's troops in New York.

Upon hearing those bold and inspirational words, the Sons of Liberty made their way to Bowling Green, where they toppled the monument. From there, the lead statue was taken to a Connecticut foundry, where it was melted down to make musket balls for the Continental Army.

According to reports, the lead from the statue made over 42,000 bullets for the Colonial guns. Therefore, it wouldn't be improper to state that the British finally got their statue returned to them.

America's history is His story!

August 15

"Sir, we have done everything that could be done to avert the storm which is now coming on. Our petitions have been slighted, our remonstrances have produced additional violence and insult; our supplications have been disregarded; and we have been spurned, with contempt. An appeal to arms and to the God of Hosts is all that is left to us." –Patrick Henry

America's History is His Story:

When Americans were captured by the British and taken to the New York prison ships, very few of them ever left their captivity alive. Death was the only release from their harsh imprisonment.

Fortunately, a relatively few number of them escaped, from whom we learn the stories of the atrocities that took place aboard these floating torture chambers.

One such man who escaped was Robert Sheffield, of Connecticut, who told his story to the *Connecticut Gazette*.

"Their sickly countenances and ghastly looks were truly horrible, some swearing and blaspheming; others crying, praying, and wringing their hands; and stalking about like ghosts; others delirious, ranting and storming, all panting for breath; some dead and corrupting. The air was so foul that at times a lamp could not be kept burning, by reason of which the bodies were not missed until they had been dead ten days."

Throughout human history, every generation has had its tyrants and despots, men so evil, that if their plans were ever fully realized, the world would witness the annihilation of freedom, justice, and any remaining shreds of human decency.

It is only through righteousness, and the bold actions of brave and selfless patriots who embrace it, that the evil is held at bay. Our nation has given birth to many of them.

America's history is His story!

August 16

"And let us not trust to human effort alone, but humbly acknowledge the power and goodness of Almighty God who presides over the destiny of nations, and Who at all times been revealed in our country's history." –Grover Cleveland

Although his skills as a fisherman made him an excellent seaman, John Glover also proved his leadership ability as an infantry leader as well.

When Washington's troops were in danger of being surrounded, Glover effectively managed to split the British forces.

Recognizing the stone walls provided him a superior field of battle, Glover located a number of his troops behind them.

The British, overly confident in their numbers, advanced on the Colonial troops.

Glover's men hid behind a couple of stone walls, waiting until the British were nearly upon them, and then they jumped up and fired a volley into the nearby troops. The men quickly retreated and the British began a bayonet charge at the retreating forces.

As soon as Glover's troops were beyond the stone wall, Glover's second bunch of marksmen came out of hiding, firing another burst into their British pursuers.

Glover's plan was devastating and greatly slowed the British attack. It also exposed a weakness of the British army, which would often be exploited in the battles yet to come. Their forces were used to fighting out in the open, against long lines of troops. They weren't prepared for the Colonial Army' shoot-and-run attacks, guerilla tactics that the Americans learned from the Indians.

America's history is His story!

August 17

"Hold fast to the Bible. To the influence of this Book we are indebted for all the progress made in true civilization and to this we must look as our guide in the future." –Ulysses S. Grant

America's History is His Story:

Recently, an avowed atheist published a secular Bible. Calling it "The Good Book: A Humanist Bible," the author decided to just compile a bunch of writings in the form of Scripture.

One can only wonder if the book's author has also decided to rewrite other works of literature, books that also refer to the one precious Deity he so readily dismisses.

In these times of turmoil and uncertainty, the last thing our nation needs right now is a Humanist Manifesto, another book, falsely calling itself a Bible, which seeks to establish fallible human beings as their own infallible god.

Every American needs to understand that it was not Humanism, but Christianity and the Word of God that gave birth to America.

Humanism gave us a land of tyranny, where the Colonists were forced to rebel and go to war, to throw off the cruelty and abuses of King George.

Humanism is the author of slavery, giving one man the right to place another in shackles. It is the philosophy that led Hitler to believe he was justified in the slaughter of six million Jews. Humanism is a High Court ruling that permits our society to allow doctors and nurses to kill the unborn. Humanism is the father of ignorance and depravity; it is the brother of Communism and terrorism; and it is the twofold child of hell.

But most of all, humanism is the polar opposite of the Bible.

America's history is His story!

August 18

"It doesn't take a hero to order men into battle. It takes a hero to be one of those men who goes into battle." –Gen. Norman Schwarzkopf

As you drive into Kenton, Ohio, you are greeted by a sign that tells you the town was the home of Jacob Wilson Parrot, recipient of America's first Medal of Honor.

For what did Parrot receive America's highest military honor?

It all started with the theft of a train.

During the Civil War, a civilian named James J. Andrews came up with a plan which he believed would hasten the end of the war.

Parrot and 21 other volunteers would infiltrate Confederate lines into Georgia and commandeer a train. Those volunteers would drive *The General* northward, stopping only to destroy telegraph lines, railroad tracks, and to commit other acts of sabotage.

However, the determined conductor of the train chased after the Union raiders, on foot and by handcar, even pursuing them backwards for over fifty miles in another locomotive. In fact, the whole incident was later portrayed in a 1956 Walt Disney movie, "The Great Locomotive Chase."

Andrews, Parrot, and the other invaders were eventually captured and tried as spies. James J. Andrews was hanged and Jacob Parrot suffered great punishment as a prisoner before finally escaping to the North.

Jacob Parrot and a number of the others were awarded the Medal for their daring actions in defense of the Union. But this one Ohio son would become its first recipient.

America's history is His story!

August 19

"I conjure you, by all that is dear, by all that is honorable, by all that is sacred, not only that ye pray, but that ye act." –John Hancock

America's History is His Story:

After just finishing a fifteen-hour surgery and barely getting any sleep, one of America's finest surgeons was called in to consult on a boy's severe hand injury. Rather than allow the boy's hand to be amputated, the physician phoned each of the weary members of his surgical team to help him in the effort.

Working many hours into the night, they were successfully able to repair the extensive damage to the boy's tissue, nerves, and tendons. Although he was exhausted from the day's labors, the doctor met the boy's nervous parents with a smile on his face.

"Your son's hand will be fine," he told the two of them.

The grateful and relieved father, with tears in his eyes, hugged the surgeon and thanked him for all he had done to save his son's hand.

The doctor shook his hand and said, "No. I should be thanking you."

Now the father was puzzled by the doctor's remark. "But, Doctor, you fixed our son's hand, when nobody else would. My wife and I are the ones who owe you."

"No, you don't," he insisted. "I must thank you for reminding me of why I became a doctor."

That is the same gratitude that every American citizen ought to give to God whenever we accomplish some great thing in our life. After all, great things are expected of us. That's why God made us Americans.

America's history is His story!

August 20

"Every step by which they have advanced to the character of an independent nation seems to have been distinguished by some token of Providential agency." –George Washington

During the American Revolution, the British took control of Stony Point, a narrow place on the Hudson River which was often used as a crossing.

Gen. Washington ordered the enemy's position taken. He selected Gen. "Mad" Anthony Wayne to lead the surprise assault on the British garrison.

Defensively, the British installed a wooden abatis, a series of felled trees with sharpened, spike-like ends, facing toward the enemy, which extended all the way to the water's edge. Wisely, however, Gen. Wayne chose to attack at low tide, which allowed his troops to get around the enemy's wooden obstacles.

Since the element of surprise was so essential to the Colonial Army's success, they elected to use only their bayonets, so as not to alert the sentries.

With white pieces of paper pinned to the hats of the troops to identify themselves in the darkness, Gen. Wayne led the daring, nighttime assault on Stony Point. Moreover, the heavy cloud cover obscured the moonlight, marking another incident of the war, in which the conditions aided the Americans' success.

The Continental Army, under the direction of Gen. Wayne, enjoyed an unlikely but overwhelming victory. Following the battle, Wayne's message to Gen. Washington contained these words: "The fort and garrison, with Col. Johnson, are ours. The men behaved like men determined to be free."

America's history is His story!

August 21

"If fear is cultivated, it will become stronger. If faith is cultivated, it will achieve mastery." –John Paul Jones

America's History is His Story:

Legendary frontier Marshal Bill Tilghman was both a friend and contemporary of Wyatt Earp, Wild Bill Hickok, and Bat Masterson.

During the course of his career, Tilghman captured many famous outlaws of his time. He chose to come out of retirement, at the age of 70, to become the marshal of Cromwell, Oklahoma.

The town of Cromwell was a corrupt place, dominated by crime, illegal liquor, prostitution, and numerous acts of violence and murder. After being there less than a year, the lawman was shot down by a crooked Prohibition officer.

Strangely enough, it was the members of the local Ku Klux Klan who demanded justice for their aged marshal's death. These white-robed avengers printed fliers and handbills that warned the criminals in their town to immediately leave their city or pay the price for their crimes.

In the days following Tilghman's death, the local bars, brothels, and pool halls were set ablaze. Not a single one of them was left standing. Moreover, nobody was ever arrested for these acts of arson, and the town never regained its status as a "wild" town.

Although Tilghman died in his mission to clean up the town of Cromwell, his murder inspired the townspeople to finish what the marshal had started. In a typically American story, the people were inspired by the efforts of one, good man, standing alone.

America's history is His story!

August 22

"In my view, the life, the teachings, the labors, and the sufferings of the blessed Jesus, there can be no admiration too profound, no love of which the human heart is capable too warm, no gratitude too earnest and deep of which He is justly the object." –William Cullen Bryant

A number of years ago, an author took his teenage son to a political event, where Jack Kemp was to be the featured speaker.

Before he went into politics, Kemp was a football player in the NFL, quarterbacking the Buffalo Bills.

After Kemp spoke, the man and his son met the former quarterback-turned-politician. Kemp gave his autograph to the man, smiled, shook his hand, and responded briefly. However, the speaker clearly personalized his autograph to the author's son and was much, more folksy in his extended conversation with the young man.

Kemp had apparently realized that the man who brought his son to the event already supported him. Yet by going the extra mile to be nice to the author's son, he not only won the dad's favor, he also earned the admiration of a young person, someone who was likely to support him for many years to come.

It is a lesson the author never forgot.

Perhaps that lesson can also be applied our spiritual lives, as well.

By simply taking the time to devote our love, praise, and special kindness to God's Son, we also please the Heavenly Father. Maybe that is a truth our country would do well to remember once again.

America's history is His story!

August 23

"A Christian is nothing but a sinful man who has put himself to school for Christ, for the honest purpose of becoming better."
–Henry Ward Beecher

Walter Carney made a lot of promises to God while flying the hostile skies over Europe in World War II.

It has been said, "There are no atheists in the foxholes." However, with flak bursting all around their B-17, perhaps there are none in the air, as well.

When his bomber was hit by enemy fire, the pilot ordered Walter and his friend to bail out of the plane. As he scrambled out of his place in the ball turret, Carney's friend, true to his word, was waiting for him there with a parachute.

The two of them left the plane together, with Carney only moments behind his friend. However, the winds would carry his friend to Allied territory. Carney's chute would place him in the hands of the German army, who repeatedly beat the young airman and interrogated him at gunpoint.

But when an armed American soldier finally liberated Carney from the prison where he'd had been kept, the vows he made to God were nearly forgotten.

Coming to a personal knowledge of the Lord, Carney recalled those promises he made as a young airman in World War II. And for the rest of his life, he kept the sacred vows he made to his wife. He honored the commitment he made to his country. And Pastor Carney kept the promises he made to God, as a faithful minister of the Gospel.

America's history is His story!

August 24

"If the stars should appear but one night every thousand years, how man would marvel and stare." –Ralph Waldo Emerson

When Neil Armstrong and Buzz Aldrin landed on the moon's surface in 1969, President Nixon's speechwriter drafted a speech to be given by the president, if the pair of astronauts failed to successfully lift off from the lunar surface.

The following is a portion of that speech:

"Fate has ordained that the men who went to the moon to explore in peace will stay on the moon to rest in peace.

"These brave men, Neil Armstrong and Edwin Aldrin, know that there is no hope for their recovery. But they also know that there is hope for mankind in their sacrifice. These two men are laying down their lives in mankind's most noble goal: the search for truth and understanding.

"In ancient days, men looked at stars and saw their heroes in the constellations. In modern times, we do much the same, but our heroes are epic men of flesh and blood.

"For every human being who looks up at the moon in the nights to come will know that there is some corner of another world that is forever mankind."

We all know that Armstrong and Aldrin did lift off from the lunar surface. They did return safely to earth. Moreover, the fact that NASA never lost an astronaut in our moon landings is just one more example of what made our nation exceptional.

And Nixon's greatest speech remained simply the printed words on a page.

America's history is His story!

August 25

"In every human breast, God has implanted a principle, which we call love of freedom; it is impatient of oppression and pants for deliverance." –Phillis Wheatley

America's History is His Story:

Kidnapped from her home in West Africa, Phillis Wheatley was only a child, when she was placed on a slave ship bound for Boston.

Everything she acquired or knew came from the depths of slavery.

Receiving her first name from the slave ship that brought her to this country, the eight-year old child's last name was selected to match the wealthy, Boston family who purchased her.

Tutored by John and Susanna Wheatley's daughter, the young child received an excellent education. Along with her studies of Scripture, Phillis became acquainted with classical writings, in both Greek and Latin.

Soon, she would develop an interest in poetry.

Becoming the first published, black poet, Wheatley proved it's impossible to imprison the minds of the educated.

Even before she gained her individual freedom, Wheatley's work supported the cause of national liberty. Moreover, her writing would be recognized and honored by Gen. Washington, Thomas Jefferson, and George Whitefield.

Although the slave-turned-poet died in abject poverty, she would be greeted in Heaven by the Great Author of Liberty.

America's history is His story!

August 26

"One cannot be exposed to the law and order of the universe without concluding that there must be design and purpose behind it all."
–Wernher von Braun

Long before Louis Leakey became the darling of evolutionary theory, he was the son of Christian missionaries in Africa.

His father and mother, who devoted their life to Christian service, trusted that their son would receive a good education at Cambridge University. His goal was also to become a missionary to Africa.

However, somewhere along the way, Leakey tragically lost his faith.

Walking away from his Christianity, in much the same way that America has drifted away from its religious moorings, Leakey willingly embraced the inane theories of Charles Darwin.

Instead of devoting his life to a higher calling, Louis gave himself to proving man was no different than the apes.

It was a tragic waste of a once brilliant mind.

The Piltdown Man and the Java Man—the skulls upon which evolutionists used to hang their hats have been disproven. In fact, nearly every great evolutionary discovery, heralded by ungodly anthropologists, has later been exposed as a hoax.

Not only did Leakey fail to prove any real link between man and apes, he also greatly undermined the Divine work and calling of his parents.

Unlike Louis Leakey, perhaps our country can return to the faith of *our* fathers.

America's history is His story!

August 27

"The race is not to the swift, nor the battle to the strong: but the God of Israel is He that giveth strength and power unto His people. Trust in Him at all times, ye people, pour out your hearts before Him: God is a refuge for us." –Abigail Adams

America's History is His Story:

Determined to help the American captives on the British prison ships, Elizabeth Burgin often visited with the men and brought them food to eat.

Upon seeing the suffering aboard these prison ships, the woman wished she could do more to help them.

At the request of one of the Colonial officers, Burgin notified the prisoners of the details of an upcoming prison escape. Her efforts and assistance led to the escape of over 200 American prisoners.

Officials of the British government were outraged and embarrassed that a woman had aided in the prisoners' escape. Perhaps they also feared the men who escaped would spread the word about the deplorable conditions aboard these floating death chambers, further inspiring the Colonists. Therefore, they put a price on the woman's head, forcing the woman to flee her home and leaving most of her belongings behind.

As a result of George Washington's letter to the Continental Congress, Burgin was later awarded with a Revolutionary pension for her service to our country.

It wasn't only the men of our country who risked their lives in the Revolution. Women also suffered, sacrificed, and offered up their homes, families, and individual lives in their quest for freedom.

America's history is His story!

August 28

"Where justice is denied, where poverty is enforced, where ignorance prevails, and where any one class is made to feel that society is an organized conspiracy to oppress, rob and degrade them, neither persons nor property will be safe." –Frederick Douglas

On this date in 1963, Martin Luther King Jr., speaking from the steps of the Lincoln Memorial, addressed a massive throng of American citizens.

King's remarks that day, in support of civil rights, is perhaps the most well-known speech in our nation's history, second only to Abraham Lincoln's Gettysburg Address.

This is merely a portion of that speech:

"I have a dream that one day this nation will rise up and live out the true meaning of its creed: 'We hold these truths to be self-evident, that all men are created equal.'

"I have a dream that one day, on the red hills of Georgia, the sons of former slaves and the sons of former slave owners will be able to sit down together at the table of brotherhood.

"I have a dream that my four little children will one day live in a nation where they will not be judged by the color of their skin, but by the content of their character."

As a result of that day's momentous gathering, America did grant civil rights to people of every color. And America has truly become the nation of which King spoke and which the King of Kings envisioned for us to reside.

America's history is His story!

August 29

"Kindness is the language which the deaf can hear and the blind can see." –Mark Twain

During his 1976 campaign to gain the presidential nomination, Ronald Reagan was to speak at a gathering in North Carolina.

America's History is His Story:

Through one of his aides, a woman sent word to Gov. Reagan that she was there with a group of blind children. And since they couldn't see the presidential candidate, they asked if Reagan would come over to their group and briefly speak with them.

Reagan immediately agreed to speak to the children, but only if the reporters weren't around when he met with them.

In order to overcome the background noise, Reagan squatted down to gently speak with the blind children on their level. He thanked them for their interest and answered their questions. Then, he did something that was quite extraordinary.

Reagan asked the assembled children, ranging in ages from eight to ten years old, if they would like to touch his face, in order to get some idea what he looked like.

For the next several minutes, Reagan allowed these blind children, one by one, to see him through their sense of touch. Their smiling faces clearly revealed their joy.

Despite the exposure that any office seeker hopes to gain from the press, Gov. Reagan insisted that this meeting should be a private moment, away from the cameras.

While on the campaign trail, Reagan's kindness to these blind children brings to mind the example of our Lord and Savior, who also made time for the little children.

America's history is His story!

August 30

"As one small candle may light a thousand, so the light here kindled hath shone unto many." –William Bradford

Approximately ten years before the Pilgrims came to Plymouth, another group of English traders and merchants came to the region. An Indian boy, who was later called "Squanto" was captured and taken back to Europe to be sold into slavery.

Squanto not only became educated in the English language, he also embraced the Christian faith of his masters. His owner kindly consented to allow Squanto to return home on the first ship bound for America. As he returned to his native shore, the young man sadly learned that a plague had wiped out all the people of his village.

When the Pilgrims arrived, they were surprised to be greeted by an Indian, Squanto, who spoke to them clearly, in their own tongue.

Squanto became a great friend and benefactor to the Pilgrims, teaching them how to fish, find game, and effective ways to plant corn and other crops. He even helped them to communicate with the other Indians who lived nearby.

When he was captured by a hostile Indian tribe, which believed Squanto's death would silence the white man's voice, the Pilgrims armed themselves and came to his aid.

Squanto took his last breath with William Bradford kneeling by his bedside.

Although Squanto was taken into slavery, like the story of Joseph, God had a special purpose for the young man. When his village was destroyed by disease, Squanto's life was spared, in order to help another people, who embraced him as one of their own.

America's history is His story!

August 31

"These are the times that try men's souls; the summer soldier and the sunshine patriot will, in the crisis, shrink from the service of his

country; but he that stands it now, deserves the love and thanks of man and woman." –Thomas Paine

During the most bitter fighting of World War I, Major Charles Whittlesey commanded a squadron of nearly 600 American soldiers in the Argonne Forest. Ordered to attack the German lines, Whittlesey's men advanced so far forward, they soon found themselves trapped in a ravine, far behind enemy lines.

For the next six days, the men of "The Lost Battalion" were surrounded by the enemy. Running low on food and water, their ammunition nearly depleted, the Americans were subjected to numerous grenade, sniper, and flame thrower attacks. However, Whittlesey boldly refused all calls for his surrender.

One of the captured troops was sent back with a message for Whittlesey:

"The suffering of your wounded men can be heard over here in the German lines, and we are appealing to your humane sentiments to stop. A white flag shown by one of your men will tell us that you agree with these conditions. Please treat Private Lowell R. Hollingshead [the bearer] as an honorable man. He is quite a soldier. We envy you."

Only about 200 men were still standing when reinforcements arrived. Rewarded for their bravery, some of the men never fully recovered from the unseen scars of battle.

The Americans' dedication and tenacity in the face of overwhelming odds was so exemplary, they even earned the respect and admiration of their German opponents.

America's history is His story!

September 1

"History is the memory of time, the life of the dead, and the happiness of the living." –Captain John Smith

Much of what you think you know about the story of Pocahontas is untrue. In fact, the real story of this Indian princess is much more colorful than the story portrayed in one of Walt Disney's animated movies.

Not long after coming to Jamestown, Captain John Smith took some of his men out hunting. The Indians, under Chief Powhatan, captured Smith and killed all the men in his hunting party. When Powhatan ordered Smith to be killed, Pocahontas, the chief's 13 year old daughter, successfully pleaded for the Captain's life to be spared.

Perhaps as a result of her kindness, Pocahontas apparently became close friends of the settlers, later warning Captain Smith of Powhatan's plans to attack Jamestown.

Five years later, the young Indian Chief's daughter would willingly embrace the faith of the settlers and make it her own. After her baptism, she chose the Christian name of Rebecca, to signify her newfound trust in the Lord.

The Jamestown settlement, established not only as a financial enterprise, but as an evangelical one as well, finally saw its first convert in the New World.

The young woman would later marry John Rolfe, have a child, and travel with them to England. During their time overseas, as a result of a letter from Captain Smith, this former Indian princess would receive an invitation to meet the Queen of England.

Jamestown was spared by God's grace, through the mercies of an Indian princess.

America's history is His story!

September 2

"A life is not important except in the impact it has on other lives."
—Jackie Robinson

When Branch Rickey signed Jackie Robinson to play for the Brooklyn Dodgers, many on the team were reluctant to welcome the first black ballplayer on their club. Some of them even got together, signing a petition that threatened to boycott the game, if Robinson joined the team.

One of the Dodgers players, Harold Henry Reese, better known by his nickname, Pee Wee, refused to go along with the boycott.

While on a road trip in Cincinnati, the crowd was particularly hateful to Jackie Robinson. Pee Wee Reese deliberately made his way over to the game's first black ballplayer. He spoke with Robinson for a moment, before putting his arm around him. As one of the game's most popular players, Reese's actions ended the heckling.

Years later, at Reese's funeral, Joe Black, another ballplayer of that era, who helped to break the color barrier, said these words about the former Dodger great:

"When Pee Wee reached out to Jackie, all of us in the Negro League smiled and said it was the first time that a white guy had accepted us. When I finally got up to Brooklyn, I went to Pee Wee and said, 'Black people love you. When you touched Jackie, you touched all of us.'"

As a result of Reese's treatment of this pioneering black athlete, Pee Wee showed the country that he wasn't only a great ballplayer, but also a giant among men.

America's history is His story!

September 3

"Children are the hands by which we take hold of Heaven."
–Henry Ward Beecher

Quite possibly the most painful thing in a parent's life is the loss of a child. However, from the earliest days of our founding, throughout the middle of the Twentieth Century, it was quite commonplace for parents to bury their children.

Families were generally large. Children often died in infancy or during the process of childbirth.

That is not to say the loss of a child was any less painful for these pioneers, settlers, and pre-World War II families. However, these hardy individuals, who often faced many instances of great personal loss, were not necessarily stronger than those from succeeding generations. But perhaps, their deep and abiding sense of faith *was*.

There were no psychiatric counselors or mental health professionals to help family members deal with the tragic death of one of their children. The grief-stricken parents were primarily on their own.

Their churches, their pastors, their love of God, and their overwhelming belief in the power of prayer served to bring them comfort, helping these Americans to bravely confront the reality of their great personal loss.

The parents wept over the grave; they remembered the loved one who had passed, and they diligently moved on with their lives, firmly trusting in the inherent wisdom of God's master plan.

America's history is His story!

September 4

"Christianity is the companion of liberty in all its conflicts, the cradle of its infancy and the divine source of its claims."
–Alexis de Tocqueville

A prominent Hollywood actor, generally opposed to conservative causes, recently crossed paths with Ronald Reagan's son, Michael.

As the two of them conversed, the actor stated that he actually missed Michael's father, the former president, and despite their profound differences in ideology, he claimed Ronald Reagan clearly had "a good soul."

A good soul—the statement was certainly true about Ronald Reagan. The same could also be said for America.

America has always had a good soul.

The soul of America was seen in the men and women who climbed off the *Mayflower*. It was seen in our rebellion against King George. It permeated the writings of our Founders. The soul of America was seen in our conflict to end the scourge of slavery. Our country's soul was displayed in the American blood that stained the sand and soil of Europe, in our quest to make others free.

Whenever there is a natural disaster, Americans are always the first on the scene, offering their service and financial help.

Throughout our nation's history, America has always had a good soul.

For almost 250 years, Christianity has been our faith, our foundation, and our fixture. The soul of a nation was clearly the product of our Godly American heritage.

America's history is His story!

September 5

"God's angels often protect his servants from potential enemies."
—Billy Graham

During World War II, heavy bomber pilots, flying in the skies over Europe, were often escorted by planes with distinctive, crimson tail markings.

These men in the "Red Tails" were the Tuskegee Airmen.

Although black pilots were accepted into the Army Air Corps, they generally weren't trusted with the flying assignments given to their white counterparts. Moreover, while other less experienced pilots were dying in the skies over Europe, the eager but frustrated Tuskegee Airmen were still left behind in the States.

However, after the Germans had exacted a deadly toll on the ranks of our bomber and fighter personnel, our generals were forced to rethink their hesitancy to employ the black pilots of Tuskegee.

Initially, the white pilots doubted the courage and skills of the black airmen. But the black pilots didn't only remarkably succeed in downing the German fighters; they also shot down the misconceptions about their abilities. It wasn't too long before the once-skeptical, white pilots were requesting "Red-Tail Angels" as their mission escorts.

In nearly 1,600 missions, the Tuskegee Airmen had a nearly perfect record of bringing their bombers home. Arguably, their exploits in the air paved the way to integrating the military on the ground, soon to be followed by the country as a whole.

Their courage inspired a segregated land to finally become one nation.

America's history is His story!

America's History is His Story:

September 6

"Enslave the liberty of but one human being and the liberties of the world are put in peril." –William Lloyd Garrison

Although training for the Tuskegee Airmen began several months before, the program might never have fully gotten off the ground, were it not for the support of the First Lady.

Having taken a keen interest in the aeronautical school at Tuskegee Institute, Eleanor Roosevelt visited the school in the spring of 1941.

While talking to one of Tuskegee's instructors, Charles "Chief" Anderson, Mrs. Roosevelt asked him if black pilots could really fly. In response, Anderson invited the First Lady to join him for a ride in his yellow Piper Cub.

Objecting to the woman taking to the skies with a black pilot at the controls, the Secret Service agents even called the President for support.

"If she wants to do it," FDR said, "there's nothing we can do to stop her."

After spending an hour in the blue skies over Alabama, Eleanor Roosevelt climbed down from the back seat of the plane. She turned towards Chief Anderson and said, "I guess Negroes can fly."

When the First Lady returned to Washington, she was extremely vocal with administration officials in support for the Tuskegee "experiment." And thanks to Eleanor Roosevelt's efforts, the black airmen of Tuskegee would prove their worth in the skies over war-torn Europe.

America's history is His story!

September 7

"It was written in their Koran, that all nations who should not have acknowledged their authority were sinners, that it was their right and duty to make war upon them, wherever they could be found, and to make slaves of all they could take as prisoners, and that every Musselman [Muslim] who should be slain in battle was sure to go to Paradise." –Thomas Jefferson

Following the attacks on 9/11, America's most recent wars have been fought against Islamic extremists in other lands. What generally isn't known by most Americans is that our nation's first war was also fought against the forces of Islam.

In the Marine anthem, you will hear the words, "to the shores of Tripoli." These refer to the United States' first war, in which Pirates from the Barbary Coast of North Africa plundered and seized the ships of our merchant sailors and held them for ransom.

Realizing that any concessions to the demands of these pirates would only lead to more kidnappings, hostages, and demands, President Thomas Jefferson ordered military action. He instructed our ships to attack their ports and blockade their harbors.

Later, a small contingent of American Marines and mercenaries, led by Gen. William Eaton, won the Battle of Dema, after they marched 500 miles across the harsh sands of the Libyan Desert.

That victory would mark the first time that the United States flag was ever raised in victory on foreign soil.

From the writings of both Thomas Jefferson and John Quincy Adams, it is obvious that they both knew the dangers that Islam posed to the United States, or any other nation that desired to be free. The threat continues today.

America's history is His story!

September 8

"As the essential principle of his [Mohammad's] faith is the subjugation of others by the sword; it is only by force, that his false doctrines can be dispelled, and his power annihilated." –John Quincy Adams

When President Thomas Jefferson ordered American forces to attack the Coast of North Africa, the forces of Tripoli took control of our ship, the *Philadelphia*, which ran aground on one of its raids.

At the time, Stephen Decatur was but a 24-year old lieutenant, when he was leading America's first Marines.

Commandeering a ship from the enemy, which he renamed *Intrepid*, Decatur planned a daring raid into Tripoli harbor, under the cover of darkness. Coming alongside the *Philadelphia*, his men quickly boarded the captured ship.

Decatur's brave Marines charged the guards, overpowered them, freed our sailors, and set fire to the vessel, so it could no longer be used against us.

As a result of his victory, Stephen Decatur would gain lasting fame as America's first military hero since the American Revolution.

In fact, British Admiral, Lord Nelson, called Decatur's raid, "the most bold and daring act of the Age."

In 1815, Commodore Decatur would lead his men once again, in a second war against the Barbary Pirates and the forces of Islam. The United States would emerge from this war, victorious once again.

America's history is His story!

September 9

"Wealth, like happiness, is never attained when sought after directly. It comes as a by-product of providing a useful service." –Henry Ford

Long before he took to wearing his trademark white goatee, white double breasted suits, and black string ties, Harland Sanders often cooked chicken for his gasoline customers in the back of his service station in Corbin, Kentucky. The man later acquired a restaurant and saw his business begin to thrive. However, the construction of a new interstate highway nearly destroyed his restaurant trade.

At the age of 65, Harland Sanders wasn't sure of what he should do.

Using the money from his social security check, Sanders started to travel around the country, trying to market his unique chicken recipe to other restaurants.

The rest is history.

By 1964, Sanders had over 600 franchises in America and Canada, making Kentucky Fried Chicken one of the most recognized and successful restaurant chains in the entire world.

Throughout our nation's history, America is a place, like no other. It is a country where men and women have often seen their dreams of success realized, often beyond their wildest dreams.

America has certainly been a unique and blessed land, where even a senior citizen, such as Colonel Harland Sanders, could acquire great wealth and become a name known to people around the world.

America's history is His story!

September 10

"Where the press is free, and every man able to read, all is safe."
–Thomas Jefferson

Ernie Pyle was perhaps the most well-known and respected war correspondent in World War II.

America's History is His Story:

In the late 1920s, Pyle got his start in journalism, writing about famous American men and women in aviation. He came to know Amelia Earhart and others of the period.

However, it was his unparalleled war reporting that would serve to bring him fame throughout the nation.

Often reporting from the perspective of the soldiers he covered, the men in battle considered him one of their own. Despite being well-connected with our military's leaders, Pyle still became the reporter of the common "foot soldier."

When soldiers were exposed to hostile gunfire, he was there beside them. When our troops stormed the beaches, Pyle made the landings with them. He slept beside them on the hard ground and joined them in the cold, wet foxholes. In fact, it was a Japanese sniper on Okinawa, firing at Pyle's beloved fellow foot soldiers, who took the life of the famed war correspondent.

Pyle died from a single bullet wound to the temple.

The writings he left for us gave America a chance to understand the true costs of preserving our liberty. It also reminded us that our nation's warriors represent our very best ideals and traditions, those for which our country was founded.

America's history is His story!

September 11

"Above all, we must realize that no arsenal, or no weapon in the arsenals of the world is so formidable as the will and moral courage of free men and women. It is a weapon our adversaries in today's world do not have. It is a weapon that we as Americans do have."

–Ronald Reagan

The phrase, "Let's roll," has become a uniquely American battle cry in modern vernacular in much the same way that "Remember the Alamo" was in the past.

Those two simple words were spoken by Todd Beamer on this day in 2001, when a number of brave, modern American patriots tried to overpower the Muslim hijackers on United Airlines Flight 93, just before it crashed into the Pennsylvania countryside.

On that day, we saw absolutely the worst that humanity has to offer and, at the same time, we witnessed the very best of the American spirit.

The orchestrated attacks on the Towers and the Pentagon were carried out by Islamic extremists, zealots who blindly swore their allegiance to Mohammed. Theirs may be the only religion which instructs the believer to give his life so that others, who do not share his faith, might die.

In contrast, Christianity inspires the believer to *live* his life so that others, who do not share his faith, might live also.

Unlike the Islamic extremists around the glove, America was established as a Christian nation. Our religious heritage causes us to attempt to convert those who do not embrace our faith; we do not try to kill them.

Let's roll!

America's history is His story!

September 12

"No power over the freedom of religion...is delegated to the United States by the Constitution." –Thomas Jefferson

We often hear people talk about a wall of separation between church and state. Unfortunately, the phrase is often misused, leading

Americans to wrongly believe that our Founders intended for people of faith to stay out of politics.

But the walls we confront today are not between church and state; they are between church and *statism*.

Not only are many of our leaders in Washington committed to assuming control over every part of our economy; they are also obsessed with legislating the message, beliefs, and practices of our churches.

All too often, our citizens have willingly surrendered the clear-cut, historical record of our Godly American heritage. We have allowed others to purge these truths from our history books. They have renounced the greatness of our Founders and our country's most sacred traditions. Routinely, they have denied young Americans the chance to truly learn their roots.

Speaking at the Berlin Wall, President Reagan told Mikhail Gorbachev to "tear down this wall!" However, as citizens of this great land, we also need to tear down some walls as well, the ones our government has erected between its citizens and their faith.

Our faith and our freedom—Americans must not allow our government to bar us from the exercise and acknowledgment of either one.

America's history is His story!

September 13

"Success is to be measured, not so much by the position that one has reached in life, as by the obstacles which he has overcome while trying to succeed." –Booker T. Washington

Following the Civil War, the United States Army created the 10th Cavalry Regiment, which was made up entirely of black soldiers.

The Indians called them "buffalo soldiers," a name which soon became synonymous for all of our country's early, black military units.

The origins of the nickname can never fully be determined, but there are two explanations for the term.

One of them was that the Indians called these troops Buffalo Soldiers, because the color and texture of the soldiers' hair reminded them of the buffalo's shaggy mane. Another possible explanation was that these soldiers were fierce fighters, and, like the buffalo, simply refused to die.

Whatever the reason for the name, the Indians certainly paid these soldiers a great honor, since they had such a high regard for this animal that roamed the Western Plains.

Throughout several wars and battles, these men served with great distinction and courage. In fact, their desertion and court martial rate was much lower than that of their white counterparts.

Their courage in battle often won them the respect of their enemies and the white officers who commanded them. Moreover, their devotion to duty eventually led to the integration of all U.S. forces.

America's history is His story!

September 14

"I prefer to be true to myself, even at the hazard of incurring the ridicule of others, rather than to be false, and to incur my own abhorrence." –Frederick Douglas

Gen. John J. Pershing led the Buffalo Soldiers of the 10th Cavalry at Cuba's San Juan Hill and also in his pursuit of Pancho Villa.

As a result of his service with these men, Pershing had witnessed their extraordinary courage and dedication in battle. The general also saw one of these men, while fighting in Cuba, give the last drops of water from his canteen to one of the mortally wounded Spanish soldiers.

Pershing's experiences made him one of the Buffalo Soldiers' most loyal and ardent supporters. In fact, his regard for them was a source of derision among some of the white cadets and officers at West Point, earning Pershing the nickname, "Black Jack."

Despite that fact, Gen. Pershing never wavered from his support of the Buffalo Soldiers, these brave men with whom the man served.

Because of the religious underpinnings of our great nation, we have always been blessed with men of immense character and moral clarity, individuals who could be counted upon to recognize injustice and strive to correct it.

These men not only gave birth to our nation; they also took the bold actions that were responsible for the United Sates moving beyond the color barriers and declaring that all men are truly equal.

America's history is His story!

September 15

"Men are what their mothers made them." –Ralph Waldo Emerson

Although the sacrifices of World War II took a toll on every family who had a loved one overseas, perhaps the experience was most difficult for the mothers.

It is definitely not a cliché that dying, young men on the battlefield often call out for their mothers. But their mothers are never around to hear their final cries.

Instead, the mothers are forced to remain behind in the States.

Mothers were the ones who worried and prayed for their children's safety in combat. They were the ones who were forced, despite their worst fears, to maintain a brave face for the children who often remained at home. They were the ones who hated to hear a car approaching their home, fearing that it might contain the military's dreadful messages of condolence.

However, one mother would see her name become synonymous with the end of the war with Japan.

The *Enola Gay*, a plane named after Paul Tibbets' mother, was to carry the atomic bomb which would be dropped on Hiroshima.

The deadly bomb that would fall on Hiroshima, would finally bring about the end of a brutal war. "Little Boy" would stop the future suffering of mothers across the country. And most important of all, it would bring Americas' young warriors home…

To their mothers.

America's history is His story!

September 16

"The time for war has not yet come, but it will come, and that soon; and when it does come, my advice is to draw the sword and throw away the scabbard." –Gen. Thomas "Stonewall" Jackson

On the fiftieth anniversary of America dropping the atomic bomb on Hiroshima, the Smithsonian Institution initially prepared an exhibit—that was later cancelled—which was greatly critical of President Truman's decision.

American apologists are often telling us that we should be ashamed of our country for unleashing this dreadful weapon upon the world.

Besides the untold number of American lives that were saved by our actions in abruptly ending the war, one must not ignore the atrocities that were committed by the Japanese Imperial Army.

When they invaded Nanking, the capital of China, the Japanese killed nearly 350,000 Chinese civilians. In the space of one month, more civilians were murdered in China than were killed at Hiroshima and Nagasaki combined.

While their husbands and fathers were forced to watch, women were brutally raped and slaughtered by Japanese soldiers. Children's bodies were tossed back and forth on the points of the soldiers' bayonets. In the aftermath, the streets of Nanking were littered with the bodies of Japanese victims, men, women, and children.

When the atomic bomb, codenamed "Little Boy," was released from the *Enola Gay*, there can be no question that the United States was acting in defense of great moral principle and once again coming to the aid of humanity.

America's history is His story!

September 17

"I must study politics and war, that my sons may have the liberty to study mathematics and philosophy." –John Adams

It is only natural for a man to wish that he can leave the world a much better place for his children. John Adams was no different.

Adams knew the actions the Founders were undertaking would place them at great personal risk. However, they went to war with Britain in order for his children to know both peace and freedom in the future.

The liberties we currently enjoy were purchased by others. In fact, there are brave Americans at this very moment holding back the forces of evil and tyranny, governments and individuals who wish to kill us or to destroy our way of life.

The thousands of brave men and women in our Armed Forces willingly *and* daily place their lives on the line for our liberties.

Perhaps George Orwell said it best when he stated, "People sleep peaceably in their beds at night only because rough men stand ready to do violence on their behalf."

If you enjoy comfort, if you know peace, and if you have tasted freedom, it is because of the selfless sacrifices of those who serve our country, or those who have gone before. It is also because our Lord has blessed Americans with a land that routinely produces these extraordinary men and women.

You can feel free to rest soundly tonight. Even though you don't see them, the watchmen are upon the walls of freedom, guarding the liberties of each one of us.

America's history is His story!

September 18

"A thorough knowledge of the Bible is worth more than a college education." –Theodore Roosevelt

Recently, the King James Bible celebrated its 400th anniversary.

At approximately the same time the first English colonies were being established in the New World, English translators were working on the Authorized Version of the King James Bible.

Perhaps there has been no other book in history that had more influence on our country's history than the King James Bible.

America's History is His Story:

In a sense, the English Bible actually became the American Bible.

The King James Bible influenced the ideals of our Founding Fathers. It inspired our westward movement across the continent. This marvelous book educated the children of our pioneers and settlers. It has also made its mark on our literature.

While taking their oaths of office, our Presidents and politicians place their hands on the Bible. Our trial witnesses swear their testimonies upon them. The misfits of the American Civil Liberties Union spend their time in seeking to banish them.

But despite the actions of many to remove it from the pages of our historical record, the King James Bible has been an integral part of our nation's history. God has blessed it; He has preserved it. He has graciously given this wondrous Book to America.

Every American should realize it was ultimately the truths of the King James that ended the reign of King George.

America's history is His story!

September 19

"In my view, the Christian religion is the most important and one of the first things in which all children, under a free government ought to be instructed. No truth is more evident to my mind than that the Christian religion must be the basis of any government intended to secure the rights and privileges of a free people." –Noah Webster

As a result of his Hollywood film and acting career, perhaps no man came to symbolize America and the Old West more than John Wayne.

While making an appearance on Dean Martin's television show, the Duke was once asked what he wanted for his young daughter.

John Wayne thought for a moment and responded with the following words:

"I'd like her to know some of the values that we knew as kids, some of those values that too many people these days are thinking are old fashioned. Most of all, I want her to be grateful, as I am, every day of my life, to live in these United States.

"I know it may sound a little corny, but the first thing my daughter's learning from me is the Lord's Prayer, and some of the Psalms. And I really don't care if she ever memorizes the Gettysburg Address, just so long as she understands it.

"And since little girls are seldom called upon to defend their country, she may never have to raise her hand for that oath, but I certainly want her to respect all those who do."

A bout with stomach cancer took his life in 1979. However, up until the day he died, John Wayne remained thankful for experiencing all the blessings of America.

America's history is His story!

September 20

"It is all over now. Many of us are prisoners, many are dead, many wounded, bleeding and dying. Your soldier lives and mourns and, but for you, my darling, he would rather be back there with his dead, to sleep for all time in an unknown grave." –Gen. George Pickett

Brimming with confidence and eager to see the world, Sid Nicholas was the product of the West Virginia farming community. During World War II, he gave that up to become the tail gunner in a B-17 bomber.

America's History is His Story:

Like many of those in his generation, Sid spent most of his adult life, seldom talking about the youthful combat experiences that formed the man he became.

These were men who were shaped in a crucible of war. They had seen people die; they saw their friends die. They had often been forced to kill others.

This acquaintance with war, death, and its gruesome aftermath forever altered these seemingly old men, scarcely out of their teens. The need to become stoic often made them appear to be cold and unfeeling.

Sadly, it often built walls between them and their children.

It was only in his later years that Sid began talking about the military experiences that shaped his war-torn youth. But until the day he died, Sid continued to shoulder the heavy baggage of his war experiences. Sid was never able to lay aside the guilt and shame he felt for returning from the war, when most of his fellow crewmen didn't.

And like so many of those who fought there, although Sid Nicholas willingly and selflessly offered up his life for these United States of America, he fought for his friends.

America's history is His story!

September 21

"Launch planes. To Col. Doolittle and gallant command, good luck and God bless you." –Admiral William "Bull" Halsey

Sixteen planes were lined up in a row on the deck of the *USS Hornet*, when they received Admiral Halsey's command to launch.

Their pilots stared off towards the blue seas, which they all expected would likely soon become their final resting place.

Their planes were not originally built to be launched from the deck of an aircraft carrier. They were not carrying enough fuel to effectively return to safety. Moreover, their pilots and crews did not expect to live out the day.

However, there wasn't a single one of them who didn't expect to live long enough to drop their payload of bombs on the Japanese mainland.

Approximately 640 miles from Japan, fearing that they were spotted, the planes were forced to leave the deck, over 200 miles early.

With his plane in front, Col. Jimmy Doolittle would have the shortest runway from which to launch. But the colonel's plane would make it, as would the fifteen others.

As these heavy B-25 bombers filled the skies, Doolittle's Raiders started their way towards Japan. Along with the bombs, these crews also carried the hopes and prayers of a wounded but resilient nation.

Seemingly against all odds, the Lord flew with them. The sixteen bombers would complete their mission, and America and its cause of liberty would not be defeated.

America's history is His story!

September 22

"No tongue can tell; no mind conceive; no pen portray the horrible sights I witnessed that morning." –Captain John Taggert

On any other day, the land was quiet and peaceful. Children often ran and played in the fields and waded through the waters of a nearby stream. The wind gently blew across the green meadows, peaceful lanes, and thriving cornfields.

America's History is His Story:

But on this one fine, September day, another wind blew through the Maryland landscape and the cool, clear waters of Antietam Creek.

The winds brought with them the crackling sounds of rifles, the gray smoke of rifles and cannon fire, and the lonely cries of the wounded and dying.

This was Antietam, the bloodiest single day in our nation's military history. In the space of little more than 12 hours, over 23,000 soldiers met their deaths. The ground was littered with the twisted, lifeless bodies of soldiers clad in both the blue and the gray.

Blood spilled upon the meadows, lanes, and cornfields of the peaceful Maryland countryside at Antietam. On this day, the once-peaceful stream, which flowed all the way to the Potomac, saw its clear waters turn to blood.

It was as if the land itself pulled a crimson blanket up over its face, so it wouldn't have to witness the scores of humanity that fell there upon it.

The Battle of Antietam wasn't a decisive victory for the North or the South. Nobody won this battle; they merely survived it. Only the rains from Heaven would wash away the stains of battle and gently smooth the troubled soil over the graves of the fallen.

America's history is His story!

September 23

"The battle of Iwo Island has been won. The United States Marines, by their individual and collective courage, have conquered a base which is as necessary to us in our continuing forward movement toward final victory as it was vital to the enemy in staving off ultimate defeat. Among the Americans who served on Iwo Island, uncommon valor was a common virtue." –Admiral Chester Nimitz

A lone flag proudly fluttered in the wind on a mountaintop of a small Pacific, black volcanic island.

Although the flag signaled a hard-fought military victory over their Japanese adversaries, there was still much fighting to be done. In the weeks to come, many more American soldiers would still die on the island. Many more would fall to the Japanese rifles and grenades. Many more of these American Marines wouldn't return home safely.

But the raising of the flag on Mount Suribachi signaled a great victory.

In our quest to take the island, American Marines were forced to confront thousands of well-armed troops, heavily fortified bunkers, and miles and miles of underground tunnels. Moreover, they confronted the Japanese Imperial Army, filled with men who thought it more honorable to commit suicide than surrender.

The picture of this flag-raising became one of the most iconic symbols of our glorious nation's history. Moreover, it inspired the hopes of those who remained at home.

Uncommon valor was a common virtue—those words are inscribed on the Iwo Jima Memorial at Arlington National Cemetery. They have come to symbolize the men of the United States Marine Corps. Those words also can be used to describe America.

America's history is His story!

September 24

"Greater love hath no man than this, that a man lay down his life for his friends." –Jesus Christ

In the midst of some of the most brutal fighting during World War II, Howard W. Gilmore was a submarine commander of the *USS Growler* in the Pacific.

America's History is His Story:

While Gilmore's vessel was surfaced, they spotted a Japanese ship, the *Hayasaki*. In preparation for a surface attack, the U.S. commander made his way to the bridge.

Upon seeing the enemy, the Japanese commander immediately ordered the *Hayasaki* to ram the *Growler*. The resulting collision of the two vessels damaged several feet of the sub's bow and hindered their ability to use the forward torpedo tubes.

A hostile burst of machine gun fire from the deck of the Japanese ship killed one of the officers and seriously wounded Commander Gilmore and a couple others. Gilmore ordered his men to "Clear the Deck!"

However, due to the serious nature of his injuries, Gilmore was unable to follow them down the hatch. Realizing that the submarine and his crew would be lost if they stayed on the surface, Gilmore quickly made a fateful decision.

In an act of great sacrifice, Gilmore issued the dreadful order, "Take her down!"

Hesitating for only a moment, the executive officer closed the hatch between them and ordered the *Growler* to dive, knowing his captain would be lost at sea.

Howard Gilmore would posthumously receive the Medal of Honor for his brave actions, his fierce duty to country, and the love he held for each member of his crew.

America's history is His story!

September 25

"A battle lost or won is easily described, understood, and appreciated, but the moral growth of a great nation requires reflection, as well as observation, to appreciate it." –Frederick Douglas

It is incorrectly believed by many Americans that there were no black soldiers fighting on the side of the Confederacy during the Civil War.

Fighting with the Thirteenth Virginia Cavalry was a black American soldier from Petersburg, Virginia, by the name of Richard Poplar.

From April 1861 until his capture at Gettysburg, Dick Poplar faithfully served his unit. He also spent over nineteen months in prison, alongside his white brothers-in-arms. And when a number of troops from his beloved Petersburg were captured in 1864, Dick selflessly offered those prisoners his dedicated aid and comfort.

A man of great faith, Poplar earned the respect and favor of his white Union jailors. However, it was often the black Union guards who frequently tormented and intimidated Dick with offers of special privileges or freedom, if he would simply renounce the Confederacy and take an oath of allegiance to the United States.

Dick steadfastly refused, choosing rather to cast his loyalties with his fellow Confederate prisoners. When questioned about his reasons for remaining incarcerated, he proudly stated, "I am a Jeff Davis man."

This proud son of the South eventually returned to Petersburg, Virginia, where he peacefully lived out the remainder of his life. Upon his death, Richard Poplar, this black former soldier, was given a burial with full Confederate military honors.

America's history is His story!

September 26

"Reason is not automatic. Those who deny it cannot be conquered by it." –Ayn Rand

Every person who is featured in these remembrances isn't necessarily a Christian. In fact, one such person is Ayn Rand, a talented writer and philosopher who steadfastly denounced all aspects of religion.

However, America is so great a country, it generally allows people to be wrong.

Francis Bacon said, "A little philosophy inclineth man's mind to atheism, but depth in philosophy bringeth men's minds about to religion."

Every nation in history has been dominated by a particular faith or a strong system of religious beliefs. Some of them exist merely on a fanatical faith in atheism, in which their bitter opposition to God eventually becomes their God.

Russia is a nation like that. It was a nation from which Ayn Rand fled, choosing rather to become a citizen of the United States.

In this country, Rand was free to challenge the ideals, beliefs and the notions of society and the government, freedoms she wouldn't have enjoyed in her native Russia.

This brilliant woman's personal quest for truth led her to embrace the counterfeit gems of the mind and overlook the priceless riches of the soul. Therefore, a philosophical journey that doesn't lead us to God ultimately fails to reach its destination.

It isn't reason that leads us to the Lord. It was reason that led us to faith, which ultimately led America to embrace those most precious treasures of the soul.

America's history is His story!

September 27

"Yes, I'm a patriotic person. For these people who disgrace the American way and burn our flag and do these things...I say, don't live here and disgrace my country. Go live in the Middle East and see how you like it." –Payne Stewart

On April 25, 1976, the year the United States celebrated its bicentennial as a nation, the Los Angeles Dodgers were playing the Chicago Cubs at Dodger Stadium.

During the fourth inning of the game, a couple of young men ran into the grass of left field. They carried an American flag, a can of lighter fluid, and a pack of matches.

As the two men were trying to burn the flag in their demented protest, Rick Monday was playing centerfield for the Cubs. Realizing what the men were attempting to do, Monday immediately sprang to action. Sprinting from his position in far center field, Monday caught up the flag in his right hand before the men could set it on fire.

As he carried the flag to safety, the scoreboard displayed the words, "Rick Monday…You Made a Great Play."

The crowd gave the former Marine reservist, turned baseball player, a standing ovation and spontaneously began singing in unison, "God Bless America."

"If that's all you're known for," Monday said recently, "it's not a bad thing at all. I think it solidified the thought process of hundreds of thousands of people that represented this country in fine fashion, many of whom lost their lives."

Over thirty-five years since the incident occurred, Rick Monday's defense of the American flag is still recognized as one of the finest moments in Major League Baseball.

America's history is His story!

September 28

"Those who labor in the earth are the chosen people of God."
–Thomas Jefferson

America's History is His Story:

Before the construction of the Panama Canal, a ship sailing from New York to San Francisco had to sail around the tip of South America, a journey of nearly 14,000 miles. The route through Panama cut the trip to less than half of that.

The first attempt to build the canal was abandoned by the French government. However, when a tough engineering miracle needed to be accomplished in the early part of the Twentieth Century, nobody succeeded like the people of the United States.

The United States not only took over the construction, they also took action to eliminate the mosquito problems, which caused malaria and yellow fever, diseases that quickly caused the French to flee the region.

The Panama Canal was completed in 1914, two years ahead of schedule.

President Theodore Roosevelt had the leftover and antiquated French earth moving equipment melted down in order to make medals for the American workers involved in the canal's timely construction.

The completion of the Canal cost the United States millions of dollars and thousands of American lives. Unfortunately, in one of the most shameful moments in our nation's history, President Jimmy Carter and members of Congress ignored the will of the American people and ceded control of the canal back to Panama in 1977. In trying to win the world's approval, they desecrated the efforts of many committed American workers.

America's history is His story!

September 29

"The highest glory of the American Revolution was this: it connected in one indissoluble bond the principles of civil government with the principles of Christianity." –John Quincy Adams

When discussing our American Revolution, it is important to understand that our Founders truly had no desire for battle. They made every effort and exhausted every means to peacefully resolve their disagreements with the British monarchy.

It also needs to be understood that most of our Founding Fathers actively opposed acts of mob violence. Moreover, some of them were greatly embarrassed and ashamed of the behavior of those involved in the Boston Tea Party. In fact, Benjamin Franklin declared that we needed to pay for the tea that was thrown into the Harbor. However, all efforts to reimburse the British for the tea were later rejected.

As further proof of the Founders' desire to inspire a Revolution built on the rights of individuals and the rule of law, one has only to look at the aftermath from the Boston Massacre.

At the risk of his own life and safety, and in fear of what the damages might be to his reputation and professional career, John Adams still dared to defend the British soldiers involved in the Boston Massacre. Moreover, Adams not only gave these men a vigorous defense, he also won their full acquittal.

It can never be stated enough that those who founded America were men of outstanding principle and overwhelming moral courage. No nation in history has ever assembled such a diverse blend of intellect, talent, wisdom, courage, principle, and faith.

America's history is His story!

September 30

"Our crew did not do the bombing in anger. We did it because we were determined to stop the killing, stop the war. I would have done anything to get to Japan and stop the killing." –Paul Tibbets

America's History is His Story:

The mission to develop and drop the atomic bomb on our enemies in Japan was shrouded in mystery and great secrecy.

In fact, the ones directly involved in the mission were prepared to do whatever was necessary to make sure those secrets remained secret.

Moments before Paul Tibbets boarded the *Enola Gay*, the flight surgeon handed the pilot a small cardboard box that contained twelve cyanide tablets, one for each member of his crew, should they be shot down or captured.

With the bomb weighing more than four tons, the plane's takeoff was much more difficult and hazardous than normal. It was only after the plane was airborne, that Tibbets fully informed the crew of their mission.

On August 6, 1945, "Little Boy" was dropped on Hiroshima, with devastating results. However, Japan refused to surrender until another bomb fell on Nagasaki.

Until he died, Tibbets steadfastly maintained his confidence in the virtue of his mission. He was convinced that his actions didn't only take lives; it also saved them.

"I sleep so well," Tibbets said, "because I know how many people got to live full lives because of what we did."

The greatness of America has always been, even when we take hostile military action against our enemies, it is to primarily stop the needless slaughter of others.

America's history is His story!

October 1

"A few year's experience will convince us that those things, which at the time they happened, we regarded as our greatest misfortunes have proved our greatest blessings." –George Mason

During those dark days of Valley Forge, when the men of our Continental Army were suffering from hunger, disease, nakedness, and frostbite, it appeared that all hope for America's Independence was lost.

Through the smoke and flames of the crippling attacks on Pearl Harbor, it looked like America's naval forces were finished.

In these two instances and numerous other times in our nation's history, it appeared that the blows of the enemy had brought our country to its knees. Although our tattered army found itself on the mat, the fight for liberty had only begun.

The cowardly attack carried out by the Japanese on Pearl Harbor would have crippled a lesser nation. However, it merely awakened a sleeping giant. America's naval forces and the power of our country's vast industrial might saw us emerge from the flame and ashes, stronger than ever before.

People often say that, in spite of the setbacks, America won. Maybe we didn't win in spite of them. Perhaps the opposite is true; America triumphed *because* of them!

Throughout our nation's history, instances of defeat, failure, and hardship have often shown our resilience and strengthened our resolve. And when circumstances drove our nation to its knees, it often brought us to our knees, and helped us find our faith.

Our country's finest hours have often followed our darkest moments.

America's history is His story!

October 2

"What preparations should we be making now? The greatest waste in all of our earth, which cannot be recycled or reclaimed, is our waste of the time that God has given us each day." –Billy Graham

America's History is His Story:

A number of years after leaving the White House, Ulysses S. Grant established a banking and investment firm with another partner. As it turned out, investment firms stealing from their clients aren't a condition reserved simply for our current day. Grant's partner was also taking money from their customers and the business.

Although Grant wasn't guilty of the crimes, the swindling of their clients caused the former president to lose his firm. Moreover, paying off the debts left Grant penniless.

Not long after this huge financial setback, Grant learned that he was dying of throat cancer. Therefore, in order to make sure his beloved wife was cared for after his death, the former general began writing his memoirs.

Fearing that he would die before the memoirs were completed, Grant often ignored his pain, working feverishly to complete them.

Fortunately, Grant won his race against death. He would die only a matter of days after completing the book. Moreover, the book would be immensely successful and his wife would be enriched unto the day of her death from its proceeds.

What a lesson this should be for every American!

Like Grant, we should all be conscious of the brevity of our lives. The individual pages of our lives are being written right now by our actions. And will the book you leave behind be something that you wouldn't be ashamed for others to read?

America's history is His story!

October 3

"Where are the warriors today? Who slew them?" –Sitting Bull

If you study his early life, there is nothing to indicate that young Ulysses S. Grant would become one of the most famous generals of the Civil War, America's bloodiest conflict. As a young man, Grant only enrolled in West Point as a result of his father's insistence. Other than excelling in horsemanship, the brilliant, young cadet did nothing special to distinguish himself in his studies, finishing in the middle of his class.

Although Grant served in our war with Mexico and was recognized for his bravery in combat, he appeared to be a reluctant soldier. Moreover, he only offered his military service to the Union Army after the future general repeatedly failed in business.

However, upon entering the war, Grant quickly distinguished himself, with his remarkable leadership in battle.

When Lincoln's other generals failed to actively prosecute the war against the Confederacy, Grant was selected as the commander of the Union forces. Lincoln responded to rumors of Grant's drinking and unworthiness for command, by saying, "I cannot spare this man. He fights."

Even though Grant would later become President, perhaps his greatest role would be the critical part he played in America's Civil War. Although his college and business career weren't noteworthy, Grant's legacy wasn't defined by them. For one brief, shining moment in history, Grant, like the nation he served, clearly found his place.

America's history is His story!

October 4

"There is a destiny that makes us brothers, no one goes his way alone; all that we send into the lives of others, comes back into our own."
–Edwin Markham

America's History is His Story:

Coming from a famous family of actors, Edwin Booth was often regarded as the finest actor of his day. However, whatever legacy he might have known as an actor was lost in the actions of his younger brother, John Wilkes Booth.

After his brother's assassination of the president, Edwin went into seclusion for nearly a year. Unsure of the reception he would receive, Edwin finally agreed to return to the stage for a production of *Hamlet*. Appearing at the beginning of one of the scenes, Booth received a thunderous round of applause.

Apparently, the people of his day didn't spend all their time focusing on the bad actors in society. They clearly recognized that Edwin wasn't responsible for the assassination of Lincoln; his brother was.

Edwin never fully recovered from the stain that his brother's action brought to the family name. However, there was no reason for him to be ashamed.

A number of years before, Edwin had been on a train that was pulling out of the station, when he saw a gentleman accidentally bumped into the space between the train and the train platform.

Edwin quickly grabbed the back of the man's shirt collar, pulling him back onto the platform. Booth's quick actions may have saved the life of Robert Todd Lincoln, the only one of Abraham Lincoln's children to live until adulthood.

America's history is His story!

October 5

"Give me your tired, your poor, your huddled masses yearning to breathe free, the wretched refuge of your teeming shore. Send these, the homeless, tempest tossed to me. I lift my lamp beside the golden door." –Emma Lazarus

A gift from the nation of France, the Statue of Liberty was originally slated for completion in 1876, to mark our country's Centennial. It was supposed to symbolize the friendship between the two nations and their cooperation in our American Revolution.

The French agreed to pay for the sculpture and its assembly. The United States was responsible for financing the statue's pedestal. The French already met their obligation in 1880; however, the funds to build the statue's base still hadn't been raised.

The statue first arrived in New York Harbor in 1884. But without a pedestal, one of America's greatest symbols of liberty was destined to remain in 350 individual pieces, rusting away in 214 wooden crates.

Joseph Pulitzer, the New York City newspaper publisher, made it his personal mission to see that the money was raised for the statue's base. He also promised to list the name of every single contributor, large or small.

Along with the large donations, school teachers across America took up the cause, appealing to those in their class rooms. Students made donations and raised funds. Children often gave the pennies they used for milk money.

Thanks to the generosity of millions of school children, Lady Liberty would finally take her place, lighting a pathway of freedom to all those who seek her.

America's history is His story!

October 6

"If I were an atheist, and believed in blind eternal fate, I should still believe that fate had ordained the Jews to be the most essential instrument for civilizing the nations." –John Adams

America's History is His Story:

Many of us know that Emma Lazarus wrote the poem on the Statue of Liberty; however, there are few of us who know the story of the one who penned those words.

Born in 1849, Emma Lazarus was the daughter of wealthy parents, among the German-speaking, Jewish community in New York City. Emma began writing poetry at an early age, seeing her first volume published while still in her teens.

Emma was deeply connected to her Jewish roots. It was through this study, and her volunteer work among the immigrants, that she learned about the Russian pogroms.

Pogrom is a Russian word that refers to hateful and violent activities directed against Jews, in order to eradicate them or drive them from the country. Moreover, it was these anti-Jewish purges that caused many of them to migrate to the United States.

Emma Lazarus became one of their most outspoken advocates, often reflecting those ideas in her poetry. As a result of her writing, she was commissioned in 1883 to write a poem to help raise money for the Statue of Liberty.

While returning from Europe in 1887, a 38-year old Emma Lazarus was dying from cancer. As her ship sailed into New York Harbor, this extraordinarily unselfish woman, who was one of the early advocates for a Jewish homeland, was too ill to see the completed Statue, which bears the words from her famous poem. One of Emma's final breaths was taken alongside Lady Liberty, a place where millions yearned to breathe free.

America's history is His story!

October 7

"This is not about land or money, but the one thing that no man should ever be able to take from another man: the freedom to make his own

choices about his life, where he'll live, how he'll live, how he'll raise his family." –William Barrett Travis

Peter Salem was born a slave in Framington, Massachusetts. He was later sold to Lawson Buckminster, who granted him his freedom. Realizing that any freedom worth having is also worth defending, Salem took his place among those brave souls who lined Concord Bridge.

On that bridge, he faced British Major John Pitcairn, who ordered the rebels to disperse. Perhaps the sight of brave men dying for their freedom inspired him to join them in this noble struggle.

Known for his skills as a marksman with a rifle, Salem enlisted in the 6th Massachusetts Regiment.

At the Battle of Bunker Hill, Salem would once again confront Major Pitcairn, who was responsible for killing his comrades at Concord. However, Salem wasn't willing to surrender the freedom that Pitcairn was now trying to deny them. Shouldering his gun, Salem shot the general out of the saddle, avenging the ones who died on Concord Bridge.

Although Salem took his final breath in poverty, this man, who had been born a slave, would die in Framington, a free man. The blessings of liberty which Peter Salem had been given, he willingly offered to his nation, purchasing America's freedom as well.

Therefore, it could be said that Peter Salem knew great wealth, great wealth indeed.

America's history is His story!

October 8

"They didn't want to go to war, they didn't want to leave their families, but when their country asked them to, they did, because they thought it was the right thing to do." –Norman Schwarzkopf

America's History is His Story:

A number of years ago, there was a car commercial on television. In this ad, the voice of the narrator said, "I refuse to be one of those old men, who sit on lawn chairs in their driveways, dreaming of adventures they never had."

At the time of that commercial, there were a great number of World War II veterans among us, men who still hadn't passed away.

Before most of us even drew our first breath, those *"old men,"* little more than youngsters, themselves, were dodging mortars, machine gun fire, and bomb blasts, in order to save our world for freedom.

Those *old men* knew more adventure than most of us will ever know. Those *old men* went around the world to fight. Those *old men* were storming beaches and trying to keep the ice from freezing around their feet, in cold, wet, lonely foxholes.

Those *old men* saw their friends die in battle. Those *old men* saw their comrades perish on the blue seas of the South Pacific. Those *old men* saw their buddies die in the sands of North Africa. Those *old men* saw their fellow sailors forever entombed inside the hulls of ships like the *Arizona*.

Each one of us should thank God for those dear old men in lawn chairs, those noble ones who preserved our freedom, those men who have nightmares of adventures *we've* never had.

America's history is His story!

October 9

"The better we understand the intricacies of the universe and all it harbors, the more reason we have found to marvel at the inherent design upon which it is based." –Wernher von Braun

When you study the lives of those twelve individuals who walked on the surface of the moon, nearly every one of them was forever altered by the experience.

In July 1971, James Irwin was the lunar module pilot on Apollo 15. As the eighth man to leave his footprints on the lunar surface, Irwin saw the blue globe of earth, this miracle of God's creation, from over 200,000 miles away.

Perhaps, Irwin also realized that the circumstances of his own life might have prevented him from walking on the moon at all.

Ten years earlier on a routine training mission, the student pilot crashed their plane. Although both men survived their injuries, Irwin was notified that his leg would have to be amputated. However, a gifted Air Force surgeon's orthopedic medical skills allowed Irwin to walk on this earth—and in space—with two healthy legs.

Irwin's time on the moon's surface only served to strengthen his individual commitment to the Lord. But his desire for exploration didn't end.

While searching for the remnants of Noah's Ark, Irwin made two journeys to Mount Ararat in Turkey. His second expedition also ended in failure, injuring his leg, when he fell on a glacier.

Despite his failure, Irwin's faith in the Biblical story was never shaken. After all, Irwin had seen the vast miracles of space, designed by Noah's own heavenly Architect.

America's history is His story!

October 10

"In vain are schools, academies, and universities instituted, if loose principles and licentious habits are impressed upon children in their earliest years." –John Adams

America's History is His Story:

During the dreadful shootings at Columbine High School, in Littleton, Colorado, a young lady, named Cassie Bernall, was brutally gunned down by one of the two diseased and evil young men.

The initial reports claimed the 17 year old was executed for her faith; because when asked about it, Cassie said, "Yes."

However, there have since been some conflicting reports as to the circumstances of her death. Some reports suggest that this verbal exchange with one of the shooters may have actually occurred with another one of the surviving students.

Perhaps we will never know the full story of what happened that day. But what we do know is this:

Apparently, Cassie Bernall was a vibrant, young woman, who treasured her personal relationship with Christ. Moreover, the initial reports of her death were readily accepted because Cassie's beliefs weren't hidden from many of her public school classmates. That makes her extraordinary.

The simple yet remarkable faith that Cassie Bernall was clinging to in the final moments of her life is the only thing that holds back the evil, contained in the hearts and minds of those two teenage killers. Perhaps we should welcome Cassie's faith back into our schools, as a means to prevent the next tragedy.

America's history is His story!

October 11

"On thy grave the rain shall fall from the eyes of a mighty nation."
                                                –Thomas William Parsons

The odds are very good that you've never heard the name of Ralph Henry Johnson. However, it is a name you really ought to know.

Johnson was born in Charleston, South Carolina, on the first day of 1949. His brief 19 years upon this earth didn't leave us a lot of information on this young, black American. Most of what is publicly known about the man involves the way he died.

However, it is clearly the manner of his death that tells you the most about the caliber of this fine, young man. Moreover, that is the reason you *ought* to know him.

While serving in Vietnam, Private First Class Ralph Johnson and the other Marines in his unit were attacked by Vietnamese troops. One of the enemy soldiers tossed a grenade into the foxhole, occupied by Johnson and two other Marines.

Thinking only of saving his brothers-in-arms, Private Johnson immediately threw his body upon the grenade, shielding his friends from the blast.

Like most of those who are awarded the Medal of Honor, PFC Ralph Johnson would not be alive to receive the award.

Today, the VA Medical Center in Johnson's hometown is named in his honor. But thanks to Johnson's noble sacrifice, another hometown in America—another family—had the privilege to see one of its own heroes come home safely. We can only hope they are aware of the cost that was paid to make that miracle happen.

America's history is His story!

October 12

"I want to be remembered as a Christian, a person that serves Him to the utmost, not as a basketball player." –Pete Maravich

From the time he was a child, Pete Maravich longed to play basketball. The son of a coach, Maravich was schooled in the fundamentals of basketball at an early age; however, it was his dedication to practicing those skills that made him a star.

He also spent long hours working on ball control skills and look-away passes, styles of basketball that were largely unfamiliar to most of the players of his time. But it was his unusual shooting style as a child that earned him the nickname "Pistol."

As a result of his hard work and dedication, Pete Maravich did realize his dream of playing professional basketball, trading in his exceptional college career at LSU for a shot at the NBA. As one of the premiere ball handlers and shooters in the league, "Pistol" Pete quickly became an all-star and fan-favorite, earning a place in the Hall of Fame.

Disheartened over a career cut short by injuries, Pistol Pete turned to alcohol, before finding the Lord. For the remaining few years of his life, Maravich devoted his nearly compulsive personality to sharing his new-found faith with others.

Maravich, who shared his faith in basketball camps, churches, and prisons, died suddenly at age 40, from an undiagnosed genital heart defect, while playing a pick-up basketball game with James Dobson, founder of Focus on the Family.

The t-shirt he wore said, "Looking unto Jesus." At the end, Maravich wore his faith on his sleeve, his commitment on his chest, and died with his basketball shoes on.

America's history is His story!

October 13

"I have full confidence in your courage, devotion to duty, and skill in battle. We will accept nothing less than full victory!"

–Dwight D. Eisenhower

Arguably, Adoph Hitler's greatest military commander was Irwin Rommel, who gained much of his fame as an expert in desert warfare.

As a military tactician and a leader, Rommel had earned a great deal of respect among the Allied leadership.

Hitler had placed Rommel in charge of his "Atlantic Wall," the Nazis' coastal fortifications and heavily-armed bunkers, which were intended to prevent the Allied invasion of Europe. And although Rommel improved upon the fortifications and armaments, they did little to slow down the Allied advance on D-Day.

Perhaps the only thing that might have given the Nazis a chance to halt the invasions at Normandy, and turn the tide against the Allies, would have been a strong and immediate counter-offensive.

However, due to Hitler's paranoid fears of giving too much power to his generals, the order for a counter-offensive could've only come from Hitler alone, or Rommel.

Although Field Marshal Rommel knew the Allied invasion was imminent, the unfavorable weather forecasts convinced him that it would not occur at that time.

As the first troops began to storm the beaches, Hitler's subordinates were fearful of waking the Fuhrer. And Rommel was home with his wife, celebrating her birthday.

Therefore, an immediate and crushing counter-offensive was never mounted.

America's history is His story!

October 14

"I love to think of nature as an unlimited broadcasting station, through which God speaks to us every hour, if we only will tune in."

–George Washington Carver

America's History is His Story:

In 1893, a young, English professor from a prominent Massachusetts college journeyed Westward by train, to teach a summer class at another school in Colorado.

Like many of those who travel across the country, she was taken with the beauty, diversity, and immenseness of this great land which God has given us. The vast farmlands and huge cities clearly left an indelible impression on her mind.

Upon her arrival in Colorado City, the woman wished to see the top of Pike's Peak, which is approximately 14,000 feet above sea level. She hired a wagon to take her up the mountain, but was forced to finish the trek on the back of a mule.

"I was very tired," Katherine said. "But when I saw the view, I felt great joy. All the wonder of America seemed displayed there, with the sea-like expanse."

It was at that precise moment, Katherine Lee Bates was inspired to write the words to what would later be known as "America the Beautiful."

However, it was still a poem without music.

The melody to "America the Beautiful" was a piece of music, which was penned several years before by Samuel A. Ward. The combination of their talents would be the perfect marriage of lyric and melody.

Whenever we hear the strains of his great song, we know that God did indeed shed His grace on thee, because the two people responsible for the song never even met.

America's history is His story!

October 15

"If perfect earthly sight were offered me tomorrow, I would not accept it. I might not have sung hymns to the praise of God if I had been distracted by the beautiful and interesting things about me."

–Fanny J. Crosby

You cannot thumb through the pages of a hymnbook without coming across a song written by Francis Jane Crosby, more commonly known as "Fanny." Moreover, if you have ever attended a church service, you've probably sung one of her songs.

Fanny Crosby was the most prolific hymn writer in history. Her numerous songs have been a blessing to many and have greatly enriched the Christian faith.

Fanny wrote the following songs: *Blessed Assurance, Near the Cross, A Shelter in the Time of Storm, Rescue the Perishing,* and *Tell Me the Story of Jesus*.

The list of her titles would go on and on. In fact, many of them are listed under her various pen names, so it wasn't so obvious that most of the songs in your hymnbook were the product of one person. Most staggering of all is the fact that all of these songs were written by a woman who was blind.

When she was only six weeks old, Fanny came down with a cold, that caused an inflammation is her eyes. With their regular doctor out of town, Fanny was treated by a man who wasn't qualified to practice medicine. The mustard poultices he prescribed were often blamed for Fanny's blindness.

Despite her condition, Fanny Crosby refused to see her blindness as a handicap. Instead, she saw it as a blessing, a blessed gift she shared with the entire Christian world.

America's history is His story!

October 16

"If it were in my power to replace my arm, I would not dare to do it, unless I could know it was the will of my Heavenly Father."

–Gen. Thomas "Stonewall" Jackson

America's History is His Story:

Feeling a responsibility to serve his country, Patrick Cleburne "Clebe" McClary enlisted in the Marine Corps. After completing officers training school, he left behind his young bride and boarded a plane for Vietnam.

While leading a recon patrol, deep behind enemy lines, Clebe's unit was overrun by enemy troops. In the course of the battle, a grenade blast blew away McClary's left eye and took his left arm. Both of his eardrums were burst and he suffered numerous other injuries, initially being told he might also lose the use of his legs.

The next two and a half years of his life were spent in military hospitals, enduring the pain, therapy, and recovery from over 30 major surgeries. With the loving support of his wife, the proud, young Marine diligently fought his way back to health.

After returning to his home, Clebe and his wife attended a local rally and heard former Yankee Bobby Richardson and a past Miss America share their faith in Christ. Although, Clebe grew up attending church, he realized his own personal need of the Lord. That night, the former Marine lieutenant accepted Christ as Savior.

Clebe now travels around the country, speaking to groups and sharing his faith. But the battles still haven't ended for this retired Marine. The Air Force Academy was recently sued to stop his invitation to speak at their prayer luncheon because they said Clebe McClary's presentation was "too evangelical."

America's history is His story!

October 17

"Winning a football game isn't the end of all things. When you accept Christ, He becomes first in your life. It's this priority that gives me peace." –Tom Landry

Whenever people hear the name of Tom Landry, they automatically think of the legendary football coach of the Dallas Cowboys, a somber figure standing on the sideline, his head always adorned with a fedora.

However, long before he led the Cowboys to a pair of NFL Titles, Landry was a bomber pilot in a B-17 Flying Fortress during World War II.

As a member of the 10-men bomber crews, Landry flew over 30 bombing missions over the skies of war-torn Europe. On one occasion, Landry survived a crash landing in Belgium, when they were forced to land a plane that ran out of fuel.

After his discharge from the military, he returned to his studies at the University of Texas, where he also played football. It marked a return to the game that would dominate his life for the next forty years.

Although Landry loved the game of football, an invitation to a Bible study group in 1958 would give his life a new priority. In his later years, Landry would arrive only moments before the kickoff of a home game, because he'd been teaching an adult Sunday school class.

Until the day he died, Tom Landry was an American, the former head coach of "America's Team," and generally just a fine example to Americans everywhere.

America's history is His story!

October 18

"Since I was a small boy, two states have been added and two words have been added to the Pledge of Allegiance: Under God. Wouldn't it be a pity if someone said that is a prayer and that would be eliminated from schools too?" –Red Skelton

America's History is His Story:

When NBC televised the third round of a major golf tournament, which was being held in our nation's capital, they began the broadcast with a montage of children reciting the Pledge of Allegiance.

However, as the children recited the words of something Americans have generally known since childhood, NBC chose to omit the words "under God" and "indivisible" from the pledge.

What started out as a beautiful and poignant display of genuine American patriotism quickly changed into something shameful and unseemly.

Outraged that the words were omitted from the Pledge, thousands of Americans began flooding the network affiliates with angry calls. Others were demanding a boycott of the network and the program's sponsors.

In a desperate act of damage control, NBC issued an apology, one in which they stated, "It was not done to upset anyone, and we'd like to apologize to those of you who were offended by it."

It's quite possible the words weren't omitted to upset anyone. It's far more likely the words "under God" were omitted because they actually upset someone at NBC, a network that routinely shows its hostility toward God and country.

America's history is His story!

October 19

"We can have no '50-50' allegiance in this country. Either a man is an American and nothing else, or he is not an American at all."
–Theodore Roosevelt

Student leaders at a California college have banned the Pledge of Allegiance from their meeting. A mayor and city council in Oregon have banned the Pledge because it might be considered "divisive." A school district in Texas has ruled that students in their classrooms don't have to stand for the Pledge.

Increasingly, we are seeing these attacks on the Pledge of Allegiance taking place all around the country.

But please make no mistake about it. These attempts to remove the Pledge from our educational systems, public forums, and the halls of power doesn't just signify an assault on the Pledge of Allegiance; they're an attack on America and your way of life.

The most vocal individuals in our society are often the ones trying the silence the voices of Americans who still value our country's precious heritage and traditions. Under the guise of "freedom of speech," these people are seeking to deny you the right to exercise yours.

The preservation of liberty may not require you to wear a uniform and shed your blood upon foreign soil. However, in gratitude for those soldiers who made that ultimate sacrifice, the least you can do is to boldly speak up in defense of the liberties they so willingly died to protect. After all, this is your country too. And the liberties you save might truly be your own.

America's history is His story!

October 20

"I can anticipate no greater calamity for the country than a dissolution of the Union." –Robert E. Lee

Emile Todd Helm was the half sister of Abraham Lincoln's wife, Mary Todd. Her husband was Gen. Benjamin Helm, a graduate of Harvard and West Point.

As blood relatives and natives of Kentucky, the two families had grown very close, as the onset of the war swept down upon the country.

President Lincoln even offered the general a position in the Union Army, but Helm declined, choosing to fight with the Confederacy. Gen. Helm was eventually killed at the Battle of Chickamauga.

Almost two and a half years before the war ended and unable to return to her native Kentucky because of her husband's status during the war, Emile Todd Helm secretly came to the White House, seeking a pardon, which she was soon granted.

Upon learning of the woman's presence, Gen. Dan Sickles, who was wounded at Gettysburg, scolded the president, for the rebel's presence in the White House

"My wife and I are in the habit of choosing our own guests," Lincoln replied. "We do not need from our friends either advice or assistance in the matter."

Apart from the terrible loss of life our country suffered during the Civil War, perhaps the most dreadful costs of the conflict were the ungodly divisions it created between family and friends. And during the Civil War, even the President of the United States wasn't exempt from the separations it created between loved ones.

America's history is His story!

October 21

"It was a little different from any I ever saw before. It rose on the side of the enemy and came up very near parallel with our line of battle, and right over us." –David Ballenger

At the Battle of Fredericksburg, the forces of the North and South engaged in some bitter and dreadful fighting. With the coming of evening, the troops pulled back.

In between the encampments were the bodies of the wounded, dead, and dying, layered from the day's slaughter. Under a flag of truce, blue and gray-clad soldiers calmly met at the spot where they'd spilled blood earlier, in order to collect the bodies of their fallen brothers-in-arms.

As the men continued the grim duty of removing the dead and making preparations for the next day's battle, they suddenly paused to stare at the heavens. Brilliantly illuminating the Virginia skies was the miracle of the Northern Lights.

Many of the soldiers from the Deep South were seeing the Aurora Borealis for the first time. Those from the North had never seen the display so radiant.

Rising over the battlefield was a dazzling, Heavenly light. Its gleaming red and yellow hues cast their brilliance upon the bloody, scarred battlefield and the mass of wasted humanity.

On that chilly December night, God's illumination of the battlefield forced everyone to see the carnage to which they had given birth. But perhaps, this wondrous reminder of God's presence in the midst of man's brutality is what inspired the great spiritual awakenings that routinely swept through their ranks.

America's history is His story!

October 22

"While we are zealously performing the duties of good citizens and soldiers, we certainly ought not to be inattentive to the higher duties of religion. To the distinguished character of Patriot, it should be our highest glory to laud the more distinguished character of Christian."

–George Washington

America's History is His Story:

During a pause in the fighting at the Battle of Fredericksburg, you could hear the moans of the wounded, crying out in thirst from the midst of the bloody battlefield.

Finally unable to stand the cries no longer, Richard Kirkland, a sergeant in the South Carolina regiment, received from his commanding officer a reluctant permission to take water to the wounded soldiers.

Grabbing as many canteens as he could carry, Kirkland paused to gather his courage and bravely stepped over the wall, which offered his only protection.

Upon seeing the Gray-clad enemy advancing their way, a hail of Union rifle fire began striking all around him. Kirkland continued on, the bullets failing to find their marks. He knelt by one of the wounded men, offering the dying soul a cool, fresh drink.

Realizing what the young Confederate officer was trying to do, the Union troops set aside their guns.

For the next hour and a half, Kirkland moved from man to man, bringing some refreshment and comfort, without any regard for uniform color or rank. From both battle lines, the men of the Blue and the Gray cheered and applauded this young man's courageous act of Christian mercy and grace. And although the fighting would eventually resume, the soldiers saw one of man's noblest acts in the middle of humanity's worst.

America's history is His story!

October 23

"Happily for America, happily, we trust, for the whole human race, they pursued a new and more noble course. They accomplished a Revolution which has no parallel in the annals of human society."

–James Madison

At the Battle of Yorktown, British Gen. Cornwallis realized that his army was in serious jeopardy. The relentless Americans were inching ever closer to his lines.

It was then Cornwallis made a bold and daring decision; he would escape.

In much the same that Gen. Washington conducted a successful, night-time evacuation of his forces from Long Island, Cornwallis prepared to do the same thing with his British army.

Assembling all the flatboats and barges under his command, under the cover of darkness, Cornwallis sent the first flotilla of troops across the York River. However, before they could safely reach the other shore, a brutal wind suddenly arose, which one person called "as severe a storm as I ever remember."

The unfavorable wind conditions quickly caused the boats to be scattered and forced Cornwallis to scrap his mission.

There would be no escape for Lord Cornwallis and his British army.

Once again, the apparent intervention of God in our Revolution thwarted the best efforts of the British officers. In three days, Cornwallis would realize their efforts were in vain and he would surrender. However, in one final act of vanity and defiance, Cornwallis remained behind and sent a subordinate officer in his place.

America's history is His story!

October 24

"Revolution was effected before the war commenced. The Revolution was in the minds and hearts of the people. This radical change in the principles, opinions, sentiments, and affections of the people was the real American Revolution." –John Adams

America's History is His Story:

As one of the most respected ministers of his day, George Whitefield's preaching was largely responsible for the Great Awakening, the great spiritual transformation which may have prepared the Colonists for the Revolution.

So great was his fame and influence, Whitefield's passing in 1770 was mourned by an entire nation. Moreover, as the Continental Army prepared to go to war in 1775, they still hadn't forgotten the late minister's influence.

Therefore, since the troops came together in Newburyport, Massachusetts, they naturally chose the tomb of George Whitefield as an inspirational gathering place.

However, as they prepared to go to war, the troops not only carried a part of the minister's influence with them; they also wanted to carry part of Whitefield, himself.

Prying open his coffin, they saw the skeleton of the celebrated minister of the Gospel. They also learned that Whitefield's clerical collar and wrist cuffs survived the years of entombment. These they removed from the minister, cut into pieces, and distributed among the men.

The soldiers wrongly believed that the key to victory was contained in small pieces of cloth, lifted from a dead minister. Instead, the success of the American Revolution had already been woven into the fabric of their souls.

America's history is His story!

October 25

"Where we love is home—home that our feet may leave, but not our hearts." –Oliver Wendell Holmes

When young wife and mother, Mary Draper Ingles was captured by the Shawnee Indians in 1755, she knew it was unlikely she would ever see her home again.

Kidnapped from her Virginia home, Mary's captors took her all the way to the area around Cincinnati, Ohio.

But the woman never gave up hope.

After winning the Indians' trust, Mary escaped. She ventured through dense underbrush and brutal conditions, making her way up the Ohio, Kanawha, and New Rivers. Ingles' daring escape from the Indians and her nearly 500 mile trek is the stuff of legends. However, it wasn't a legend. The story is real.

Surviving on little more than berries, bugs, and roots, Mary was forced to scale rocky inclines and wade through dangerous river crossings. The shoeless woman endured weeks of hunger, hiding from her enemies, and the constant dangers of exposure.

Her family scarcely recognized the naked and emaciated figure, whose weak and tired voice spoke to them, when she arrived home. But Mary Ingles *did* come home. This brave and committed woman completed her desperate journey and lived out the rest of her life with her friends and family.

Perhaps as much as anyone else, Mary Ingles displayed that one remarkable quality our nation has always had: a driving, insatiable need to find our way home.

America's history is His story!

October 26

"There are no great men—just great challenges, which ordinary men, out of necessity, are forced by circumstances to meet."

–William "Bull" Halsey

America's History is His Story:

In times of war, circumstances and strange twists of fate occasionally lead to decisions and choices that are critical to the eventual outcome of a battle.

One such instance was the condition that elevated Raymond Spruance to power in the Pacific during World War II.

When Admiral "Bull" Halsey was hospitalized due to a tropical skin disease, he recommended Ray Spruance to replace him. Although Spruance had proven his skills as an excellent commander of a cruiser division, there were still some in the Navy who questioned his ability to head up the American carrier force.

They needn't have worried.

Spruance provided calm, critical, and decisive leadership during the Battle of Midway, which turned the course of the war in favor of the United States.

While leading our carriers at Midway, Spruance was responsible for the sinking of four Japanese aircraft carriers, which greatly crippled the Japanese fleet, erasing much of the advantage they had previously gained in their surprise attack on Pearl Harbor.

Although Admiral Raymond Spruance never knew the fame of "Bull" Halsey, our nation was once again blessed to have a man such as Spruance elevated to a critical leadership role. In times of crisis, America has always witnessed seemingly-ordinary men step forward. By guiding us through troubled times, these men have achieved greatness.

America's history is His story!

October 27

"With reasonable men, I will reason; with humane men, I will plead; but to tyrants, I will give no quarter, nor waste arguments where they will certainly be lost." –William Lloyd Garrison

It was a quiet Sunday morning in Hawaii when the first Japanese planes began the attack on Pearl Harbor.

Due to the time difference between Hawaii and the continental U.S., many Americans had just returned from Sunday morning church services when the first torpedoes began to fall on our naval fleet.

The attack was planned and executed by Japanese Fleet Admiral Yamamoto, who at that moment became a target of U.S. forces.

"Operation Vengeance" was the military's plan to locate and kill the Japanese admiral.

Not only would the man's death help to avenge the lives of our young sailors at Pearl, it would also be seen as a devastating blow to Japanese morale and greatly hinder their naval leadership.

Our naval code breakers finally located the precise time and location that Yamamoto's plane would be in the area of the Solomon Islands. The surprise attack worked to perfection, as the American strike force fired on their target, sending the Japanese admiral's damaged plane to crash in the island jungle. Yamamoto was dead.

On that day also, many Americans had just returned from Sunday morning church services. It was Palm Sunday.

America's history is His story!

October 28

"I freed a thousand slaves. I could have freed a thousand more if only they knew they were slaves." –Harriet Tubman

No doubt some of you will remember lawn jockeys, the figurines that often adorned people's yards, featuring a young black man, in brightly colored clothing, normally holding a lantern or hitch ring.

Rarely do you see them these days, because many people feared that their display might brand them as racists. However, these statues have a remarkable history.

It has been claimed that the lawn jockey was created to resemble a young man named Jocko Graves, who reportedly froze to death, while holding a lantern, to aid in Gen. Washington's nighttime crossing of the Delaware.

While some question the story's authenticity, the lawn jockey's history is well established. When slavery still existed in this country, these figures were often located outside of houses that were part of the Underground Railroad, an intricate network of locations, where people helped runaway slaves escape from their masters.

Those trying to escape their slave holders were instructed to take note of the clothes the lawn jockey was wearing, which were often an indication to the runaway whether it was safe or risky to approach the house.

Today, the display of a lawn jockey certainly isn't racist. However, the myths and history regarding these figures should stand as a glorious reminder of the costs that were paid to guarantee freedom for every American.

America's history is His story!

October 29

"It is hard to see how a great man can be an atheist. Without the sustaining influence of faith in a Divine power, we could have little faith in ourselves. We need to feel that behind us is intelligence and love. Doubters do not achieve; skeptics do not contribute; cynics do not create. Faith is the great motive power, and no man realizes his full

possibilities unless he has the deep conviction that life is eternally important, and that his work, well done, is a part of an unending plan."
–Calvin Coolidge

Recently, an atheist group tried to contract with an aircraft advertising company to promote their views on the Independence Day holiday.

Agreeing to spend several thousand dollars on the project, the atheists wanted the pilots of this advertising company to drag their banners across the skies in a number of American cities on the 4th of July.

The banners were emblazoned with the following phrases: "God-LESS America" and "Atheism is Patriotic."

However, when the idea was presented to the company, eighty percent of the pilots employed by them sternly refused to fly the banners.

It was just one more proud moment for the United States, a country which was founded on Godly principles.

Increasingly in America, we see people who will do almost anything or routinely sell out their principles in the pursuit of profit. However, it is certainly refreshing to learn that there are still people in America who won't trade their consciences for currency.

America's history is His story!

October 30

"You have the highest human trust committed to your care. Providence has showered on this favored land blessings without number, and has chosen you as the guardians of freedom, to preserve it for the benefit of the human race." –Andrew Jackson

America's History is His Story:

Whenever people hear the name Reuben James, they often think of a song by Kenny Rogers. However, it is so much more. The name, Reuben James has a rich and glorious tradition in American military history.

During America's first war, when we were fighting Islamic pirates from Africa's Barbary Coast, Reuben James served alongside Commander Stephen Decatur. It is also known that, during the midst of the hand-to-hand fighting, an already wounded James bravely threw his body in front of a sword, and was pierced by the blade that was intended to kill his commander, Stephen Decatur.

Although James later recovered, so great was his contribution to our nation, the Navy later commissioned one of their ships in his honor.

Less than two months before America declared war on Japan and Germany, the *USS Reuben James* was giving protection to a British shipping convoy. A German U-Boat torpedoed the ship, taking the lives of 115 brave, American seamen.

This ship, named in honor of one who would give his life for another, positioned itself between a British ammunition ship and the enemy, which might seek to attack it.

As a result of the crew's brave actions, the *USS Reuben James* became the first U.S. Navy vessel to be sunk by hostile enemy actions in World War II.

America's history is His story!

October 31

"We must, indeed, all hang together or, most assuredly, we shall all hang separately." –Benjamin Franklin

During America's Civil War, President Abraham Lincoln often grew frustrated by Gen. George McClellan's multiple failures to take bold and decisive action to quickly end the conflict.

During one such instance, Lincoln wrote the general a letter, in which he stated, "If General McClellan doesn't want to use the army, perhaps I may borrow it for a while."

In this letter, the great President Lincoln displays a gentle, but biting sense of humor that Americans have been characteristically known for throughout our history.

The Scriptures tell us that there are occasions when God laughs. Perhaps that is also one of God's attributes that America has inherited.

In fact, this remarkable, uniquely American sense of humor, clearly reflected in the writings of Ben Franklin, is often misunderstood by those from other countries.

During times of great national and personal crisis, Americans have routinely displayed a sense of humor, a quality that often sustained us during those trying times of life. Not only does it sustain *us*, an American's ability to laugh and find humor during periods of war, calamity, or great personal loss is something that lifts the spirits of others and often gives them the courage to face their trials as well.

America's history is His story!

November 1

"Those interested in the future of the country, not only from a national defense standpoint, but from a civil, commercial, and economic one as well, should study this matter carefully, because air power has not only come to stay but is, and will be, a dominating factor in the world's development." –Col. Billy Mitchell

America's History is His Story:

Long before anyone else in the Army saw the possibilities of aerial warfare, Billy Mitchell was urging his superiors to look to the future. However, Mitchell's innovations and foresight in the area of aerial combat weren't fully recognized until after his death.

Col. Mitchell's insistence that the military adopt his suggestions was often met with skepticism. Moreover, this visionary's stubborn and passionate writings regarding the subject eventually led to a military court martial, which Douglas MacArthur opposed.

Mitchell wasn't only a proponent of the benefits of aerial warfare, he was also a prophet of its potential dangers to America.

In a 325-page report, written in 1924, Mitchell predicted the Japanese would start their war in the Pacific with an attack on Pearl Harbor.

Mitchell predicted the attack as follows: *"Bombardment, attack to be made on Ford Island (Hawaii) at 7:30 A.M..... Attack to be made on Clark Field at 10:40 A.M."*

Seventeen years before the "date which will live in infamy," Mitchell was only off by 25 minutes on his prediction of the attack on Pearl Harbor and less than two hours off on the attack on Clark Field in the Philippines.

America has always remained free because ours is a land of visionaries like Billy Mitchell, men who risked everything to bring their wisdom and ideas to this nation.

America's history is His story!

November 2

"Had the doctrines of Jesus been preached always as pure as they came from His lips, the whole civilized world would now have been Christians." –Thomas Jefferson

After competing in the 1936 Olympics as a youngster, many believed that Louis Zamperini would be the first man to break the four-minute mile. However, his once-promising track career would be put on hold with the coming of World War II.

As a bombardier on a B-24, mechanical problems caused Zamperini and his crew to put down their plane in the Pacific Ocean. Only three of them survived the crash. And only two of them survived the forty-seven days they spent adrift on the sea.

The two men survived on captured rainwater and raw fish. On more than one occasion, they were subjected to random strafing attacks by Japanese pilots.

When Louis and his fellow crewman were finally discovered at sea, they had the misfortune to be picked up by a ship from the Japanese navy, which placed them in brutal captivity.

He ended up in the same prison camp with legendary airman, Major Greg "Pappy" Boyington, who stated that Zamperini helped them survive with imaginary descriptions of Italian recipes he created for the prisoners' enjoyment.

Eventually coming to know Christ through a Billy Graham Crusade, Zamperini returned to Japan in 1950, preaching the Gospel through an interpreter to the imprisoned Japanese war criminals, who committed the worst atrocities of the war.

America's history is His story!

November 3

"You don't raise heroes, you raise sons. And if you treat them like sons, they'll turn out to be heroes, even if it's just in your own eyes."

–Wally Schirra

America's History is His Story:

Upon learning her son had been killed while defending the Alamo, Jim Bowie's mother replied, "I'll wage they found no bullets in his back."

Her plain-spoken statement was as much a declaration of how she raised the child as it was a comment on his character.

Bowie's mother knew Jim had been raised to be brave and strong. Moreover, his mother was confident that Bowie hadn't run from danger and died a hero in the battle for Texas independence.

America has always been a nation that produced seemingly-ordinary young men, who often proved their extraordinary heroism, when faced with danger.

In his quest to establish new frontiers and settlements, Daniel Boone saw his sons fall to Indian attacks and the American Revolution. In the preservation of freedom, Mrs. Alleta Sullivan lost all five of her sons with the perishing of one ship in World War II.

These three parents, Alvina Bowie, Daniel Boone, and Alleta Sullivan, didn't raise their sons to be heroes. But that is what they became. The same special and unique qualities that make a great son often produce a great citizen.

Americans seldom raise their sons to be heroes. However, it is often impossible for us to escape our nation's destiny. A great nation often gives birth to great offspring.

Is it any wonder that great circumstances often reveal them to the world?

America's history is His story!

November 4

"Do not pray for easy lives. Pray to be stronger men."
–John F. Kennedy

Before the final day of the 1941 baseball season, Boston's Ted Williams was proudly sporting a .3996 batting average, which rounds up to .400 for the season.

As any baseball fan can tell you, hitting .400 is the dream of everyone who ever donned a major league uniform.

Desperately wanting to see his ball player achieve the magic mark of .400, Joe Cronin, Ted Williams' manager, suggested that the Boston outfielder sit out the season's final day. Ted Williams quickly rejected the idea.

As much as he wanted to hit .400, Williams had no desire to achieve this milestone cheaply. Ted didn't believe he deserved the record, if he had to sit out to win it.

Not only was it the final day of the season, the Red Sox were forced to play a doubleheader. Moreover, with his record at stake, Ted insisted on playing both games.

Ted *did* take his place in the lineup that day. Williams was superb, getting six hits in eight at bats and raising his season average to a staggering .406.

For most of America's history, the attitude exhibited by Ted Williams, on the final day of the 1941 season, has traditionally been a part of our nation's character.

Americans only wanted those things that they could acquire themselves. They didn't desire those things from others which they failed to earn. And whenever we lose this part of our national character, then we may forever risk losing this nation.

America's history is His story!

November 5

"Courage is doing what you're afraid to do. There can be no courage unless you're scared."–Eddie Rickenbacker

America's History is His Story:

After attending a Christmas party and dance in Hawaii, followed by an all-night poker game, Lt. George Welch and Lt. Kenneth Taylor were just outside the barracks at Wheeler Field, when the first Japanese Zeros began sweeping down upon them.

Seeing the attack, they called ahead and told the men at nearby Haleiwa field to have their planes ready. Their frantic, nine-minute drive was fraught with great danger, with Japanese fighters repeatedly strafing their speeding Buick.

Upon their arrival, Welch and Taylor, found their pair of P-40 Tomahawk fighters fueled, armed, and running. The two men sprinted to their planes. Without waiting for orders, Welch and Taylor took off to confront their Japanese attackers.

Once airborne, the two Army fighter pilots immediately began engaging the enemy in the skies over Hawaii.

Welch and Taylor would eventually land their planes to refuel, load up on more ammunition, and quickly return to the skies. They were waiting for the second wave of Japanese attackers, downing at least four Japanese planes that day.

With little thought for their own safety, George Welch, Ken Taylor, and at least three other American pilots managed to take to the skies on December 7th and recorded at least one "kill" on their Japanese attackers. It was this brand of individual courage and self-sacrifice that made it possible for us to triumph over our enemies in World War II.

America's history is His story!

November 6

"I always consider the settlement of America with reverence and wonder, as the opening of a grand scene and design in Providence for the

illumination of the ignorant, and the emancipation of the slavish part of mankind all over the earth." –John Adams

If anybody questions the fact that America has clearly been blessed by God, then they need only to look at our geographical boundaries.

Our eastern and western borders are shielded by vast ocean bodies, which places an essential, strategic barrier between America and those who would routinely seek to do us harm. Our northern and southern borders are connected to Canada and Mexico, countries which are not openly hostile to us.

In our nation's past, there have been brief wars and hostilities with both Canada and Mexico. However, the nations to the north and south of us have been at peace with the United States for these many years.

Although we share some great political, philosophical, and cultural differences with the nations to our north and south, they are not desperately seeking to destroy us.

Most of the nations in Europe and Asia are bordered by countries, which openly declare their hatred for their neighbors and are dedicated to their ultimate destruction.

America has certainly been blessed.

Every single peace-loving American should thank God we live in a nation, not confronted with the challenges of Israel, our great ally in democracy; for Israel is surrounded on all sides by nations who desire to wipe them off the face of the earth.

America's history is His story!

November 7

"The human soul is God's treasury, out of which He coins unspeakable riches." –Henry Ward Beecher

America's History is His Story:

In 1982, Air Florida Flight 90 was taking off from a Washington D.C. airport, when it crashed into the 14th Street Bridge. Most of the passengers died on impact, but there were only a handful of survivors, who were subjected to the icy, frigid waters.

As news people filmed and spectators watched from the bridge, and just when it appeared there would be no rescue for the survivors, a helicopter arrived on the scene.

As the helicopter dropped a life ring to the survivors, to hoist them out of the water, a 46 year old federal bank examiner, Arland Williams, repeatedly passed his life line to someone else.

After lifting another woman from the frigid Potomac, the helicopter finally returned for Williams, the former military graduate of the Citadel. However, Williams had already succumbed to hypothermia, slipped beneath the water, and drowned.

Williams was not the only hero on that day. The brave helicopter pilot and a paramedic nearly died also, when the added weight of the survivors momentarily pulled the skids of the chopper beneath the surface of the water.

The 14th Street Bridge saw the last moments of an unknown bank examiner's life, his selfless dedication to saving others, and the man's final acts of incomparable courage. Today, that bridge bears the name of Arland D. Williams, one more man who displayed the courage and characteristics that have come to be known as uniquely American.

America's history is His story!

November 8

"A man who hasn't found something he is willing to die for is not fit to live." –Martin Luther King

When Air Florida Flight 90 failed to achieve lift-off and plunged into the chilly, ice-covered waters of the Potomac River, the rush-hour travelers were lined across the length of the 14th Street Bridge.

These people witnessed the accident occur right before their eyes. In fact, four of these motorists were crushed and killed when the plane collided with the bridge.

As the six survivors of Flight 90 struggled out of the sinking plane, spectators lined the bridge, watching the drama play out before them.

Lenny Skutnik was one of them.

Lenny watched in horror, as one of the women survivors was growing weak and unable to hang on to the helicopter's life line.

While others merely watched, Skutnik acted.

Taking off his coat and boots, clad in only his pants and short sleeves, this unknown governmental worker dove from the bridge to help.

Ignoring the icy waters, Skutnik swam to the struggling woman's aid, helping her to reach the shoreline.

During times of crisis, it has never been unusual for Americans to display great courage and come to the aid of others. And although it isn't unusual, it certainly isn't any less extraordinary. Seemingly, it is a quality that God has placed in our nation's DNA.

America's history is His story!

November 9

"How little do my countrymen know what precious blessings they are in possession of, and which no other people on earth have."

–Thomas Jefferson

America's History is His Story:

The settlers who first came to this country discovered a land that God had remarkably blessed with a vast supply of natural resources.

The trees from our forests provided the lumber that would build a fledgling nation. Our great rivers gave us an efficient mode of transportation and provided the means to transport our supplies and products to other markets.

The oil, coal, and ore, underneath our soil, drove our westward and industrial expansion. These resources helped to fuel our locomotives, and provided the ribbon of steel upon which they traveled. They also powered our vehicles.

These great resources, and the innovation to go get them, made possible the cheap and abundant energy that transformed our country into the envy of the world.

However, in our willingness to bow down before Mother Nature, we have deliberately turned our back on Father God.

Coal and oil are just a couple of the abundant natural resources, which God graciously provided for us. Is it any wonder that America is suffering economic hardship, when we fail to employ those blessings He has already placed in our hands?

The religion of radical environmentalism has become a deluded form of self-worship. If we continue to bow before this false altar, then we willingly deny ourselves the Divine birthright that we were granted as Americans.

America's history is his story!

November 10

"The doctrines and miracles of our Savior have required nearly two thousand years to convert but a small part of the human race, and even among the Christian nations, what gross errors still exist!"

–Robert E. Lee

God is real—His existence is written into our founding documents. The fact has influenced our laws and system of government. His name is engraved in Washington's greatest buildings and monuments. Our trust in Him is also printed on our currency.

Moreover, the existence of God is a fact acknowledged by every individual homeowner in the United States.

Written into every policy is a provision explaining that insurance companies often will not pay for any incident which they call "an act of God."

Apparently, the existence of God and His almighty hand in the affairs of men is a common practice, acknowledged and accepted by our insurance companies. And since our insurance industry is strictly regulated by our government, apparently they also recognize the fact that God often intervenes in our daily lives.

Routinely, we have seen numerous lawsuits filed by atheist groups, trying to remove any mention of God from our society. However, they have apparently forgotten this common provision in their insurance policies, which recognizes the acts of a Divine Power, they have deliberately chosen not to recognize.

God is certainly real; our churches know it. Our government and Founders acknowledged it. And our insurance companies currently maintain their profits through it.

America's history is His story!

November 11

"Although no sculptured marble should rise to their memory, nor engraved stone bear record of their deeds, yet will their remembrance be as lasting as the land they honored." –Daniel Webster

America's History is His Story:

On this day we celebrate as Veterans' Day, it is important to know that the holiday was first known as Armistice Day, which marked the ending of hostilities in World War I.

Approximately 20 million people died in World War I, often referred to as "the war to end all wars." Would to God that it had of been! Of course, we know this war was only a precursor for the numerous wars to follow

The cease fire was to begin at the "eleventh hour of the eleventh day of the eleventh month." That is the reason we remember this specific day.

But on this day, let us remember the men and women who served. Let us remember the sacrifices that were made to keep us free.

Let us give praise to the fallen, the returning, and those forever missing in action. Let us not forget a single person who donned the uniform of the United States of America. Each one of them gave up so much to keep us free.

And on this day, let us momentarily look to the flag, that precious emblem for which they were willing to give their lives. Let us take the time to remember.

On this Veterans' Day, look to the flag, say "thank you" to a vet, and give just a moment of praise to the God who made this great nation our home.

America's history is His story!

November 12

"I pray that our Heavenly Father may assuage the anguish of your bereavement, and leave you only the cherished memory of the loved and lost, and the solemn pride that must be yours to have laid so costly a sacrifice upon the altar of freedom." –Abraham Lincoln

While U.S. forces were fighting in Europe and the Pacific, it was commonplace to find a flag, adorned with a blue star, hanging in the front window of houses all across the country.

The simple blue stars told everyone who saw them that a child in the household was serving in the military. Often, there were multiple stars displayed, signifying that more than one child was in the armed forces.

Wherever these blue stars were displayed, inside the house was a mother, desperately praying she wouldn't receive a visit from a black sedan, which typically brought the news from the War Department, the somber notifications that a family member had been killed or was missing in action.

Unfortunately, it was also much too commonplace for a home to replace one of their blue stars with a gold one, meaning that someone in the family had paid the ultimate price in defense of their nation. It also indicated that there was a woman, inside the home, suffering the indescribable pangs of a broken heart.

Two thousand years ago, another heartbroken mother saw her Son die on a cross, knowing that the sacrifice of His life was for the good of all mankind. Perhaps there is nothing on this earth more godly than these women we call "Gold Star Mothers."

America's history is His story!

November 13

"The bitterest tears shed over graves are for words left unsaid and deeds left undone." –Harriet Beecher Stowe

Morgantown, West Virginia, is the football home of the West Virginia University Mountaineers, with some of the most spirited and vocal fans in the country.

America's History is His Story:

As a result of their loud and loyal crowd, opposing teams have found the city to be one of the toughest venues in which to play a college football game.

However, following the stabbing death of University of Connecticut's Jasper Howard, the Connecticut Huskies were scheduled to play a game in Morgantown.

The administrators of the two schools arranged to honor young Jasper Howard's memory, with some-on-the-field ceremonies, prior to the kickoff.

As the Huskies' players, carrying Howard's jersey, came out onto the field, they were not greeted with jeers and boos from the loyal Mountaineer fans. Instead, the Huskies were welcomed with spirited applause and a standing ovation. And during the on-the-field remembrance for the dead college player, the stadium was eerily silent.

A book by James Webb recently claimed that West Virginia had the highest proportion of volunteers and veterans in all the wars of the 20th Century. Therefore, the people of the state are closely acquainted with the grief and loss of good, young men. It was that spirit, reflected by the Mountaineer faithful on that football Saturday, a quality that should make every American proud.

America's history is His story!

November 14

"A baby is God's opinion that the world should go on." –Carl Sandburg

The organization that Americans now know as Planned Parenthood was founded by a nurse named Margaret Sanger.

Despite their name, Planned Parenthood has absolutely nothing to do with bringing a child in the world, and everything to do with preventing their birth, or aborting the lives of those already conceived.

While many of the leaders of the organization seek to disassociate themselves from its origins, there can be no denying that Planned Parenthood has its roots deeply planted in the soil of racism.

Margaret Sanger openly advocated the use of birth control or sterilization to limit the populations of American Blacks, Hispanics, Asians, and Jews. In fact, Sanger's racist views were so openly known, she was even invited to address a women's version of the Ku Klux Klan.

There can be no question that Planned Parenthood in America shares the same evil hatred for the family that dwelt in the mind and heart of its founder, Margaret Sanger. But, perhaps, the seeds to her views on the world were planted at the tender age of twelve years old, when a she heard a prominent speaker come to her town.

The man's name was Robert Ingersoll, who was greatly renowned for his skepticism and hatred of God.

America's history is His story!

November 15

"Thou shalt not be a victim; thou shalt not be a perpetrator, but above all, thou shalt not be a bystander." –Yehuda Bauer

A Polish-born Jewish immigrant, Haym Solomon became a great believer in America's Revolutionary cause, becoming one of its most prominent financiers.

Believing him to be a spy, Solomon was captured by the British, when a fire destroyed much of British-occupied New York City. They planned to employ Haym, who was fluent in several languages, to communicate with their German troops. Instead, Solomon told the Hessians to desert their British allies.

He was later captured again and sentenced to death. However, Solomon escaped, probably with the aid of his acquaintances in the Sons of Liberty.

Solomon repeatedly raised money to finance the Revolution, and guaranteed that Gen. Washington's troops would have what they needed to defeat the British.

However, Haym Solomon's fund-raising efforts for the United States didn't end with the surrender of the British. His was the country's first financial bailout, providing the funds to meet the debts of our young and struggling new government.

Like many of those who gave so much to America's Revolution, he was never fully reimbursed by his government. However, it is believed that the stars, representing our thirteen original colonies, which form the shape of Israel's Star of David on our dollar bill, was George Washington's gift to Jewish-born American, Haym Solomon.

America's history is His story!

November 16

"Abraham Lincoln recognized that we could not survive as a free land when some men could decide that others were not fit to be free and should therefore be slaves. Likewise, we cannot survive as a free nation when some men decide that others are not fit to live and should be abandoned to abortion or infanticide." –Ronald Reagan

It is quite common to hear people lament the destruction of the rain forests, claiming that we are potentially destroying trees and plants that might contain the ingredients to our future life-saving drugs.

However, these same people never agonize over the millions of abortions that have been legalized in our country, potentially destroying the young men and women who might be our next Jonas Salk or Madame Curie.

Throughout the annals of history, governmental attempts to limit the population are always untaken for evil purposes, or are followed by evil ends.

In Egypt, Pharaoh tried to limit the population of the Hebrews, not knowing that, Moses, their deliverer, would be nourished right in his own house.

Herod, who feared losing his kingdom to the King of the Jews, killed great numbers of male Jewish children, in his attempts to eliminate Christ.

From Pharaoh, to Herod, to Adolph Hitler, you cannot find one incident of the wholesale slaughter of large numbers of infants and children that turned out well for its perpetrators. In fact, you will see that God often raised up a deliverer for His people.

After nearly 40 million abortions, since its legalization in 1973, we can only pray that God still cares enough about the United States, to raise one up for us as well.

America's history is His story!

November 17

"I believe a long step toward public morality will have been taken when sins are called by their right names." –Billy Sunday

In the last two decades of the 1800s, Billy Sunday was a great outfielder and base stealer in Major League baseball. However, in the first two decades of the 1900s, Billy Sunday became a great force for the Gospel in America.

Upon hearing a sermon in Chicago's Pacific Garden Rescue Mission, Sunday repented, surrendered his life to Christ, and abandoned his prominent baseball career.

Sunday turned down offers of $400-500 a month from the Philadelphia Phillies and the Cincinnati Reds for a salary of $83 a month from the YMCA, back when it was still an evangelistic organization.

While in the pulpit, Billy Sunday was a spirited and enthusiastic messenger of the Gospel. He traveled all over the country as an evangelist, holding week-long or extended meetings in tents and tabernacles. Sunday's fame was widespread; the crowds that came to see him, enormous.

A harsh opponent of alcohol, it was commonplace for the saloons in a town to permanently close their doors, for lack of business, following one of Sunday's revivals. Moreover, it is commonly believed that it was the preaching of Billy Sunday that led to the institution of Prohibition in America.

So great was Billy Sunday's legacy, it is not surprising that his name is repeatedly mocked in the song, "Chicago," often performed and made popular by Frank Sinatra.

America's history is His story!

November 18

"The Creator has not thought proper to mark those in the forehead who are of stuff to make good generals." –Thomas Jefferson

George Washington first became acquainted with Daniel Morgan, and the man's great courage, during their time serving together during the French and Indian War.

Years before the Revolution, a British general struck Morgan with the flat of his sword. Angered by the actions of his superior officer, Daniel Morgan yanked the man from his horse, and knocked the officer to the ground with a single punch.

For his act of insubordination, a court martial sentenced Morgan to receive 500 lashes with a whip. Weary and bloodied from the harsh beating, with strips of flesh hanging from his back, Morgan laughed and told the man that he had miscounted and only administered 499.

Perhaps it was a result of these actions, from the hands of his former British allies, which made Daniel Morgan such a great general and fierce opponent of the forces of King George.

In the American Revolution, Morgan led an effective and deadly band of rifle marksmen, who deliberately targeted the British commanding officers and the Indians who often guided them.

At the Battle of Cowpens, "Morgan's Riflemen" fired on the British, and then faked a retreat, compelling the overconfident British to charge their lines. Morgan's strategy worked to perfection, leading to a stunning British entrapment and defeat.

America's history is His story!

November 19

"Try not to become a man of success, but rather to become a man of value. He is considered successful in our day who gets more out of life than he puts in. But a man of value will give more than he receives."

–Albert Einstein

America's History is His Story:

In the early part of the 20th Century, milk chocolate was a luxury item, produced only in Switzerland, and largely unavailable to the masses.

With a dream of making milk chocolate and selling it to Americans, Milton Hershey built a factory on 1,200 acres of land near Lancaster, Pennsylvania.

Hershey was also a man of great vision.

Not only did he dream of mass-producing the delicious treats that would be loved and purchased by all Americans; Hershey also recognized the need to nationally market his product. In addition, he visualized an entire community springing up around his enterprise.

One other thing that made Milton Hershey different from many of the captains of industry was his extraordinary concern for the individual worker. Hershey believed that happy and satisfied people made better and more productive employees.

He provided them with proper housing, educational opportunities, convenient transportation, recreational activities, adequate medical care, and places of worship.

Until the day of his death, Milton Hershey not only cared about the product, whose recipe he struggled to perfect; he also concerned himself with the lives and futures of the families who manufactured the Hershey bar, one man's sweetest dream.

America's history is His story!

November 20

"For this blessed mission to the nations of the world, which are shut out from the life-giving light of truth, has America been chosen."
–John L. O'Sullivan

During World War II, the company founded by Milton Hershey produced over one billion milk chocolate bars, which were placed in the ration packs of American soldiers going to war.

When American forces drove the Nazis out of cities all across Europe, it was commonplace for compassionate GIs to share their milk chocolate bars with the young children in the cities they liberated.

In a sense, the Hershey bar became the symbol of America, an emblem of freedom to the world.

This simple gift, from these brave and lonely, young warriors, far away from their own homes, showed the world that America was truly an exceptional nation. Not only were we capable of saving Europe from a godless Nazi regime; America also brought mercy and a little sweetness to those who knew only the bitter taste of war.

In 1912, Milton Hershey and his wife booked a first class ticket on the doomed British luxury liner, *RMS Titanic*. However, in another act of mercy, their lives were spared when Milton's wife, Kitty, came down with an illness and could not make the trip.

The creator of the Hershey bar didn't perish in the treacherous, icy seas of the North Atlantic. Perhaps this one incident may be the explanation why the rest of his life, and the profits from his business, were sweetly dedicated to the service of others.

America's history is His story!

November 21

"If you will not fight for the right when you can easily win without bloodshed, if you will not fight when your victory will be sure and not too costly, you may come to the moment when you will have to fight with all the odds against you and only a small chance of survival. There

may even be a worse case: you may have to fight when there is no hope of victory, because it is better to perish than to live as slaves."

—Winston Churchill

North of our border is the nation of Canada, a country that passed a version of "Hate Crimes" legislation, making it a crime for pastors and churches to preach against the practice of homosexuality.

Unfortunately, there are way too many misguided souls in this country who think this same legislation should be instituted in the United States.

In day-to-day conversation, you will often hear Americans say that "you should never talk about politics or religion."

However, please allow me to point out to you that our country was founded on the discussion of politics and religion. Our First Amendment is primarily about the rights of our citizens to freely and openly discuss the topics of politics and religion. Another thing the First Amendment protects is our precious right to assembly.

If you don't like the message coming from the pulpit, you have the precious right to go elsewhere. You don't have a right to silence those who deliver a message you don't like. You can assemble where you choose; that same right extends to your neighbors.

Our country was largely founded by our churches and pastors, men of God, whose pulpits openly flamed with fearless calls for righteousness. These were the leaders in the Revolution, which gave every minister the right to preach the truth of God, as he sees it.

America's history is His story!

November 22

"There is a certain enthusiasm in liberty, that makes human nature rise above itself, in acts of bravery and heroism." —Alexander Hamilton

His early interest in flying inspired by a local appearance of Charles Lindberg, young Joe Foss longed to soar above the clouds. With the coming of World War II, the South Dakota native would certainly realize his dream.

As a Marine fighter pilot, Foss was credited with downing 26 Japanese planes, five on just one day. Moreover, he shot down a Japanese Zero on his first day in aerial combat. For his service to America, Foss was awarded the Medal of Honor.

Even after returning from the war, the life of Joe Foss continued to be filled with challenges and excitement, which are uniquely American.

The South Dakota war hero, who appeared on the cover of *Life* magazine, would be elected the governor of his state. In addition, Foss would also become the commissioner of the American Football League, the president of the National Rifle Association, and the television host of ABC's program, *The American Sportsman*.

The story of Joe Foss's life reads like it could have been the inspiration for a Hollywood movie, which it might have been. Always a man of great honesty, Foss turned down the opportunity to see his life portrayed on the big screen, with John Wayne playing the title role, simply because the producers wanted to add a fictional love interest.

Joseph Foss, who served his country so nobly in war, and who also was an inspiration in peace, is honorably buried in Arlington National Cemetery.

America's history is His story!

November 23

"The battle is lost, and many of us are prisoners, many are dead, many wounded, bleeding and dying. Your soldier lives and mourns and but

America's History is His Story:

for you, my darling, he would rather, a million times rather, be back there with his dead, to sleep for all time in an unknown grave."

–Gen. George Pickett

Whenever people think of the Civil War, they rarely stop to think about the carnage these battles left behind at places like Antietam or Gettysburg.

The battle at Gettysburg lasted three days. However, when the final cannon blast was heard, at the moment when the last rifle sounded, then the surviving generals and troops marched away.

The 2,400 citizens of Gettysburg were left to remove the 7,000 bodies from the battlefield, often burying them in shallow graves or in long, crude trenches.

And before we become too critical of their seemingly-harsh treatment of the fallen, please let us imagine the blood, the stench, the flies, and the great potential for disease these remaining unburied corpses could create. Sanitary conditions required that the burials be conducted quickly, before the brutal summer heat could make conditions even worse on the once-peaceful, Pennsylvania countryside.

The dead were certainly not the only problem faced by the locals. Wounded soldiers, of both armies, were still being treated in one of the field hospitals on a local farm, for the next six weeks.

In short, the Civil War wasn't only a hardship on the soldiers and their loved ones; it also affected the nearby citizens of these towns where the battles were waged.

America's history is his story!

November 24

"We have fought this fight as long, and as well as we know how. We have been defeated. For us as a Christian people, there is now but one course to pursue. We must accept the situation." –Robert E. Lee

Less than a week after Gen. Robert E. Lee surrendered to Gen. Ulysses S. Grant at Appomattox, President Abraham Lincoln was assassinated by John Wilkes Booth.

The conspiracy to kill the president also included attempts on the lives of the Secretary of State, Vice President Andrew Johnson, and possibly Gen. Grant.

With their champion dead and the government in disarray, Booth believed the generals and soldiers of the Confederacy might be inspired to once again take up arms.

However, with Lincoln dead, one man was solely responsible for the continued preservation of the Union that the president was martyred to restore.

That man was none other than Robert E. Lee.

As a result of his service with the Confederacy, Lee's Arlington home and property had been confiscated. This act of treason had also stripped the man of his citizenship. However, the general's remarkable sense of honor was still fully intact.

The words and actions of their beloved general carried great authority with the Confederate forces. Had Lee chosen to once again take up arms against Federal troops, then there would have been no shortage of gray-clad soldiers for him to command.

Robert E. Lee sternly rebuffed any efforts to get him to lead another attack against the Union. When America needed another champion, an unlikely hero came to the aid of the United States, a country that no longer recognized Gen. Lee as one of their own.

America's history is His story!

November 25

"Whereas it is the duty of all nations to acknowledge the providence of Almighty God, to obey His will, to be grateful for His benefits, and humbly to implore His protection and favor." –George Washington

America's History is His Story:

Perhaps more than any other national observance, Thanksgiving is a distinctive American holiday, in which our nation pauses to remember our blessings.

Thanksgiving was first celebrated by the Pilgrims in a 1621 celebration at Plymouth Plantation. The settlers thanked God for their preservation and the bountiful harvest He bestowed upon them.

Following the defeat of the British and the ratification of our Constitution, George Washington urged our nation to recall God's mercies to America, when he called for a National Day of Thanksgiving in 1789.

However, it took President Abraham Lincoln to make the holiday official, when his national proclamation was ratified by an act of Congress. Lincoln declared that the last Thursday in November would be observed as Thanksgiving.

And although Thanksgiving has been celebrated every year in our country since 1863, the date wouldn't be fully settled until Congress acted in 1941, when they chose to make it the fourth Thursday of November.

Throughout our nation's history, declarations of thanksgiving have been issued and observed by any number of our presidents and our Continental Congress. However, the date we choose to thank God for the marvelous blessings He has given our nation isn't nearly as important as the need for Americans to actually take the time to do it.

America's history is His story!

November 26

"We shall defend our island, whatever the cost may be. We shall fight on the beaches; we shall fight on the landing grounds. We shall fight in

the fields and in the streets; we shall fight in the hills. We shall never surrender." –Winston Churchill

Although the United States had to violently throw off the reins of the British government, our country has been blessed to have them as an ally for these many years.

It could be said that the United States had no greater friend, outside our shores, than former British Prime Minister Winston Churchill.

Long before anybody else truly understood the threat that Adolph Hitler posed to the world, Churchill knew. Although his warnings were ignored, the prime minister clearly recognized the man's evil intentions. Churchill urged President Roosevelt's involvement for quite some time before America finally chose to enter the war.

Through the sheer strength of his will, Britain found the courage and resolve to stand against the Nazi onslaught. Churchill had the will to fight; moreover, he inspired a nation to follow his example.

In fact, the more you study the courage and resolve of Winston Churchill, the more you are reminded of our Founding Fathers, those who bravely stood against the might of the British Empire.

Perhaps Churchill's exceptional character and courage didn't have its origins in the land of his birth. However, the man may have still been a product of his upbringing.

After all, Winston Churchill's mother was an American.

America's history is His story!

November 27

"Our armament must be adequate to the need, but our faith is not in these machines of defense, but in ourselves." –Admiral Chester Nimitz

America's History is His Story:

Although we should in no way minimize the great and noble sacrifices made by the brave men who gave their lives in combat, it must be stated that the Battle of Midway may have also been won by those who sat alone in a room, with a headset over their ears, listening, analyzing, and deciphering Japanese communications.

Joseph Rochefort was one such man.

Rochefort's commanding officer, Laurance Safford, wisely told Rochefort to spend whatever money was necessary in seeking out the best personnel and equipment to crack the Japanese codes and determine their battlefield intentions.

Rochefort quickly assembled a crew, who were experts on Japanese linguistics and the art of encryption. As a result of his team's expertise, they came to believe they had intercepted the plans of the Japanese to take Midway Island.

Confident they had correctly determined the enemy's intent, the American code breakers instructed Navy officials to deliberately communicate a false message. Then, they nervously listened for the Japanese response to follow. The resulting Japanese communications clearly confirmed their discovery. The Japanese codes had been broken.

The work of Joseph Rochefort, and other dedicated members of his team, prevented a devastating, surprise attack on Midway Island. Moreover, it gave America the means to determine the goals of their enemy and brought about a final end to the war.

America's history is His story!

November 28

"Character, in the long run, is the decisive factor in the life of an individual and of nations alike." –Theodore Roosevelt

One of the greatest things about America is the fact that nobody's destiny is solely determined by the circumstances of his upbringing. Some of the most remarkable men in our history have been the products of bad environments and poor family influences.

One such man was Butch O'Hare, after whom Chicago's great airport is named, who was a fighter pilot, assigned to the *USS Lexington*.

Only minutes before Japanese bomber pilots could drop their weapons on the *Lexington*, O'Hare was forced to engage them alone. The daring US pilot waded into the enemy fighters, quickly downing five Japanese planes in little more than four minutes.

With his ammunition depleted, O'Hare continued to attack the enemy, trying to clip their wings, or break their attack any way possible, even at the loss of his own life.

Although he would be killed in action about a year later, Butch O'Hare's courageous actions on that day made him the US Navy's most famous fighter ace and earned him the Congressional Medal of Honor.

However, if our destinies are only determined by our background, then there is no earthly reason why Butch O'Hare served his country with such distinction. His father was Edward "Fast Eddie" O'Hare, a mob attorney for Chicago crime figure, Al Capone.

The United States is a land of redemption, a place that gives each individual a chance to make his own way in life, regardless of the circumstances of his upbringing.

America's history is His story!

November 29

"I will ever conduct war with a view to perfect and early success. But, my dear sirs, when peace does come, you may call on me for anything.

America's History is His Story:

Then will I share with you the last cracker, and watch with you to shield your homes and families against danger from every quarter."

–Gen. William T. Sherman

Perhaps no general in American history has been more hated and misunderstood than William Tecumseh Sherman.

Gen. Sherman believed that war should be hard and total, requiring an army to quickly and thoroughly crush their enemy, both economically and psychologically.

Sherman's harsh method of prosecuting the war earned him the hatred of many in the South. However, Sherman's extraordinarily charitable terms of surrender, to Confederate Gen. Joseph Johnston, also earned him the hatred of some in the North.

In the wake of Lincoln's assassination, Secretary of War Edwin Stanton refused to go along with the terms Sherman negotiated with Johnston. In Sherman's mind, he was simply carrying out the wishes of his fallen Commander-in-Chief. However, at Stanton's directive, Grant ordered Sherman to renegotiate the terms of Johnston's surrender, an order that forever earned Sherman's bitter contempt for the cabinet secretary.

But the negotiation meetings between Sherman and Gen. Johnston only seemed to deepen the growing sense of respect and admiration these two men held for each other.

William T. Sherman was certainly a harsh opponent in war; however, the general was an incomparable gentleman in peace. Moreover, upon his death, Gen. Johnston would proudly serve as one of Sherman's pallbearers.

America's history is His story!

November 30

"Courage is not simply one of the virtues, but the form of every virtue at the testing point." –C.S. Lewis

On the day of the attacks on the World Trade Center, the terrorists also flew an airliner into the Pentagon.

During the resulting explosion and fire, a number of civilians saw the crash and immediately rushed to the scene. With no thoughts for their own safety, they came to the aid of the wounded and helped with the evacuation of the survivors from the burning military facility.

It is certainly not uncommon during times of crisis for those in uniform to run to meet the danger, while civilians flee for their lives. However, this was one of those rare occasions, when some of those in uniform were forced to flee from danger, while civilians ran to meet it.

On that day, the entire nation was under attack.

In Washington and in New York, and in the skies over Shanksville, Pennsylvania, thousands of American civilians were enlisted in the battle for liberty.

On that one tragic and memorable day, men and women in uniform stood alongside their brothers-in-arms, the men in women adorned in shirt sleeves and business suits. Together, they responded to danger, faced down their attackers, and upheld the very best qualities of the American spirit.

America's history is His story!

December 1

"I'll be grateful for the rest of my life that I had a chance to do something in this war that was not destructive. Nothing for me can ever compare with the satisfaction I got from helping to free our prisoners."

–Robert Prince

America's History is His Story:

During World War II, about 500 American survivors of the Bataan Death March were sent to Cabanatuan Prison in the Philippines.

Like most of the POWs held by the Japanese, the Americans were subjected to malnourishment, thirst, torture, and cold-blooded murder. And with MacArthur and the Allies closing in on the Philippines, the prisoners feared they would be executed.

That fear was also shared by the men of the Sixth Army, who already knew about the incident involving 150 POWs, driven into air raid shelters, covered with gasoline, and burned alive by the Japanese in other sites, just before the Allies arrived.

Boldly deciding that wouldn't be the ultimate fate of those at Cabanatuan, Lt. Col Henry Mucci chose Capt. Robert Prince to come up with a plan for their rescue. The plan called for the 6th Ranger Battalion, assisted by Filipino guerillas, to conduct a surprise attack in a daring, nighttime assault on the prison.

Against all odds, God truly smiled on the mission.

Despite the fact that many of the prisoners were sick or wounded, nearly all of them were successfully liberated from Cabanatuan, with only a minimal loss of life.

The Rangers daring raid on Cabanatuan Prison would prove to be the most successful rescue mission in U.S. military history.

America's history is His story!

December 2

"Today we did what we had to do. They counted on America to be passive. They counted wrong." –Ronald Reagan

When Army Rangers were planning their raid on the Japanese prison camp at Cabanatuan, they were faced with what appeared to be a nearly-insurmountable obstacle.

As the rescuers approached the camp, they would have to crawl across several feet of open field without the aid of darkness. Capt. Prince and Lt. Col. Mucci believed the Rangers were certain to be spotted by the Japanese guards, eliminating any remaining element of surprise.

Hoping to minimize the likelihood that they would be seen by the guards in the open field, it was decided that a P-61 Black Widow would repeatedly fly over the camp, creating a diversion.

Capt. Kenneth Schrieber and 1st Lt. Bonnie Rucks flew the plane over the camp several times. They momentarily cut the power to one of the engines, like the aircraft was in distress, making the guards look, as the plane barely cleared the distant hill.

"I didn't think it would work, not in a million years," Prince said. "But the pilot's maneuvers were so skillful and deceptive that the diversion was complete. I don't know where we would have been without it."

Although they didn't face any of the brutal fighting on the ground, Schreiber and Rucks played an essential role in one of the greatest feats in military history.

America's history is His story!

December 3

"If there must be trouble, let it be in my day, that my child may have peace." –Thomas Paine

America's History is His Story:

During the Revolution, the British were determined to stop the aid to the colonists in Georgia and the Carolinas, which was coming from those hardy settlers who moved into the Appalachian Mountains.

British Major Patrick Ferguson boldly sent them a letter, ordering them to cease their rebellion or he would "march his army over the mountains, hang their leaders, and lay their country waste with fire and sword."

With an army of nearly 1,100 Tories, American citizens who were loyal to the British cause, Ferguson formed an encampment on Kings Mountain, near the North Carolina/Tennessee border and stated that "even the Almighty cannot drive me from it."

Apparently, the Lord failed to receive the memo.

A pair of American militia colonels, Issac Shelby and John Sevier, decided they would act without authorization and attack the British commander. Leading their force of "Overmountain Men," buckskin-clad, American sharpshooters, who had gained their wartime experience fighting the Indians, the militia marched all night through driving rains and then made a surprise attack on Ferguson's camp.

In the space of one hour, British Major Patrick Ferguson was killed and every member of his army was either killed or captured in the Battle of Kings Mountain, which Theodore Roosevelt called "the turning point of the American Revolution."

America's history is His story!

December 4

"Only those are fit to live who are not afraid to die."
                                            –Gen. Douglas MacArthur

No story of God's marvelous intervention for America during World War II would be complete without mentioning the help given to American troops by the brave people of the Philippines.

It must also be stated that, after the fall of the Philippines, the Filipino people were prisoners in their own country. The cruelty inflicted upon the Filipinos by the Japanese was every bit as severe as that visited upon American servicemen. Over one million Filipinos lost their lives as a result of the Japanese Imperial Army.

Therefore, the people of the Philippines became some of our greatest allies.

The raid, to free American POWs in Cabanatuan Prison, wouldn't have succeeded without the aid of the Filipinos. They supplied us with surveillance and intelligence reports. They provided food and carts, to help with the sick and wounded. Moreover, many of them died in a brutal firefight with the Japanese, endeavoring to stop the American raid.

It must also be stated that many Filipino civilians, members of the resistance, were involved in smuggling food to American POWs or supplying them with quinine, to treat malaria, a disease which swept through the ranks of the already-weakened prisoners.

The brutal Japanese army tortured and executed many of the Filipinos, who were discovered providing these items to American POWs. These great and noble acts of mercy by our Philippine allies must never be forgotten by the people of the United States.

America's history is His story!

December 5

"Would that I was an artist and had the material to paint this camp and all its horrors, or the tongue of some eloquent statesman, and had the

America's History is His Story:

privilege of expressing my mind to our honorable rulers at Washington, I should glory to describe this hell on earth, where it takes seven of its occupants to make a shadow." –Sgt. David Kennedy

Joining the Union army at the age of 16, Dorence Atwater was captured and became one the first Union soldiers to be sent to Andersonville Prison in Georgia.

Andersonville had been built to house approximately 13,000 prisoners; however, at one point, the number contained within its walls would swell to 32,000.

The Confederate government, which saw its already-limited resources depleted by the war, was incapable of adequately providing the food, medicine, and supplies for the nearly 400 Federal prisoners a day, who came within its walls.

Therefore, many of the emaciated dead of Andersonville may have been unknown to their relatives, lost to history, and forever listed as missing in action.

And perhaps that would have been the case, had it not been for the daring and covert actions of Dorence Atwater.

Working as a surgeon's clerk, Atwater kept a detailed list of the prison dead and the locations of their burials. Fearing the list would be lost or destroyed, Atwater secretly prepared a duplicate list, which he later smuggled out of the prison and protected, even from some of those in the government's own War Department.

Thanks in large part to Dorence Atwater's secret lists, only 460 men, out of the 12,000 who died in Andersonville, were never identified.

America's history is His story!

December 6

"Don't fire unless fired upon, but if they mean to have a war, let it begin here." –Captain John Parker

Our national military cemeteries are full of white stone markers or simple white crosses, each one representing a man and woman who offered up their life in the cause of America's freedom.

Many of these markers signify a person who paid the ultimate price so that you might know the blessings of liberty.

As a result of their noble sacrifices, most of us have been the beneficiaries of their efforts. However, every generation of Americans are called upon to make at least some small contribution to the cause of liberty.

For most of us, liberty doesn't demand that we put on the uniform of the United States military. Independence doesn't require us to shed our blood on foreign soil. The preservation of your freedoms calls for very little from each one of us.

Liberty does, however, demand our vigilance and willingness to speak up, whenever we see an infringement upon those liberties. When so many have given so much, how can you not be willing to speak out, something that costs you so very little?

To remain silent, to ignore the threat, and to leave that responsibility to others is a dereliction of your duties as a citizen. Moreover, remaining silent in the face of threats to your liberties is the moral equivalent of defecating on the gravesite of every person who wore that uniform and risked their lives to preserve your God-given rights to freedom.

America's history is His story!

December 7

"Praise the Lord and pass the ammunition." –Howell M. Forgy

December 7, 1941, was a peaceful Sunday morning in the territory of Hawaii. The blue, calm waters of Pearl Harbor were home to most of America's Pacific naval fleet.

Suddenly, without any warning, the harbor was under attack.

Sleepy sailors were just starting their duties, having breakfast, or climbing out of their racks. As the hundreds of Japanese planes torpedoed the ships and strafed the sailors with gunfire, men aboard the ships scrambled to man their guns. The cries of the dead and the dying were all around them.

Howell Forgy, a chaplain on one of the cruisers, shouted encouragement and helped the men to hand out the ammunition.

America's pastors and ministers have always been in the forefront in times of war. During the American Revolution, these men often recognized that freedom from tyranny was indeed a righteous cause. Their pulpits often flamed with the words of liberty. Some of these ministers even led their congregations to take up arms.

Many of these religious patriots paid a high price for their leadership. It was not uncommon for pastors, who were captured by the British, to routinely be hanged for treason. The offending pastors sometimes saw their churches burned.

In the earliest years of our nation's history, men of God often paid a high price, lifting up the standard of liberty at the same time they lifted up the Cross.

America's history is His story!

December 8

"Some Americans need hyphens in their names, because only part of them has come over; but when the whole man has come over, heart and thought and all, the hyphen drops of its own weight out of his name."
—Woodrow Wilson

Raymond Harjo was an American Indian from the state of Oklahoma; Sidney Nicholas was a white farm boy, from the state of West Virginia.

However, the two of them would become brothers.

These two individuals were as different as any two people could be. They grew up in different states, different surroundings, and vastly different home lives. Under normal circumstances, these two people would never have even met.

But there was certainly nothing normal about America, during those turbulent years of World War II.

Raymond Harjo and Sidney Nicholas were people of two different races, brought together by one man's arrogant and evil obsession with creating a Master Race.

People of all nationalities and cultures, whose families came to our country for freedom, left these peaceful shores, in a noble quest to establish freedom in many of the countries they once departed. This situation happened repeatedly in the war.

Thrust together as part of a bomber crew, flying a B-17 over the skies of Europe, Harjo and Nicholas would often face death together. Their experiences bonded them together as friends, warriors, and brothers-in-arms. Moreover, it should remind us all of the words on the official Seal of the United States: *E pluribus unum*, out of many, one.

America's history is His story!

America's History is His Story:

December 9

"I leave you, hoping that the lamp of liberty will burn in your bosoms until there shall no longer be a doubt that all men are created free and equal." –Abraham Lincoln

For too many years, black athletes weren't permitted to play in Major League baseball. However, their exclusion gave rise to the Negro Leagues, in which black baseball players were able to show their skills to the world.

Almost everybody has heard about Satchel Paige, whose pitching skills were legendary, eventually earning this athlete his rightful place in the big leagues.

Another great black player of that era was Josh Gibson, often known as the "black Babe Ruth." According to those who saw him play, Gibson hit approximately 800 home runs, one of which sailed clear out of old Yankee Stadium.

Then there was James "Cool Papa" Bell, who once scored from first base on a bunt. One legend states that Bell ran so fast, he once slid into second base, at the same time he was hit by his own batted ball.

Fortunately, America and Major League baseball finally rectified its great injustices to these remarkable black athletes, placing all three of them in the Baseball Hall of Fame in Cooperstown, New York.

Most importantly, baseball also threw open the doors to black athletes, when Branch Rickey, a devoted Christian gentlemen, signed Jackie Robinson to a contract with the Brooklyn Dodgers in 1947. Rickey's courageous actions truly opened the floodgates of Major League baseball to athletes of all colors.

America's history is His story!

December 10

"A man's character always takes its hue, more or less, from the form and color of things about him." –Frederick Douglas

Many of those in the black community fiercely claim Jamaican-born Samuel Fraunces as one of their own. However, the man's true racial identity, which is still a great source of debate, truly matters little. It does matter what he accomplished.

Often known as "Black Sam," Fraunces was the proprietor of an inn and tavern, which often served as a clandestine meeting place for the Sons of Liberty. Along with becoming a close friend of Gen. Washington, Fraunces also provided food to the 13,000 Americans held captive on the deplorable British prison ships.

In one of his most providential decisions, Washington obtained the services of Samuel Fraunces and his family as stewards of his temporary wartime headquarters.

Posing as a British deserter, Thomas Hickey was employed by Gen. Washington as his personal bodyguard. However, unknown to the general, Hickey was conspiring with the British to assassinate him.

History isn't clear whether Hickey truly loved Samuel's daughter, Phoebe, or if she was simply another pawn in his elaborate plot. However, Phoebe discovered Hickey's attempt to poison Washington's plate of peas and kept the general from eating them.

As a result of their brave actions, Samuel Fraunces and his family were responsible for the punishment of a traitor, the protection of a general, and the providential founding of our nation.

America's history is His story!

December 11

"I know this world is ruled by infinite intelligence. Everything that surrounds us—everything that exists—proves that there are infinite laws behind it. There can be no denying this fact. It is mathematical in its precision." –Thomas Edison

Whenever you blindly accept the claim that only ignorant people believe in Creation, then you have fallen victim to one of the greatest injustices ever perpetrated on the American people.

If only the ignorant believe in Creation, then how do you simply dismiss the learned minds of the past, those who clearly believed in a Creator, or in some sort of Intelligent Design? Are we simply to label them as kooks and crackpots?

These were men who gave us the wonders of the incandescent light bulb. They enabled our rockets and astronauts to touch the distant reaches of space. These were men who gave us over one hundred uses for a single item, such as the peanut.

These are only a few of the innovations and inventions made by our great scientists and inventors, people who believed this earth wasn't a random act of fate.

Perhaps it's time we begin to investigate the credentials of today's scientists, who openly scoff at the idea of creation. Where are their inventions? What great contributions have they given to mankind? What special lights have they brought to society?

Moreover, it isn't the believers in Creation, who are seeking to plunge our nation back into the darkness, a goal that's already been embraced by the disciples of evolution.

For they are the ones who sought to ban the incandescent light bulb.

America's history is His story!

December 12

"We must not conclude merely upon a man's haranguing upon liberty, and using the charming sound, that he is fit to be trusted with the liberties of his country. It is not unfrequent to hear men declaim loudly upon liberty, who, if we may judge by the whole tenor of their actions, mean nothing else by it but their own liberty." –John Adams

When John Adams spoke on this subject, he was describing people all over this country today, many of them walking the halls of Congress.

We often hear people eloquently praising the greatness of America, at the same time they're apologizing for our country and ashamed of our heritage. They pontificate on the need for tolerance, while they openly mock people of sincere and abiding faith. They loudly proclaim the blessings of liberty for themselves, while they endeavor to remove those same freedoms *from* others.

These so-called defenders of freedom desire to remake America in *their* own image. They wish to give birth to a nation that readily embraces any and all forms of deviancy, while it scoffs at those who seek to lead a moral life. They lecture us on mercy and demand that we spare the lives of evil, convicted murderers, but offer no protection whatsoever to the innocent soul in a mother's womb.

It isn't enough for Americans to simply praise our country; their actions should clearly reflect the words they speak. Those who truly love our country will embrace its ideals, value its heritage, preserve its foundations, and elevate its truths.

Just because a person's lips might peal the bells of liberty doesn't mean that their words will ring true.

America's history is His story!

America's History is His Story:

December 13

"Far better is it to dare mighty things, to win glorious triumphs, even though checkered by failure, than to rank with those poor spirits who neither enjoy nor suffer much, because they live in a gray twilight that knows not victory nor defeat." –Theodore Roosevelt

When the Colonies went to war with Britain, the troops of our Continental Army fought the war and returned to their homes and farms. When America went to war with Mexico and Cuba, we won the battles and then went home. In World War II, the United States sent troops overseas. In four years, they won the war and happily came home.

All of these wars had one thing in common: there was no "exit strategy."

Exit strategy is a recent term, coined by politicians, men who won't let our troops do what they must do, in order to fully win these wars and return home. Exit strategy is a term loved by the leadership of the United Nations, an institution dedicated to national impotence and world dominance. Exit strategy is a preparation for failure.

Ulysses S. Grant and Robert E. Lee had no exit strategy. Gen. William Tecumseh Sherman knew nothing but total war. Gen. George Patton couldn't conceive the idea of doing anything less than fully defeating the enemy. He obviously had no exit strategy. Gen. Douglas MacArthur was ordered away from the Philippines; he did not choose to leave. But true to his word, MacArthur did return. He had no exit strategy.

In the person of George Washington, America was led and guided by a general who also had no exit strategy. His only strategy was victory, an idea that gave birth to our country and has made us invincible in battle, back before we had an exit strategy.

America's history is His story!

December 14

"Yonder are the Hessians. They were bought for seven pounds and ten-pence a man. Are you worth more? Prove it. Tonight the American flag floats from yonder hill or Molly Stark sleeps a widow!" –John Stark

During the American Revolution, John Stark spoke these words and rallied his troops at the Battle of Bennington, in which America gained a crucial victory.

This battle was waged against the forces of British Gen. John Burgoyne, aided by the Hessians, Tories, and their Indian allies. Moreover, the devastating losses suffered by the Indians, caused them to return to their native Quebec, eliminating their assistance to the British as scouts and allies.

Another factor that contributed to the stunning American victory was the fact that the German-speaking Hessians knew very little English.

They had been instructed to not fire upon the Tories, American-born British loyalists, who were supposed to be wearing slips of white paper tacked to their hats.

Upon learning this information, John Stark wisely used this knowledge to his troops' advantage.

The Americans won the battle because they were able to successfully flank their enemies. Their strategy was aided because the American troops were able to move in close proximity to the Hessian mercenaries, who would not fire upon them, because their hats were adorned with white pieces of paper.

America's history is His story!

December 15

"Wars may be fought with weapons, but they are won by men. It is the spirit of men who follow and of the man who leads that gains the victory." –Gen. George Patton

Although the Confederacy lost the Civil War, the contributions they made to naval warfare are still with us today.

In his desire to help the South win the war, Horace Lawson Hunley designed and built a submarine, which he called the *H.L. Hunley*.

Early on, the *Hunley* sank during a training exercise, killing all five members of her crew. Two months later, the *Hunley* sank again, killing eight members of her crew, including the ship's inventor.

Apparently, these tragic failures and great losses of life didn't dissuade the Confederates of the submarine's limitless capabilities in naval combat. And once again, undeterred, they brought the sunken vessel to the surface.

Four months later, the *Hunley* would finally prove its worth in battle, when it successfully attacked the *USS Housatonic*, a steam-powered Union ship, which blockaded the harbor in Charleston, South Carolina.

Although the *Hunley* became the first submarine to ever successfully sink a ship in battle, the destruction of the *Housatonic* also led to a final loss of the *Hunley* as well.

Although its crew perished in the attempt, the United States submarine fleet can trace its roots to the Confederacy and one man's groundbreaking idea, that a submarine could be a crucial vessel for winning the war at sea.

America's history is His story!

December 16

"I look back to the early days of our acquaintance and friendship, as to the days of love and innocence." –Abigail Adams

Just before her sweetheart went off to fight in the Civil War, Queenie Bennett gave Lt. George E. Dixon a $20 gold piece, to carry in his pocket for luck.

At the Battle of Shiloh, a Union soldier's bullet struck Lt. Dixon. It mangled the gold piece in his pocket, but mercifully spared his leg and possibly saved his life.

Pleased by his good fortune, Dixon had an engraving placed on the distorted, life-saving $20 gold piece. However, the lieutenant never returned to his home and sweetheart, and was lost during the war.

Over the years, the members of the Dixon family had passed down the details of this story, which was never confirmed.

However, when scientists and researchers raised the Confederate submarine, the *H.L Hunley*, they were able to conclusively identify the remains of Lt. George Dixon, who commanded the vessel.

Near his body's location, they discovered a mangled $20 gold piece, engraved with the words *"Shiloh April 6, 1862, My life Preserver G. E. D."* Moreover, a forensic anthropologist confirmed that his body had once suffered an injury to the hip bone.

Like others who saw their sweethearts go to battle, Queenie Bennett would never know what happened to the one she loved. But the simple token of her affection reminds us that love is a golden treasure, which often survives the scars and losses of war.

America's history is His story!

America's History is His Story:

December 17

"I've learned from experience that the greater part of our happiness or misery depends on our dispositions and not on our circumstances."
—Martha Washington

During the Revolutionary War, it was not unusual for women to follow their husbands to war.

After marrying John Casper Hay, a soldier in the Continental Army, Mary Ludwig chose to follow her husband into battle. She helped with the cooking and washing duties, and also assisted with treating the sick and wounded.

In the midst of the fighting, at great risk to herself, the woman carried water to the thirsty troops, earning Mary her more famous nickname, "Molly Pitcher."

During the Battle of Monmouth, John Hay was one of the men responsible for manning the cannon. However, from her place on the battlefield, Mary would see her husband go down in battle.

Dropping her water pitcher, Mary rushed to her fallen husband's side. Then, in an extraordinary act of courage and self-sacrifice, Mary regained her composure and assumed his position on the cannon line. And there the woman stayed, helping to fire the cannon until the battle was finally won.

For her brave and noble actions, the woman known as Molly Pitcher was awarded a sergeant's commission by Gen. Greene.

Throughout American history, battles have often been won because brave men and women willingly rose to the occasion and unselfishly met the needs of their country.

America's history is His story!

December 18

"In the beginning of a change, the patriot is a scarce man, and brave, and hated and scorned. When his cause succeeds, the timid join him, for then it costs nothing to be a patriot." –Mark Twain

Many Americans falsely believe that all of the early Colonists supported the Revolutionary cause. However, that simply isn't the case.

When the first sparks of liberty began to be kindled, a great majority of the Colonists were loyal to the British and did not wish to be separated from them. In addition, a great number of the Colonists wished the rebels to be silenced or hanged.

America's Founders not only had to fear the actions of the British government; they also had to face the scorn and hatred of many of their own countrymen.

Yet that has always been the way of liberty.

It should come as no surprise that patriots, pioneers, and statesmen are often forced to stand alone. They are often hated and feared by those who do not understand them; or they often face dangers from those who are much too fearful to take the bold and noble actions from which patriots are born.

The men who founded our country were extraordinary individuals, the likes of which few generations ever see.

The United States has been blessed to have been given them. Moreover, their boldness, their courage, their love of liberty, and their deep, abiding faith have made us the country we became.

For everyone becomes a patriot, when there is no longer any threat to face.

America's history is His story!

December 19

"When it is dark enough, you can see the stars."
–Ralph Waldo Emerson

In the 2011 storm that struck the town of Joplin, Missouri, a massive tornado tore through the city, leaving a grisly path of death and destruction wherever it touched down.

Over one hundred of Joplin's citizens were killed.

The people of Joplin wept. They embraced their loved ones. They searched for survivors among the rubble. They comforted their friends and family.

However, in the midst of all this death and devastation, a single cross remained silhouetted against the sky.

The church to which the structure was attached would be obliterated by the storm; however, the cross continued to stand.

In much the same way that a cross survived the carnage at the World Trade Center, this cross survived the worst forces of nature that were unleashed against it.

The Lord chose to leave a reminder to the people of Joplin, that, even in the midst of their darkest days, He was still with them. Structures might be shaken. Lives could be lost. Homes and businesses can be destroyed. But faith continues to stand.

Americans instinctively know this; they have always known it.

At moments when nature does its worst, the enduring spirit of faith causes us to do our best. The people of Joplin proved it once again, as they bravely rebuilt their lives.

America's history is His story!

December 20

"As we honor their memory today, let us pledge that their lives, their sacrifices, their valor shall be justified and remembered for as long as God gives life to this nation." –Ronald Reagan

Whenever you think of the Navy SEALs, you think of America's most elite and secretive fighting force. From the rescue of a young, female soldier in Iraq, to the liberation of a ship captain from Somali pirates, to the assassination of the world's most dangerous terrorists, the SEALs are there.

Every time they undertake a mission for the United States military, these men bring honor upon themselves and their government.

However, despite their reputation for taking on the world's toughest missions, we often forget these brave and determined warriors are simply fine, young men.

When their helicopter was shot down over eastern Afghanistan, thirty Americans perished in the crash, many of them Navy SEALs.

Not only were these young men some of our nation's finest warriors, they were also sons and nephews. They were brothers and uncles. Among the fallen were grandsons, husbands, and fathers.

The men who perished on that helicopter were the finest products of some of our nation's most outstanding families. Moreover, our nation can never fully repay the debt we owe them for offering up their loved ones in the protection of our sacred liberties.

The people of the United States can never fully understand the loss suffered by these families; but the gratitude many of us feel for them can never be fully expressed.

America's history is His story!

December 21

"May none but honest and wise men ever rule under this roof."
  —John Adams

When we were children, many of us were brought up with a reverence for the office of the presidency. It was nearly a sacred position to us. Americans saw their presidents in much the same way that we viewed our ministers. In our young minds, only the very best men occupied the Oval Office.

Our parents held them up as examples; they wanted us to be like them. Moreover, many of our presidents did their best to live up to this sacred trust. Our country's presidents often were not perfect men; but they did their best to elevate their stature to match the honor of their station.

Before the eyes of a watching world, the reputation and honor of our Commander-in-Chief should be without blemish. The sanctity of life and the sanctity of marriage should be given an elevated status by our Chief Executive. We should elect a president who will guard the vows he made to his wife with the same diligence as the oath he took to his country.

But most of all, we must always choose a president who will treat the office with the same respect that it rightfully and historically deserves.

To some, the words of John Adams, upon moving into the White House, may sound archaic and outdated, but they are the timeless birthright of every American. It is high time that we reclaimed them.

America's history is His story!

December 22

"Oh poor, New England! There is a deep plot against your civil and religious liberties, and they will be lost. Your golden days are at an end. You have nothing but trouble before you." –George Whitefield

These words from George Whitefield were spoken nearly two hundred and fifty years ago. However, many would say that they were still true today. Others would say these words are not only true about New England; but they are also true about the United States as well.

There can be no question that there are no shortages of loud and destructive forces in this country, people who are dedicated to destroying our traditions, rewriting our history, and permanently obliterating the civil and religious liberties that we have enjoyed since our founding.

Despite the claims you often hear from our militant environmentalists, the earth certainly isn't fragile; however, the liberties we enjoy most certainly are!

President Ronald Reagan said, "Freedom is never more than one generation away from extinction."

The people of the United States must come to understand the fact that, if we continue to squander the blessings of liberties, then there will be no inheritance of freedom to pass down to our own children.

And should that ever happen, then George Whitfield's prediction will have proven true. Our golden days will come to an end as a nation, and there will be nothing but trouble before us. Let us all pray that it never happens to the United States.

America's history is His story!

December 23

"No man in the wrong can stand up against a fellow that's in the right and keeps on a-comin'." –Texas Ranger Bill McDonald

America's History is His Story:

In 1987, a felon named Brent Beeler kidnapped a wealthy rancher's daughter and murdered her young, female caretaker. The killer barricaded himself inside their house, demanding a ransom and a car in exchange for the young girl's safety.

A pair of Texas Rangers, Stanley Keith Guffey and John Aycock, determined that they wouldn't let the criminal escape with the two-year old child.

When the Lincoln Town Car and the $30,000 ransom were delivered to Beeler, the outlaw tried to flee with the money and young child. However, hiding in the trunk, with the rear seat removed, were the brave pair of Texas Rangers.

As he threw the money in the backseat, Beeler spotted the Rangers. In the ensuing shoot-out between them, Ranger Guffey would be mortally wounded. But Aycock would successfully pull the child away from danger and kill Brent Beeler.

Throughout their history, the Texas Rangers have become legendary for their heroism and exploits. And for his remarkable sacrifice, Ranger Stanley McGuffey would forever be enshrined in the Texas Rangers Hall of Fame

America has always been blessed with law enforcement personnel, who would willingly place themselves in danger, in order to save the life of another. It is just one more of the qualities that makes our nation exceptional before the world.

America's history is His story!

December 24

"If the historian of the future should deem my service worthy of some slight reference, it would be my hope that he mention me not as commander engaged in campaigns and battles, even though victorious to

American arms, but rather as that one whose sacred duty it became, once the guns were silenced, to carry to the land of our vanquished foe the solace and hope and faith of Christian morals."

–Gen. Douglas MacArthur

Following the Japanese surrender in World War II, Gen. Douglas MacArthur was placed in charge of their government.

MacArthur believed that Japan's willingness to blindly follow and worship their emperor had been largely responsible for their war atrocities and ultimate defeat. Therefore, he wisely determined that Japan was suffering from a spiritual vacuum and that Christianity would prove to be the key to Japan's future success.

The general repeatedly called for American missionaries to saturate Japan with the Gospel message. These preachers of the Gospel were awarded temporary military commissions, which allowed them to move freely throughout the country.

MacArthur also sought to introduce the Word of God to the conquered nation. Apparently, the strategy worked, as the Bible would soon become a best-seller among the Japanese people.

The Christian faith, which made the United States an economic power, was responsible for transforming the nation of Japan into an industrial powerhouse as well.

There can be no question that the introduction of Christianity not only transforms the heart and soul of an individual; in addition, those same truths, when properly followed, can also place even the most beleaguered nation on the path to greatness.

America's history is His story!

December 25

"For unto you is born this day in the city of David, a Savior which is Christ the Lord." –Saint Luke

Much like the Lord we serve, the United States was certainly a land of humble beginnings.

Our Savior was born in humble circumstances, a lowly stable, surrounded by farm animals and the provisions to feed them. This king wore no crown; he was not arrayed in purple or adorned in fine, linen garments.

Our nation was also born of meager circumstances as well.

The earliest settlers who came to this country were often trying to escape the religious persecution they suffered elsewhere. Many of them began their time in America as indentured servants and the subjects of the king.

The Colonists were opposed by the greatest military power in the world, an army and navy that had never known defeat. On paper, the soldiers of the Continental Army were clearly no match for their British adversaries, troops which were better equipped, better clothed, better fed, better armed, and better trained than their Colonial counterparts.

However, as we learned in the Gospels, humble beginnings are certainly no indication of future success. Christ and His message would not be stopped or silenced, even by the Crucifixion. Moreover, the Gospel He preached would change the world.

A humble land of servants would become the greatest nation in the world, by following the words of a humble Servant, who would become the Savior of the World.

America's history is His story!

December 26

"I may be compelled to face danger, but never fear it; and while our soldiers can stand and fight, I can stand and feed and nurse them."
–Clara Barton

As the Founder of the American Red Cross, Clara Barton began her service to American servicemen on the battlefields of the Civil War.

Refusing to remain behind on the battlefield, Barton was eventually given permission to come to the aid of wounded soldiers on the front lines of conflict. She instructed her drivers to follow the sounds of the cannon blasts, taking her to the places where men injured in battle most needed her help.

On one such occasion, while helping a wounded soldier to his feet on the battlefield, Clara Barton was nearly killed.

"A ball had passed between my body and the right arm which supported him," Barton said, "cutting through the sleeve and passing through his chest from shoulder to shoulder. There was no more to be done for him and I left him to his rest."

The woman later stated that she never felt led to mend the bullet hole in her garment. Moreover, she wondered if any soldier ever did.

Clara Barton's close call with death apparently didn't persuade her to change her behavior or to stop coming to the aid of those wounded in battle. However, the hole in her garment made her fully appreciate the dangers faced by those in combat.

It also served as a constant reminder that God spared her life and that He won't allow His servants to be killed until they have fulfilled their sacred purposes on this earth.

America's history is His story!

America's History is His Story:

December 27

"America will never be destroyed from the outside. If we falter and lose our freedoms, it will be because we destroyed ourselves."
–Abraham Lincoln

When we look at the economic condition of our troubled nation, it isn't hard for any thinking American to see that our nation's greatest danger isn't the threat of a foreign army; it is the danger of unrestrained federal spending.

An unsustainable federal debt is not only irresponsible behavior; it is also the greatest threat to America's national sovereignty.

Abraham Lincoln was right.

In fact, almost one hundred years later, President Eisenhower reaffirmed the truth stated by President Lincoln, when he said, "Only Americans can hurt America."

America became the greatest nation in the world, because we paid our debts, both financially and morally.

Traditionally, the United States has been good to her friends and allies. Moreover, our country has thrived because it hasn't generally been abusive to its citizens.

The government our Founders established derived its powers from "the consent of the governed."

Increasingly, however, those in Washington ridicule the citizens they claim to serve and behave like British Lords, from which we fought to achieve our liberty.

America's future will only be bright again when our citizens realize that our greatness is not a product of ourselves; it is a precious gift bestowed upon us by the Lord.

America's history is His story!

December 28

"The Holocaust was the most evil crime ever committed."
–Stephen Ambrose

When Dwight D. Eisenhower was Supreme Commander of the Allies in World War II, he went to visit the Nazi death camps, one of the most ghastly discoveries of American troops in the liberation of Europe.

Appalled by the nearly-unspeakable atrocities that he witnessed in Buchenwald, this future American president was morally outraged. Moreover, he didn't believe that the German citizens of Gotha had been ignorant of these depraved and deplorable acts, which were taking place this close to their beloved city.

Therefore, Eisenhower ordered his troops to forcibly bring the townspeople to the camps. He made them observe the mounds of burned, tortured, and emaciated bodies; the general also required them to witness the smell of death, filth, disease, and charred flesh.

Obviously disturbed by what they witnessed at the prison camp, the local mayor and his wife returned to their house and hanged themselves.

Eisenhower also ordered every available American soldier in the area to visit the camp, so that they might know why they were fighting the war. In another wise decision, Ike also brought in the media, urging hundreds of journalists to photograph and chronicle the unspeakable acts of evil that took place inside the camp.

His crucial insistence on photographic evidence made it impossible for evil men to credibly gain any traction when they deny the evil truth of the Holocaust.

America's history is His story!

America's History is His Story:

December 29

"What students would learn in American schools above all is the religion of Jesus Christ." –George Washington

Increasingly, Americans who devotedly cling to their faith, often find themselves the object of scorn and derision from many of those in Hollywood, politics, or the media. However, in America, it is not the Christian who should hang his head in embarrassment.

If you believe you are entitled to only those things which you can earn with your own hands, then you share the wisdom of William Bradford.

If you recognize that mankind and this earth are not the random acts of fate, but rather, the products of a Divine Creator, then you share the brilliance of Samuel Adams.

If you know that our sacred rights are not granted to us by the power of governments, but come to us as endowments from God, then you have touched the intellect of Thomas Jefferson.

If you believe that soldiers and citizens become better at their duties, when they seek to become better Christians, then your thoughts run parallel with the ideas of George Washington.

If you acknowledge that a nation cannot rise to prominence without the aid of the Almighty, then you have been blessed with a portion of Ben Franklin's insight.

If you believe in the ideas and traditions that made our country great, then you share the soul and brilliance of our Founders. You certainly aren't the one who is ignorant, unlearned, or un-American. That dubious honor belongs to your detractors.

America's history is His story!

December 30

"We have no government with power capable to contending with human passions unbridled by morality and religion. Our Constitution was made only for a moral and religious people. It is wholly inadequate to the government of any other." –John Adams

Our nation was built on a foundation of faith. However, whenever that foundation begins to crumble, then so will our nation. You are already seeing that happen today.

The loudest voices in Washington today are those that cry out about the "evil" influence of faith on our government. They are the same people who refuse to call terrorists by their proper name, but repeatedly use that same term for honest American citizens, who wisely demand that the government should live within its means.

Atheism and agnosticism not only poison the soul; they are also toxic to the American spirit.

Washington is dominated by religious skeptics, who wish to punitively tax our citizens into a form of morality, solely dictated by the state. At the same time, they seek to destroy a man's natural inclination to seek God's help in times of trouble or to share his excess with others in need.

These skeptics bow their knees only to the State. They have betrayed those they claim to serve. And they have changed the truth of God *and* America into a lie.

Over two hundred years after those words were first spoken, John Adams' simple truth about government has not changed. The Constitution was written only for a moral and religious people. It is wholly inadequate for any other.

America's history is His story!

America's History is His Story:

December 31

"Finally, let us not forget the religious character of our nation. Our fathers were brought hither by their high veneration for the Christian religion. They journeyed by its light and labored in its hope. They sought to incorporate its principles with the elements of their society, and to diffuse its influence through all their institutions, civil, political, or literary." –Daniel Webster

When we consider the United States of America, the nation which we know as home, there can be no question that ours is a Christian nation.

The only people who can challenge the fact of our religious heritage are the ignorant, the uninformed, or the deceitful.

America *is* a Christian nation.

We have been blessed by God. In looking at our history, we can witness His gentle guiding hand orchestrating the events of our founding. We are able to see His awesome power over nature, directing the winds and rivers to rescue or rally the seemingly overmatched forces of Gen. Washington.

Most of all, any thoughtful reading of our founding documents clearly reveals the evidence of Divine influence in their authorship. Their words, their principles, and their spirit were guided by the pages of Holy Writ.

The men who founded our country, the authors of our liberty, the ones who conceived this great experiment in democracy were some of the finest minds ever assembled in one room. And without exception, these extraordinary and learned men knew that the establishment of the United States couldn't be accomplished without the blessing and assistance of our Creator.

America's history is His story!

Author's Note

The book you have just read is the *only* project I ever took on as a favor to a friend.

Although he was born in Texas and I'm a West Virginia native, Oliver Araiza and I have known each other since our teenage years. He is indeed a good and trusted friend.

When Araiza was starting a Christian radio station near Clarksburg, West Virginia, and was seeking to present a patriotic message to his listeners for every single day of the year, my name was one of the people that came to his mind and he asked me to pen this book.

As a child, I loved to listen to Paul Harvey on the radio every day, a kind, decent man and superb radio personality who always ended his broadcast with the same tagline, "And now you know the *rest* of the story."

When I first began to pen this book, like Paul Harvey, I also sought to have a unique tagline for each day's broadcast. That was when I decided to add the phrase, "America's History is His Story!"

This is perhaps the most difficult project I have ever undertaken, but also the most satisfying. I trust that you will love it and our nation as much as I do.

R.G. Yoho

About the Author

R.G. Yoho is a West Virginia native with a passion for history and tales of the American West. Raised on a cattle farm, he is the prolific author of multiple Western novels, along with works of fiction and non-fiction. Yoho is a former president of the West Virginia Writers. Living with his wife near the banks of the Ohio River, Yoho is also a proud member of the Western Writers of America.

Now Available!

R.G. YOHO'S
ACTION / ADVENTURE WESTERNS

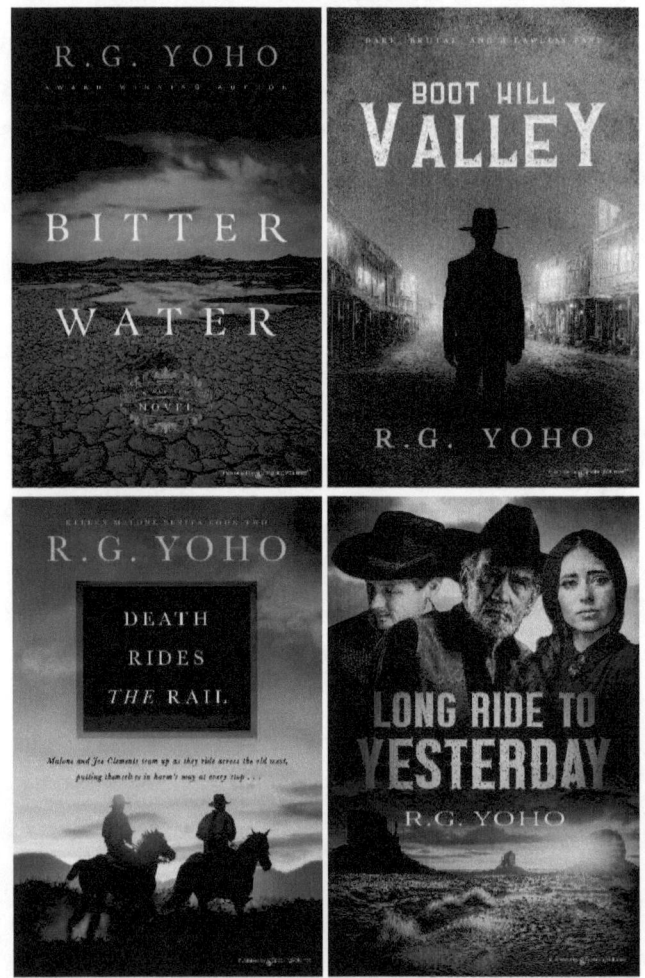

**For more information
visit: www.SpeakingVolumes.us**

www.ingramcontent.com/pod-product-compliance
Lightning Source LLC
LaVergne TN
LVHW041741060526
838201LV00046B/872